.142

NO
BED
OF
ROSES

NO

BED

OF

ROSES

by JOAN FONTAINE

WILLIAM MORROW AND COMPANY, INC.
NEW YORK

For

Lilian, Tim,

Kit, Gams . . .

that

extraordinary lady

I called Mother

INTRODUCTION

WHY DOES ONE WRITE THE STORY OF ONE'S LIFE, SPREAD IT OUT LIKE a well-worn carpet for unknown feet to tread upon? Every actor is supposed to have one book inside him; every woman has a thousand disappointments, joys, sorrows, heartaches she carries around within her secret self. Being both an actor and a woman, I cannot feel that my life has been a bed of roses. It has had many vicissitudes, many frustrations, many rewards. I write about it for many reasons, not the least of which is the hope that it may be a guidepost to others.

When my mother died in 1975, I was not invited to her memorial service. Only after burning the telephone wires from coast to coast were my daughter and I permitted to attend. It was then that I felt I must eventually straighten out misconceptions, erroneous conclusions, ill-considered judgments concerning my relationship to my family.

When I had read several biographical obituaries of my film career, read the inaccuracies, the false assumptions, the downright unrealistic appraisals of various stages of my contractual life in Hollywood,

I felt that someone had to set the record straight. It might as well be me.

I have no wish, within the covers of this book, to air the family linen, to resurrect ghosts from studio closets or broken marriages, to malign, blame, diminish. I shall simply start at the beginning of my life and continue to the present time. I shall write of events as I saw them. I shall pull no punches.

There is much in my life that might make me the envy of many . . . fame, fortune, romance, self-expression, independence. Yet I have found no lasting romance, no marriage that I could salvage without jeopardizing my own happiness or freedom, my own brand of integrity. My career is the result of opportunity and luck as much as anything else.

Being a woman, I have found the road rougher than had I been born a man. Different defenses, different codes of ethics, different approaches to problems and personalities are a woman's lot. I have preferred to shun what is known as feminine wiles, the subterfuge of subtlety, reliance on tears and coquetry to shape my way. I am forthright, often blunt. I have learned to be a realist despite my romantic, emotional nature. I have no illusions that age, the rigors of my profession, disappointments, and unfulfilled dreams have not left their mark.

I am proud that I have carved my path on earth almost entirely by my own efforts, proud that I have compromised in my career only when I had no other recourse, when financial or contractual commitments dictated. Proud that I have never been involved in a physical liaison unless I was deeply attracted or in love. Proud that, whatever my worldly goods may be, they have been achieved by my own labors.

My regrets are the what-might-have-beens. The personal or business relationships that went awry, the misunderstandings, the turning-to-ashes of love and friendship. The needless waste of what now, at my point in life, might provide comfort and solace, pleasure and delight. On the brighter side, many friends reward my days. The memory of those I loved who have departed this earth still warms me.

I have dedicated this book to my mother . . . the one person who, fully aware of my shortcomings, nevertheless appeared to forgive them.

NO
BED
OF
ROSES

———————————

1

FATHER FELL OUT
OF THE FAMILY TREE

FATHER SAID I SHOULD HAVE BEEN NAMED ONYX BECAUSE I WAS UNEX-
pected. Mother said I was conceived on her chaise longue one Saturday afternoon. Father had come home from his chess club with a
moment to spare before dressing for dinner.

A large revolving atlas is entirely responsible for my being born in
the Orient. After attending Harrow, then reading theology at Cambridge to follow in his father's professional footsteps, young Walter
de Havilland became disillusioned by the mistranslations in the
Bible, which, he told me, he had discovered by reading the Sacred
Book not only in Latin and Greek but Aramaic as well. He maintained that to swear on it was a farce.

His one desire was to put not only religion but England as far
away from him as possible. He blamed his dissatisfaction with his
countrymen on my grandfather's limited income, which, nonetheless,
was sufficient to educate the large family well. Father would have
preferred to have gone to Eton and Oxford, which, he felt, were
more *de rigueur* than Harrow and Cambridge. Nor was he satisfied
with Trinity College at Cambridge when he wished to be at King's

College . . . all subtle refinements suitable in a "poor parson's son," as he liked to call himself, who would, one day, marry a genteel lady of equal fastidiousness. He was a victim of the rigid class system of his day.

So, after receiving his M.A. degree, my father placed the index finger of his left hand on the mouth of the Thames, his right index finger at the same latitude on the opposite side of the globe. He found he was pointing to Hokkaido, a remote island in the Sea of Japan, where the tall, blue-eyed aborigines, the Ainus, lived. With perfunctory good-byes, if any at all, to his family, young Walter boarded the next P. & O. boat bound for this windswept no-man's-land. His Cambridge oar, inscribed with his name and the date of the winning race in 1893, his M.A. degree, and his passport were among his few possessions.

In Hokkaido he taught English and French, eventually doing the same in Kobe and finally in Tokyo. Former students of his have told me that he was very strict, autocratic, and given to ridicule, and generally behaved with supercilious hauteur. No doubt he was avenging himself upon a society which had inflicted the same treatment upon him as an undergraduate.

Father was a genuine eccentric. Six feet tall, blue-eyed, undeniably handsome. Walter Augustus de Havilland was a crack shot, a formidable tennis player, and had earned his "blue" on the rowing team at Cambridge. Born on August 31, 1872, in Lewisham, Kent, raised in Guernsey in the Channel Islands, he was the youngest of ten children by my prolific grandfather, the Reverend Charles Richard de Havilland. On Guernsey his ancestors, the de Havillands, the de Beauvoirs, the de Saumarezes, and the de Carterets, had intermarried for centuries. They probably found little else to do on this tiny island but fight for King and Country, save souls, and propagate.

Father's brothers and sisters were acquired in two batches. The first Mrs. de Havilland, exhausted from childbirth, departed this world to make room for my grandmother, the Honorable Margaret Letitia, sister of the eighth Viscount Molesworth. The title is an Anglo-Irish one, and a street in Dublin bears the Molesworth name, for, I gather, one of the black sheep was crass enough to go into trade.

The de Havilland side of the family was proud of its heritage. One ancestor embarked for the wars in England with William the Conqueror, while another accompanied Richard Coeur de Lion to Palestine.

One day in 1949, on my first trip to England, I happened to be driving through Oxford when I remembered I had a relative nearby. Over the telephone, Irene Ollard, a de Havilland from the distaff side, acknowledged that she would be delighted to receive me for tea, but was concerned that I should find her disheveled . . . she had been "working on the tree" all day. Naturally I pictured her overall-clad, up a ladder with saw in hand. Not at all. Upon arriving at her cottage, I found my cousin immaculately tweed-encased, as befits a proper English spinster, with photographs, family chronicles, marriage licenses, yellowed newspaper clippings, *Burke's Peerage* and *Landed Gentry*, as well as *Debrett's* spread about her study like paper napkins after a cocktail party.

Irene's mission in life was to update the family tree, though not to add to it with progeny, and she had abstained from marriage. Undoubtedly she felt the Reverend Charles had borne fruit enough.

Irene gave me two clothbound, shield-embossed volumes of her beloved tree on which admirals, generals, people of accomplishment dangled from every limb, and, on my paternal grandmother's side, with two Plantagenets firmly embedded at the roots. One genealogy I gave to my sister, Olivia, for her son, Benjamin, the other I took home to Brentwood, California, for my daughter, Deborah. After riffling through Deborah's copy, her father, Omaha-born William Dozier, threw it down and scoffed, "You couldn't sell it for fifty cents." Irene would have said he couldn't have bought it for a million pounds.

On this trip I also met my cousins Geoffrey and Hereward de Havilland. Two of Geoffrey's sons had been killed testing planes of their father's manufacture (a third son had sagely stuck to the ground and the design board). Knighted in 1954, shy, introverted Geoffrey senior refused the responsibilities of a higher title, much to Irene's disappointment. He did, however, accept the Order of Merit, for the de Havilland Aircraft Co. contributed illustriously to aviation history with planes such as the Tiger Moth, the Gipsy Moth, the Vampire, the Mosquito, the Albatross, and eventually the Comet, the world's first jet airliner.

In 1949 my newfound family and I flew in a D.H. Dove for my first visit to the Island of Guernsey, where we visited Havilland Hall, once the family home.

* * *

I was to go back to this almost tropical island in the English
Channel in 1968, accompanied by my mother and sister. Our mission then was to scatter my father's ashes into the sea at dusk. But
we managed to smuggle only two-thirds of Pater into St. Peter Port.
In Canada, his third wife, Rose Mary, had been adamant: the other
third should nurture flowers in the soil near Vancouver where he had
lived with her so happily, dying there at the age of ninety-six. I remonstrated with her, suggesting Father was not a birthday cake to be
parceled out in such a manner. Nevertheless, she divided his remains
meticulously into three packages, one for each daughter, the third for
herself and British Columbia.

2

THE TOSS OF A COIN

MOTHER'S ANCESTRY IS LESS WELL-DOCUMENTED. BORN LILIAN AUgusta Ruse, on June 11, 1886, she hated her last name and insisted upon an accent over the final vowel. Reading, in Berkshire, was her birthplace. That it was "an industrial town" was a considerable blot on her escutcheon, she felt. I gather that her father was comfortably off, for she was convent-schooled, tutored in piano and voice, and she practiced long hours each day while her brother, Ernest, earned his degree at the University of London. She adored her father, loathed her mother, and seldom corresponded with her only sister, Ethel. No doubt about it, Mother preferred men.

Lilian was a snob, which is to say she had exquisite taste in all things, selectivity, a rigid code of behavior, and not one mediocre thought in her head. She also had an unswerving sense of class distinction which was eventually to cause her much anguish in the democratic United States. Like most Victorian girls, she was not allowed to "go on the stage," but she taught at Reading University before her marriage in 1914.

Five feet tall, auburn-haired, with a decided aquiline nose, she thought she was beautiful. Justly proud of her legs, inclined to weight, she bemoaned the fact that "you girls ruined my figure." She never passed a mirror or shopwindow without looking at her reflection. She had the world's most beautiful speaking voice. As I am not a musician, I can only say her singing voice was melodious and well phrased, and as a child I was in heaven when her soprano notes in "A Little Brown Bird Singing" or "Who Is Sylvia? What Is She?" would come floating up the stairs to my sickroom. Her diction, her choice of words, the timbre of her voice could make angels weep with jealousy.

Before the outbreak of the First World War, Lilian had left her native England for Japan, where her brother, Ernest Ruse, taught at the Waseda University. As Walter de Havilland also taught there, as well as at the Imperial University, it is quite likely my parents-to-be met at a faculty gathering. Though by now father's main profession was that of patent attorney (the late Lawrence Langner, founder of the Theatre Guild, was a New York partner), his M.A. degree from Cambridge was accepted as the equivalent from a Japanese university. Evidently, he was fluent in French and Chinese as well as Japanese.

A year later, on her return trip to England via the Panama Canal, Mother discovered her by now ardent suitor was also on board. Weary of his pursuit, she found herself standing by the rail of their ship as it steamed out of the harbor of New Orleans being proposed to for the umpteenth time. "Let's toss for it," she gaily mocked. A silver coin was flipped into the air. She lost. Upon docking at New York City, on November 30, 1914, they found a justice of the peace to officiate. Mother was to say the marriage was Father's way of avoiding the draft! After a brief honeymoon at Niagara Falls, the voyage was resumed, this time in one cabin instead of two.

On their return to Japan, my parents settled comfortably in a large, attractive house in an exclusive residential section of Tokyo. Later the house became the Swedish Embassy. Eventually it was razed, and the land where it stood is now occupied by a new wing of the Hotel Okura.

Mother had studied acting at the Royal Academy of Dramatic Art in London, singing with the Master of the King's Musick, Sir Arthur Parrott, and had toured England with composer Ralph Vaughan Williams, illustrating his music. Thus she was in great demand in the European colony. After a dinner of countless courses, served by white-gloved, kimono-clad butlers, she would be called upon to sing and play the piano, much to the annoyance of Father. He felt that all women should be seen, preferably undressed, and not heard at all.

Their marriage was doomed from the start. As a husband, Father felt that the proper life of an Englishman in Japan was to spend his leisure hours at his chess and go clubs. (He wrote a book on the intricate Oriental game: *The A.B.C.'s of Go*.) He played tennis and the stock market and delighted in upsetting the social smugness of the British colony as much as possible.

Father was geisha-trained. I was sixteen when he took me through the Yoshiwara, a quarter that specializes in catering to masculine desires. I had to agree with him that the grounds of the compound were indeed magnificent with their dwarf gardens and carp-filled pools, while the kimonoed girls, combing their long black hair on flowered balconies, were seductive and utterly feminine. He explained to his virgin daughter that the Western habit of kissing on the mouth was ridiculous and unsanitary, whereas the Japanese centuries-old tradition of coping with sex in red-light districts was highly civilized and a great art. As we turned from the gardens, he muttered to the sky, "I say, if one wants something done expertly, one consults an expert, what!"

That Lilian Rusé, cultivated, artistic, flirtatious, should toss a coin into the air and find herself at twenty-eight pledged for life to this particular forty-two-year-old antisocial bachelor seems incongruous. Let me not quibble . . . but for their ill-made bed there would be no Olivia Mary or Joan de Beauvoir.

3

MADE IN JAPAN

FOR ME, BEING BORN IN JAPAN HAD MANY REWARDS AND FEW DRAW-backs. Only during the first days of World War II did I find it inconvenient. One day in December 1941, the F.B.I. knocked on my Beverly Hills door in search of sequestered guns and shortwave radios. Evidently, all Japanese-born were suspect and, therefore, so was I. Later I was almost arrested while returning across the Mexican border from Tijuana. In those post-Pearl Harbor days, the guard did not think my reply to his question as to my place of birth was at all amusing.

Olivia Mary was born one year, three months, and three weeks before her only sibling. She was still too young to accept the arrival of a competitor for the affections of her parents and adoring staff when I made my appearance on October 22, 1917. As amahs were plentiful in those days, both de Havilland children had their own day and night nurses. Obviously there would be rivalry over their charges.

Also, because of eczema from a diet of goat's milk, I was swathed in cotton wool from head to toe until I was almost two. Mother was highly "germ-conscious" and insisted on strict nursery procedures, a fact which kept the baby sisters apart, creating a breach we were never to span.

Brown-eyed, olive-skinned Olivia, Mother told me, never toddled near the crib of her tow-haired, hazel-eyed baby sister. Her horoscope suggests that Olivia would have fared better as an only child. Born July 1, 1916, she has always been a stout believer in the rule of primogeniture. Perhaps my being a puny child had a great deal to do with her resentment, as I am sure I was a fretful infant, and in the nursery she was no longer preeminent with the servants or her parents.

We were not to remain in that nursery long. Mother's whole attention was absorbed in us, in amateur theatricals, and in entertaining the European social set. Father felt slighted and sought other playmates. Soon Mother's breakfast trays were being served by an upstairs maid who was wearing increasingly beautiful and costly kimonos. Though Victorian, Mother was no fool. It was Yoki-san who had to go . . . or us. It was us.

With Father, February 1919 found mother and daughters aboard the S.S. *Siberia Maru* bound for San Francisco, en route to Italy, where Mother felt the climate was suitable for rearing her two English roses. After we landed in California, Father, nursing his wounded pride, returned to Japan and Yoki-san. We were not to see him again for several years. While Mother consulted lawyers, she temporarily nestled her brood in an apartment edging Golden Gate Park. My earliest memory is of the eucalyptus trees and the greenest of flower-fringed lawns. For some reason I remember particularly the sound of foghorns from the bay and the "bufflo," as I pronounced that hairy beast in the zoo . . . just like the one on an American nickel I was shown.

Mother's haunting fear was that we would be taken from her, as Father had already threatened. (Years later when I was to go through the same legalities with my own daughter's father, I knew the sensation well.) After Mother's lawyers told her that California laws were more sympathetic to the maternal parent—far more than Japan or Italy—we stopped our hegira and went no farther. Besides, both small girls were in and out of hospitals with assorted childhood maladies.

The first time I "died" was in St. Francis Hospital in San Francisco. German measles plus streptococcal throat with a raging, unceasing fever had put me into a coma. I was given up for dead. Mrs. de Havilland was told that she could go into the patient's room, as all hopes of survival had passed. With her, waiting in the corridor, was an acquaintance (Mother never had "friends" in America then) who was a devout Unity practitioner. The lady asked if she might go into the room alone and pray by the bedside of the dying child. Though not religious herself, Mother consented. In minutes the door opened. Mother entered to see her three-year-old daughter sitting up in bed, the fever miraculously vanished, her color restored.

As a child, I prayed quite regularly, for, being ill most of the time, whom else did I have to talk to? I played it safe. To petition some-one "on the other side" to assist me, to deliver my messages person-ally as it were, seemed the pragmatic thing to do. Whom did I know up there? Well, Mrs. Bruiner, an aunt of two of my playmates, had died. I vaguely remembered seeing her from time to time when we played tag in their garden. Mrs. Bruiner would have to do. Thus, for years, it was nightly and several times a day, "Dear God and Mrs. Bruiner, please . . ." Only five years ago, when we were discussing the German measles experience, I asked my mother the name of the practitioner who had performed the miracle of prayer attributed to saving my life. "Mrs. Bruiner," she said.

The second time I "died" is as clear to me this day as when it oc-curred at age ten. I had rheumatic fever. For months I was forbidden to turn in bed without assistance. Injections were administered into the peritoneum by white-clad nurses every four hours around the clock. I was given no solid food for two months. Late one afternoon, as the sun was setting, I remember soaring above my bed, seeing my body lying below me. As I rose through the french door overlooking our poplar-edged garden, I was met by a group of friends, as I can only call them. Possibly there were ten. Though they were facially unrecognizable, the sense of loving understanding and familial affinity was pervasive. Their images were colorless, white on white. As though in unison, the figures conveyed to me that I was welcome to join them immediately, yet first there was something they would like me to do. I felt no fear, only gratitude at being acceptable, pleased that I might please them by doing their bidding. With a sense of serenity and purpose, I turned back and reentered my body.

A previous religious experience had occurred at the Notre Dame Convent in Belmont, California, where I was enrolled at the age of nine. Up at six-thirty each day, the small children were shooed, bleary-eyed and hungry, rain or shine, to Mass. Despite colds or tummy-aches, we threaded our way in the dark through the maze of covered paths that led to the chapel. This particular day was Good Friday, so the 7 A.M. Mass was attended not only by the entire convent, but by Catholic neighbors as well.

I remember kneeling on the mosaic floor. There were no prie-dieus for the little ones as all the pews behind us were filled. Close beside me, smiling down from her niche, stood the Virgin Mary. Weak from hunger, from trying to balance on my knees through the long prayers, I keeled over halfway through the service. The next thing I knew I was being dragged from the scene of my disgrace by two black-robed nuns and placed in a white iron cot in the infirmary. I was later told that I insisted I had had a visitation from the Holy Mother. That very day, the nuns having less faith than I, Joan was removed from the convent. Olivia finished the term.

It was blissful returning home. I had missed my mother desperately and had been excruciatingly homesick. The Virgin had indeed performed a miracle. In gratitude, I placed a small statue of her on my dressing table in a makeshift shrine. Soon it disappeared. Philosophically, I figured that Mother couldn't stand the competition.

Another confirmation of the proficiency of my hot-line-to-the-great-switchboard-in-the-sky occurred when I was twenty-two. I was playing at the Cypress Point golf course in northern California. It was only my sixth game of golf. This exquisite and difficult oceanside course shares honors with Pebble Beach during the Bing Crosby annual tournament. My partner that day was Marion Hollins, once winner of the Women's U. S. Amateur, who, with Sam Morse, had developed this seventeen-mile golfers' paradise. The other two players were Charles Boyer and my husband at the time, Brian Aherne.

My golf game was nonexistent. I could not even be called a duffer. On the short fifteenth hole, which spans a sea-churned cove, we found William Powell and his wife, "Mousie," and two or three other friends who had stopped by to watch our tee shots. Frozen with fear and embarrassment, when my turn came I placed my ball on the turf-embedded tee. Addressing both golf ball and God simultaneously, I put my head down and closed my eyes, and with no time for preliminaries, I sidestepped Mrs. Bruiner and placed an emergency call to the Almighty. "Please, God, don't let me make an ass of myself." Opening my eyes, I swung my three wood. Looking up, I heard shouts of triumph. There below me on the sloping turf I saw my ball ring the pole and drop into the flag-marked cup. A hole in one on my sixth game of golf? Some people would say it was because I had kept my head down during my swing. If she's forgiven me for bypassing her, Mrs. Bruiner and I know better.

Brian Aherne was of frugal nature. After the eighteenth hole was played, he bundled me, still in my golf shoes, into our waiting station wagon. Admonishing me to keep my head well down under the dashboard, he sped away. The traditional round of champagne proffered to club members and guests by the lucky player was thus circumvented. Whenever I am asked, "What's your handicap?" the same reply always comes to mind: "Men."

4

FATHER FIGURE FOUND

WITHIN MONTHS OF OUR ARRIVAL IN CALIFORNIA, MOTHER MOVED US south from foggy San Francisco to the Vendome Hotel in sunny San Jose. Surrounded by gardens of yellow and red cannas, lawns, and giant oaks, it was the perfect place for a lady who knew no domestic arts to nurture her children. One day, while Mother was sitting on a tree-shaded bench, embroidering yet keeping a watchful eye on her gamboling twosome, Olivia skipped up to her and tugged at her skirt. The eager child chirped, "Dana-san, Dana-san!" She pointed to a mild-looking American gentleman, reading the newspapers on a nearby bench. As we still spoke Japanese to some extent, Mother recognized that her four-year-old daughter was saying, "Father, Father." Thoroughly unabashed, the determined little ambassadress made the introductions, presenting our future stepfather, George Milan Fontaine, to his next bride.

"Danny," as we were allowed to call him, rather than Dana-san, was a recent widower, having lost his wife and only daughter within the year. A son, George, had been placed in military school, leaving the father a lonely and sorrowing man. Mr. Fontaine managed the O. A. Hale department store in San Jose for many years. Later he became an investment counselor. Then Mother would say, "Thank God, he's no longer in trade."

I remember Danny with mixed emotions. Of medium height, pink-cheeked, a salt-of-the-earth American, he smelled of castile soap, Harris tweed, and soda mints, and was hypochondriacal. A stern disciplinarian, his reaction to humor was only a slight upcurve of his lips and a heightening of the blue of his eyes.

He delighted us with awesome stories of his childhood on his father's trading post in Minnesota, where he was born. He told us he often spent the night bedded on a shelf in the store which was constructed of logs. He slept with his gun beside him, on vigil against possible attack by marauding Indians.

Catholic by birth, he had trained for the Jesuit priesthood, and, like Walter de Havilland, the more he studied, the more violently he turned away from religion. Years later, on his deathbed, refusing the last rites of the Church, he whispered to the hovering priest, "I've lived my adult life without religion and I shall die without it."

He was an intellectual, shunning the society of man as a waste of valuable time, eschewing all sports or pursuits that were not "constructive." I can well see why Mother chose him to be her partner in raising these two girls who were just reaching the precocious age when a strong paternal hand was needed.

I doubt if it was a love match on either side. Rather, a sober, well-thought-out, second marriage for a displaced divorcee on short rations, then in her mid-thirties, and a serious-minded widower in his forties. We two children were to resent bitterly her choice and to balk at the heavy yoke of his authority. That resentment was to shape our destinies and take both of us, eventually, to Hollywood.

From the Vendome Hotel Mother and her girls moved to the foothills of the Santa Cruz Mountains, to the prune- and apricot-orchard country of Saratoga, California. In the early Twenties this sleepy hamlet was inhabited by farmers, artists, and "comfortable" retired couples. The authors Charles and Kathleen Norris lived not far away; violinist prodigy Yehudi Menuhin and his family settled in nearby Alma, as would the Alfred Hitchcocks in later years. Zoë Akins, the playwright, once served me fresh peaches and vanilla ice cream for lunch at her home in Atherton, thus becoming my first culinary idol.

A family called Leis owned a vast Japanese summer place named Hakone in the wooded hills, complete with shoji, tatami-carpeted floors, and Oriental help, making us feel close to the land of our birth. We children delighted in playing on the high-arched, red-lacquered bridges overlooking the ornamental pools, spearing the too numerous frogs with bamboo poles.

Tojo, their gardener, was my first conquest. He would often bring wicker baskets laden with fresh-picked string beans, curling lettuce, and fruit to our door. He openly declared his devotion by presenting me with a white china Siamese cat. I realized at six that I was marked to be a femme fatale.

Often at Hakone weekend guests would be Alfred "Poppa" Hertz, conductor of the San Francisco Symphony, Gaetano Merola, conductor of the opera, and numerous opera stars and musicians. A buffet lunch would be set out on wooden tables under the overhanging madrone trees. We children, seated on benches, were rapt in attention while listening to backstage stories and anecdotes from the music world. After lunch the guests would enter the Japanese house, where they sang and played various instruments. Hakone was a child's paradise.

Until Mother could get her divorce, we lived for a time at The Lundblads, a gray-shingled, paying-guest-and-meals boardinghouse on Oak Street. Our temporary home was run by the Swedish couple, their daughter Hazel, and her husband, Joseph Bargas. Mr. Paul Lundblad, or "Grandpa," as we were permitted to call him, often took us in his horse-drawn hay wagon up the dirt trails to the mountaintop, while Grandma Lundblad let me watch her knead dough, roll out the flat Swedish *bröt* to be served for tea. Often I was allowed to garnish the rows and rows of salads awaiting the next meal. The best treat of all was turning the handle of the ice cream churn in peach season.

How comforting was that big Swedish kitchen with its great round table where the family met for tea each afternoon! We children were allowed our cambric tea of hot milk, flavored with tea and sugar, while the adults were served coffee from a gray-speckled enameled pot. A whole egg, shell and all, went into the pot just before serving to clarify the fragrant, steaming beverage. Then came the sugar-sprinkled rolls, the flat bread, and homemade jams and honey. Tea over, I sat on Mr. Bargas' lap while he read aloud "Little Orphan Annie" and "The Katzenjammer Kids" from *The San Francisco Chronicle*.

It was Mr. Bargas, with pillow tucked into his white-cotton-trimmed red suit, who played Santa Claus at Christmas, dispensing Swiss cuckoo clocks and animal-shaped soap to us children from under the ceiling-tall fir. We helped trim that great tree with glass birds, looping garlands of cranberries and popcorn, shiny ornaments marked "Made in Bavaria." Wax candles of various colors were twisted into holders on the outer branches and lit on Christmas Eve, when the family and guests assembled in the living room. No other occasion has ever been so exciting to me as that solemn moment when Santa Bargas would pick up the first brightly wrapped package from under the laden branches.

Though I have long ceased to believe in the stork or the Easter bunny, I still find Christmas a time of magic and awe. In the film script of Daphne du Maurier's *Rebecca*, there is a line spoken by "I" de Winter: "I wish I could save this moment like scent in a bottle." My childhood Christmases at The Lundblads were such as these.

It was at this boardinghouse that I first knew Olivia and I were destined to become actresses. The Lundblad attic contained huge steamer trunks of clothes, musty, yellowed with age, saved for no particular reason other than thrift and nostalgia. We two delighted in sneaking up the creaking wooden stairs, in dressing up in the elaborately flowered hats, whaleboned lace-and-satin gowns with tippets and furbelows. A precocious mother's boy of approximately our age, a boarder like ourselves, was unusually obnoxious one particular day. Set on revenge, Olivia and I hurried to our secret cache, donned our borrowed finery, and, with much affectation, assumed what we felt was grown-up conversation. Promenading before the pest, we completely ignored him as we strolled up and down the long hall, waving fans and twirling petticoats. Darting after us, the bewildered brat remonstrated, "You're Joan, you're Olivia, aren't you? Aren't you?" His final query, his lack of total conviction persuaded me that we had found our métier.

As Olivia was approaching school age, we moved from the boardinghouse into two green cottages, connected by a latticed stile, that still stand today opposite the playground of the Saratoga Grammar School. Obviously Mother and her suitor wished privacy in the evenings when Danny would motor out in his dark-green Chevrolet with its two runningboards, returning before midnight to his home in San Jose. One cottage was Mother's "suite," while the other was shared by Olivia, myself, and our governess, a forbidding lady called only by her surname, de Belville.

This was not a particularly happy time for me. Mother was frequently absent, going to "the city," as San Francisco is still called by those living on the peninsula, squired to concerts and plays by Mr. Fontaine.

Olivia had learned to read before she was six. For some reason, de Belville had left us alone the evening my sister chose to flaunt her erudition. Listening to her read aloud the crucifixion from the Bible in mounting gusto, I not only experienced man's inhumanity to man, but that of sister to sister.

When she read of the crown of thorns and the soldier's stab in the side of Jesus, my screams were heard down the entire row of cottages. Gleefully persisting, Olivia continued reading of Christ's journey up the Via Dolorosa, and only when she had reached the part where the nails were being driven into His flesh was I rescued by a neighbor from the last cottage on the row. Years later, when I walked the same route that Christ had traversed, the incident returned in all its horror. To this day I cannot look at a statue of Christ on the crucifix or pass the Stations of the Cross without that same anguish recurring.

Olivia's precocity in reading had its humorous side. I was madly infatuated with film star Ramon Novarro, whom I had just seen in *The Prisoner of Zenda* at a showing in the grammar school auditorium. Not to be outdone, my sister maintained that she was madly in love with the world's most famous man, since Nosmo King's name was written on walls, over doors, wherever the eye fell. When I learned to read I realized she was right . . . NO SMOKING signs were omnipresent. I was not "myzzled," to use her favorite word . . . she had not *misled* me!

I remember being in my high chair, bib-bound, with Page & Shaw's fig jam spread on buttered bread on the tray before me. Junket, apple betty, tapioca pudding. "Oh, Mr. Gallagher, Oh, Mr. Shean" on the phonograph. I remember my shiny black patent-leather cat, Felix, with his red felt bow tie and green bolero jacket. When Felix disappeared I was inconsolable. Mother had tossed him into the Franklin stove when his excelsior stuffing refused to stay in place. No doll, no other toy, ever conquered my affections like Felix.

Except a pink balloon. One Saturday afternoon Danny and Mother had brought us back helium-filled balloons from the city to placate us for their continued absences. Olivia and I, thrilled by our presents, trotted up the tree-lined road beyond the school, the balloon strings tightly clenched in our chubby fists. Being of scientific mind, I let go my string, despite earlier parental warning, to see what would happen. Up and up soared my new treasure, up into the clouds, pink-tinged with sundown. After Felix's demise, the pain of this loss was too great to bear. As I stood, tear-stained, I saw one rosy cumulus cloud, luminescent in the sunset. It would have to be my balloon. It just had to be. My balloon had turned into a pink cloud and would float, forever and ever, high in the heavens for all the world to see.

5

GROWING PAINS

OUR BEING SICKLY CHILDREN WAS PARTLY BECAUSE OF OVER-ATTENTIVE nurses and an overconscientious mother. Oh, those scratchy wool sweaters, those long stockings attached to a pantywaist. The high-button boots. I still feel the buttonhook cutting into my flesh as the monstrosities were fastened each morning, one leg at a time resting on de Belville's lap. The agony of humiliation and embarrassment at sunbaths, stark naked on the front porch for all passersby to witness, timed by a stopwatch, so many minutes on each side, like a broiling lamb chop. The castor oil and orange juice chaser, the Scott's emulsion, administered by the tablespoon as I stood on a steamer trunk which still bore labels from foreign lands.

With tears streaming I gagged down the bitter licorice cough medicine, manufactured by the Smith Brothers in cigar-shaped portions to be melted on the back of the black-iron, potbellied stove in the living room. And the mustard plasters that took the skin off with them as they were removed after an exact twenty minutes. Constant temperature-taking, tongue-checking, too public queries about elimination. All sorts of indignities done to the colon. (How modest children really are and how easily humiliated.) Milk of Magnesia. I can still hear the ominous shaking of that "family-size," white-labeled,

Madonna-blue bottle. My earliest memories are of bathrobe-clad women approaching my bed in the middle of the night with instruments of medical torture.

By age six, I had endured so many afflictions that I was selected in first grade to be the guinea pig. The visiting nurse, as I stood by the teacher's desk, gave me the school's first smallpox vaccination to show the trusting class that the injection didn't hurt. Of course it did, but I'd long since learned that screams of protest begot slaps or Coventry in dark closets or trunks.

Our mental health was also under constant scrutiny. My coordination was checked by Danny tossing pennies onto the lawn; then, stopwatch in hand, he would time how quickly I could pick them up. To this day I drop more objects than I retrieve in defiance of that examination, the purpose of which I was thoroughly aware.

At Stanford University in Palo Alto, Dr. Lewis Terman was originating his genetic studies of genius, scouring the area for gifted children. His tests were later known as the Stanford-Binet Intelligence Quotient tests. The de Havilland girls were taken to his office to be rated, as were many other California children (one of whom, Alfred Wright, I would marry in 1964). Olivia, on the day of her test, had a fever. I tested higher than she—so high, as a matter of fact, the examiners called me back. The only thing I can remember was that when asked what I did at night, I answered logically, "Wet the bed." For goodness sake, they didn't want some obvious answer like "sleep," did they?

What damage is done to many children informed of the outcome of those tests. Not only are the results changeable from year to year, but they can fluctuate according to many external circumstances. A child told of a high I.Q. may become indolent and conceited, while another, if informed of a low rating, may become discouraged, defeated, and despairing. Unfortunately, Olivia was told the results of both our tests. Joan was undeniably her enemy. Besides the inexcusable intrusion into her life—that of Joan's birth—this latest display of arrogance was the last straw for the older sister. I regret that I remember not one act of kindness from her all through my childhood.

My life in the Green Cottages reminds me of a sea creature, struggling from the mire to exist on alien land. I must have been five when one summer's evening, the sun not yet down, I was taken from my bed and, in my Japanese kimono, led outside by Danny. There under the oak trees, in the fallen leaves, he had dug a shallow grave. "This is where I shall put you if you don't stop biting your nails," he warned.

My continuing terror only made the habit worse. I soon chewed my Kleenex-thin nails to the elbows. Undaunted, Mr. Fontaine brought home a pair of leather handcuffs. I was ordered, hands shackled behind me, into the school yard for all the children to witness my shame.

Eczema, too, caused me humiliation. Periodically, my skin would break out in a rash resembling poison ivy, and just as itchy. To stop my scratching one day, my entire face was bandaged with only slits for eyes and mouth. I was commanded to school with dire warnings of excruciating punishment if I, for one moment, removed the white gauze mask before returning home. I didn't, but with two hands I stretched a child's handkerchief across my unsightly face. All through classes, in the corridors, at recess, I never once lowered my hands. As no one snickered, I assumed my eccentricity had gone unnoticed. Later I learned the teacher had warned the students not to deride me for my affliction.

Olivia did not get off scot-free from the Draconian discipline, either. One day, after telling a fib at home, she went off to school, relieved at not being spanked on the spot. Before noon, the third grade door opened and Mrs. de Havilland strode up to the teacher's desk. Having obtained permission from the startled schoolmistress to address the class, Olivia's parent told them that they had a liar among them who was, unfortunately, her daughter. "Prevaricators should be shunned," said Mrs. de Havilland, expecting the class to take her advice and act accordingly.

I doubt if they did. Olivia was a ringleader, captain of "The Fearless Five," a group of "A" students whose days were spent in harassing and exasperating the teachers to the point of resignation. Olivia's seventh-grade class was notable, having six teachers in one year. I participated in one prank. The girls' lavatory in the old school was in the basement, lit by high windows near the ceiling. One summer, before it was torn down, several of us broke into the building. We stuffed the toilets with rags, flushing them continuously until the whole area was flooded. Rub-a-dub-dub, in metal washtubs we rowed about our child-made lake in high glee. Fortunately, we were never caught and, like staunch comrades in crime, were utterly incredulous when the school superintendent interrogated us. Goodness, what terrible things some children will do. We shook our heads in unison at the thought of what the world was coming to.

Mother was building a house for us. We were frequently taken after school to watch its progress. I loved the smell of the new-sawed wood, the tar paper. The miracle of chicken wire, stucco, and shingles all combining to shape my palace, so long dreamed about, and now soon to be realized. As I played among the upright beams, the curls of wood shavings, the scraps left over from the carpenters' lunch pails, my delight was boundless. No longer nomads, we would have a permanent home. "Befitting our station," Mother said.

Danny supervised the plans. He was meticulous: a solar water-heating system on the roof (in 1924!), two feet of soil removed from the surface of the garden and replaced with sieved loam. To promote proper pollination, two trees of each variety stood like soldiers in the orchard. It is reputed he baked a cake before designing the kitchen to learn how best to conserve time and motion. A laundry chute, a coal chute, an electric dishwasher, a clothes washer, a hidden ironing board that came down from its closeted hideaway, a "receivador" so that the milkman and grocery boy need not enter the house with deliveries. The stove was both electric and coal-burning should there be a power failure. The effect was totally efficient, totally charmless. The house motto should have been "A place for everything and everything in its place . . . or else."

Astride three half-acre lots along its ginkgo-edged sidewalk, La Paloma Avenue soon had a two-storied, awkward-shaped Tudorish house. For privacy, one lot was left uncultivated; the house occupied the middle lot, while the corner one nurtured the fruit trees, lippia paths between them, as well as a play yard with a slide and sandbox for us and ground enough for my horticultural pursuits. The property was surrounded by a tall pyracantha hedge. Though the grandest one on the street, our new home was never to open its doors to most of the neighbors, and their children passed through them only for an occasional birthday party.

Neither Mother nor Danny had any interest in the "locals." Mother's infrequent bridge games with socially acceptable ladies were considered frivolous in the extreme, even by her daughters. I often think of how lonely, how displaced Mother must have felt in our rural community which had turned her into a housewife, nurse, chauffeur . . . this laughing, gay creature who should have been an enchantress in Lotus Land. And I often think, How was I, a six-year-old, to know of the difficulties my mother had encountered with my father? Letters show that he cut off all maintenance for his wife and his children. Mother's only recourse was to go to Japan and figure a way out of her marital cul-de-sac.

After consultation with lawyers in America as well as England and Japan it became clear the only way to handle the situation was for Father to sue for divorce.

So when we were firmly established at 21 La Paloma Avenue, Mother sailed for Japan and the year-long divorce proceedings, knowing that Danny, with the help of a housekeeper, would be a diligent overseer of her brood.

The day she sailed, I was inconsolable. I clutched the legs of the dining-room table and would not come out until nightfall. Olivia went out to play.

The motherless year of 1924 was torture to me. Only when Danny lit the living-room fire at night and, with me on his lap, read from *The Animal Book* would I forget the white-cold ache which lived under my left collarbone. Life was simply suspended, a vacuum until Mother's return.

This period, however, contained an episode that was to change our lives. Mr. Fontaine bathed us little girls in the tub each night. The washcloth would tarry too long in intimate places. Olivia and I, never given to confidences, did agree that something was odd. We were to have the same discussion eight years later, this time joined by Mother, with more serious consequences. Fathers and daughters, stepfathers and stepdaughters. The story is not new.

6

DISCIPLINE TIME

MOTHER WAS COMING HOME.

She had established herself in the residence of a respected lady friend in Tokyo, and when Father tried to get her to come and live with him, she refused. Mother's psychology worked. Humiliated, Father went to court as the plaintiff. Judgment was handed down on February 23, 1925. The plaintiff accused the defendant of willful desertion. The decree, granted by the First Civil Department of Tokyo District Court, gives no provision for alimony . . . the children of the marriage were not even mentioned. Mother was ordered to pay the court costs.

After almost a year away, Mother was coming home. What's more, she was bringing Japanese dolls, one for each of us. My ecstasy was fever-pitch. On *the great day* we were dressed carefully in our navy-blue reefers, matching hats with streamers down the back, white gloves, strapped, patent-leather Mary Jane shoes. The new four-door Chrysler inched its way along the Bayshore highway to the Embarcadero, to the bustle and excitement of the pier. With a clank of the gangplank, Mother's argosy docked. At last my only friend, my living madonna, my ministering angel would soon be in the car with us, heading home forever.

But not so. A strange lady in unfamiliar and fashionable clothes was flirting outrageously in the front seat with Danny. The promised doll was not cuddly like Felix, not blond and hazel-eyed like me, but a stiff, ceramic Japanese geisha, chalk-faced, in ceremonial wig and robes. She even came in a sandalwood coffin, lined in red silk. We children were told to sit more quietly, to stop quarreling, trying to attract attention. Dear God and Mrs. Bruiner, the sky is falling.

April 1925: soon another separation of mother and children. Mrs. de Havilland became Mrs. Fontaine in Santa Barbara.

After the honeymoon, the house on La Paloma smoothed into an unshakable routine. Mother learned to cook, Danny to garden. The housekeeper was replaced by an adorable Japanese lady, who laundered and ironed, waxed the floors, and did the heavy cleaning.

After school and weekends, we children were given assorted chores: shoes to polish, lawns to weed, fruit to pick before we could swim or ride the pony cart of our "acceptable" neighbors, the Chauncey Goodrich family. Their estate, Hayfield House, abutted on La Paloma Avenue; their stone gates faced our hedge. The driveway wound through orchards until it reached a large fieldstone house, webbed with 'Paul Scarlett' roses, surrounded by lawns and gardens. It was in their pool that I learned to swim.

Unrelieved discipline reigned at La Paloma. If we were good, the reward was a Saturday-night movie in neighboring Los Gatos. If bad, the miscreant remained at home to contemplate the adage that crime does not pay. Upon the family's return, the plot of the film was not to be disclosed to the disobedient sister.

Other than movies, our treats were the Saturday opera over the Stromberg-Carlson radio, "The Palmolive Hour" with Paul Oliver and Olive Palmer, and "Amos 'n' Andy," as well as trips to San Francisco, with museums, aquarium, symphonies, and theatre. How exciting it was to see Otis Skinner in *The Merchant of Venice*, Betty Bronson in *Peter Pan*; to be terrified, too close to the timpani section, while Poppa Hertz conducted Wagner; to go backstage to visit Queena Mario after her performance in Humperdinck's *Hansel and Gretel*.

One great treat was being piped aboard the U.S.S. *Saratoga* as the aircraft carrier lay at anchor in San Francisco Bay. Admiral and Mrs. Fredrick Horne had been stationed in Yokohama and were "Aunt Alma" and "Uncle Freddie" from our babyhood.

One San Francisco "treat trip" recalls an incident that makes me cringe to this day. We'd been staying the weekend at the Clift Hotel, and had packed our bags. I was told to wait in the lobby while the car was brought round. Spying all that lovely white notepaper, embossed envelopes, the miniature bars of soap in our rooms, I hastily stuffed all I could find up the front of my slipover sweater. I buttoned my reefer, donned my white gloves, and innocently whistled my way to the lobby. Sitting alone in a straight-back brocaded chair, my feet not touching the floor, I saw the newsstand lady beckon me. She held up the funnies. Eagerly I skipped toward her, only to hear peals of laughter on all sides. My cache was dislodging itself, cascading like snow in a blizzard along the flowered carpet. The more I stooped to retrieve my stolen goods, the more fell to the ground. The laughter became guffaws. I've never stolen anything again, anywhere. That lesson was quite enough, thank you.

At La Paloma, it was always learning time. Perfection was the least expected of us. No faculty, no talent, no hidden attribute must lie fallow. Real education was at home, not at school, "Especially not American schools," said Mother. Danny concurred.

What? *Walking* lessons? Yes! We were drilled up and down the tree-lined sidewalk, toeing out on the center line. Not STRAIGHT, not IN, but OUT, OUT, OUT! That was the way nature intended, said Danny's latest copy of *The American Medical Journal*. Obedient Joan now walks in a permanent ballet fifth position, while defiant Olivia's toes point straight ahead.

Diction lessons? To be sure. Around the dining-room table sat the seven- and eight-year-old sisters, reading aloud from Shakespeare. After a slurred or mispronounced word, a ruler was smartly applied to taut knuckles by Mother of the golden voice.

Manners? All sorts. Friends of our parents, of whom there were few, could be addressed by their first names only if requested and if "Uncle" or "Aunt" came first. "Sir" and "Ma'am" were subservient and never used by "persons of rank," said Mother. Curtseying was obligatory. No Christmas package could be unwrapped before a thank-you note was written on hand-ruled paper to the donor of the last opened gift.

And table manners: One does not butter bread in the air, but on the butter plate, that's what it's for. Knife and fork are left together, side by side, slightly right of center on the dinner plate. A soup bowl is never tilted while the soup is spooned. Knife and fork are used together, none of this American juggling of the fork from left to right hand. Salad comes between the entrée and dessert course, as in Europe. A finger bowl is used not to swim in, but for dipping the fingers. One does not leave the table without permission. A flick of Danny's thumb and middle finger would force an errant elbow off the table with alacrity. And sit up straight!

Dinnertime was for conversation. It was for abstract ideas. It was for lessons, too. Danny would extol the virtues of having adequate life insurance. For example: That day a widow with three hungry children had come into his office, selling pencils. He had refused her with a stern lecture that her fate was her own fault, as she should have had more foresight. We had to "finish the plate" with tears falling into it, our stomachs knotted with pity and compassion for the three starving children.

To teach us the value of thrift, we were taken to the local bank, where savings accounts were opened for both of us. Our pin money, saved from neighborhood chores or an occasional allowance, was dutifully deposited there. In the Depression, Mr. Fontaine closed out both our accounts and used the money to pay bills. Nothing could have taught me more about letting a man handle my finances. I only wish I had remembered that lesson in future years.

Each afternoon after school ("Come directly home, no loitering, please"), I was confronted by a white-haired spinster who instructed me in arithmetic as well as piano. The multiplication tables were graphed in variously colored crayons, drawn over and over again until I could recite them by heart. And oh, MacDowell's "To a Wild Rose," beaten out to the tick of a metronome. Again, the ferule on the knuckles for a misplaced note.

And the ballet lessons. A Miss Johnston held weekly classes in Los Gatos. Olivia and I, clad in black bloomers, green crepe-de-Chine tunics tied with black ribbons at the waist, danced to the tune of Chopin waltzes. We executed endless entrechats, jetés and pliés, one hand on the back of a gilt music chair. We even performed the maypole dance at the Annual Saratoga Prune Festival. Humorously, I liked to allude to us as "The Belles of the Prune Belt."

A Miss Johnson, without the *t*, gave us domestic-science lessons. These included not only the culinary arts but the chemical side of cooking as well. Why a soufflé expands, why it falls. Why Hollandaise sauce curdles, why butter burns.

Once, after the appropriate lesson, we sisters were to surprise our parents with an omelette, the fluffy kind. Halfway through the cooking process, we realized we had left out the cream of tartar. Back into the mixing bowl went the half-cooked mess, the missing ingredient was added, and the whole mixture was again plopped into the black-iron skillet. The result was disastrous. This was the last time Olivia and I shared chef's caps.

I soon learned to curry favor with the grown-ups by mastering the mighty cookstove. My ego rewards were tied to my apron strings. Olivia was smarter. She just wouldn't learn.

Cooking came to me by instinct and observation. Those hours in the Lundblad kitchen, where Grandma never used a recipe, were not wasted. And Santa had left a toy electric stove for me under one of those Christmas trees. I baked my first apple in it, bear a scar on my left hand today from cutting a green quince and missing, tried baking a potato (all of this in my clothes closet) and gave up after four hours and little success. However, when I eventually attended *cordon-bleu* classes in New York under the eagle eye of Dione Lucas, I knew my onions and had learned that creative talent and imagination can find substantial and rewarding outlet in the kitchen.

Long absences due to illness set me apart in classes and playground. I had lost the contact necessary for friendship with my own age group. I hung round the adults, observing and learning. By the time I was ten, I could graft a limb on a tree, splice wire, and mend an electric plug. Having backed the Chrysler up and down La Paloma Avenue when no one was looking, I could rightfully brag that I could drive a car. I could use a soldering iron, change a tire, make an entire dress on the Singer sewing machine. I learned to set up and work a loom, use a hacksaw, wrap caramels professionally at Patty Charlesworth's candy shop ("Made by a Maid at Home"), and put the books back on the public-library shelves after school. Earnings from my odd jobs went to buy white saddle shoes for school. My favorite pastime was picking wild flowers and arranging them, Japanese-fashion, in open wicker baskets with rocks and ferns. These I sold to friendly "aunts" for fifty cents each. Best of all, I cooked for the Prince of Wales. . . .

An illness at the beginning of my first year at Los Gatos High School had resulted in orders from the doctor that I was to have only a half day of classes, no strenuous activities, no social life. Noons found me home in a deserted house, my lunch to prepare, with long afternoons alone. Glorious! First, pull down all the shades. Set the table for two with the best linens, add candles, cosmos and delphiniums from the garden for the centerpiece. Get into my apron, empty the icebox of its leftovers, and, with the aid of herbs and spices, concoct delights never dreamed of by Lucullus or Epicurus. Next, on the phonograph, put on records of Haydn and Mozart, even "My Silent Love," "Night and Day," "Stardust." Now all was ready.

At the stroke of one, I'd open the door and there on the brick steps would be standing H.R.H. the Prince of Wales himself, impeccably dressed in a suit of Glenurquhart plaid, Tyrolean hat in hand. (I'd seen copies of *The Sketch, The Tatler, Illustrated London News.*) Soon he'd be behind my dining-room chair, and after he had seated us both, a two-way conversation of utter sophistication and world-shattering import would ensue as we consumed the embellished leftovers. The champagne glasses held lemonade. H.R.H. pronounced it "a very good year."

My royal guest having departed, promising to return the next day and the next, the dishes done and all traces of our tryst concealed, I'd get out my watercolors and copy the Japanese prints hanging on the living-room walls. These, too, like my wild-flower arrangements, I sold for fifty cents each, though they'd be worth a million times that when my engagement to the Prince was announced. Anyway, it helped pay for the candles.

In France, in 1957, I visited the Duke of Windsor, as he had then become, and his Duchess, at their Moulin de la Tuileries at Gif-sur-Yvette. At lunch, I confessed to my host my earlier fantasies. The Duke was so amused at this story of my childhood crush that he took me for a stroll through their gardens. Giving each flower its botanical name, he unconsciously lapsed into German, which he had spoken as a child. I noticed he was wearing a suit of Glenurquhart plaid.

Another illness at La Paloma occurred in my second year at high school. I had been given a hand-me-down, a green watered-silk dress and short bolero jacket belonging to an "acceptable" neighbor's child about my own size. The first day of the new term found me coatless, proudly sporting my new acquisition. On the school bus coming home that September afternoon, the chills and fever struck.

Mother was sitting at the dining-room table, playing solitaire, an empty teacup, a finished crossword puzzle from the San Jose *Mercury-Herald* beside her, awaiting our return. She took one look at my flushed face as I entered the room and sighed in resignation. "Well, have a cup of tea and then I'll call the doctor." Double pneumonia and pleurisy. During those pre-penicillin weeks Mother was condemned to endless trips up and down the stairs, carrying special diets, fresh linens, trays of medicines up to my sickroom. And I never wore the green dress again—I had outgrown it when I was allowed out of bed three months later.

Danny would visit my bedside each evening on his return from his investment counsel office in San Jose. His conversation dealt with high finance, stock market manipulation, inflation, unemployment, the elected idiots in Washington. Despite my fever, I fell asleep each night worrying about the national debt. Danny had nothing trivial to talk about: I should be made aware of how much my illness was costing him. To save money, I separated my Kleenex tissues, using only one sheet at a time. Danny's visits, though instructive, were nonetheless depressing. I don't remember Olivia visiting me at all except to return to the bed next to mine when I was considered free from contagion.

Every afternoon Mother took the car and picked up my daily book from the library. Holding on to the steering wheel with her right hand, she brought back, in her left, a dripping ice cream cone from the drugstore for her patient. The books, ice cream, her singing and piano-playing, the top-level discussions on politics and finance were my only respite from the discomfort and confinement of illness . . . except pillow fantasies.

In my darkened room I would envision a whole make-believe world. In a continuous imaginary soap opera, I invented friends, lovers, husbands, children. I traveled to exotic lands, dined—exquisitely gowned and bejeweled—in fashionable restaurants, aboard yachts. I played endless scenes of romance, passion, jealousy, rejection, death. I built and decorated houses, steamships, ballrooms. I designed sets and costumes, cast roles . . . and played them all myself.

As I had been forced to be a perfectionist under Danny's tutelage, there were endless retakes of my fantasy movies. I must have been preparing myself for working with George Stevens, the director of films such as *Shane* and *A Place in the Sun*. Years later, when I worked with him in *Gunga Din*, *A Damsel in Distress*, and *Something to Live For*, I felt quite at home with his meticulous technique, his camera shooting from every conceivable angle.

Yet, on the stage or screen, attention to minute detail has its draw-backs. There isn't a single performance of mine that totally pleases me. Not one line that is spoken, one gesture given that couldn't be improved upon. Only rarely do I feel I have given a consistently acceptable performance. And there are no retakes on the stage, but, thank God, there *is* tomorrow's performance.

Years later a psychiatrist told me that the pillow fantasies probably saved my sanity. They may have given me objectivity and drive, the ability to live alone, be independent, and love it. Perhaps I've spent my whole life trying to fulfill my pillow dreams.

7

REBELLION IN THE RANKS

WE HAD LITTLE DIVERSION IN OUR TUDOR FORTRESS. DANNY WAS THE drill sergeant, Mother his corporal. The large bedroom shared by Olivia and me, with its two walk-in closets, was a military barracks. Two single iron cots, scarcely graced by their white seersucker spreads, were painted khaki color like the Chrysler. Danny said, "Tan shows the dirt less."

Two bureaus, two straight-backed chairs of the same khaki color were the only furniture other than the night table and the single lamp between Olivia's bed and mine. A taupe carpet lay on the yellow oak floor. The curtains were beige linen with a small geometric pattern. They did not close.

Inspection could take place at any time, but Sunday afternoon was the most dreaded time of the week. Then "G.M.," as we now secretly called our stepfather for his initials, would survey our closets, our bureau drawers. Each item of apparel must be in the place designated by him or the penance was wrathful. And if we failed to pass the test of daily tasks on a school morning, we were yanked off the school bus. If, after an hour later and our chores redone, we failed again, the process would be repeated. One morning he placed a small white thread on the edge of our bedroom carpet which the vacuum cleaner failed to pick up. It was not found until after the third aborted trip to the bus stop.

Sunday morning was a time of moratorium. We "cuddled" in our parents' bed. Danny had read that all young cubs, puppies, kittens, or children must have affection in the form of physical contact. We got our allotment on the Sabbath day of rest. For half an hour. Then G.M. would cook the breakfast: finnan haddie poached in milk, sausages, kippers, popovers, blueberry gems, waffles. He mastered cooking all of these; this one weekly hour of kitchen chores he accomplished with habitual thoroughness and competence. By 10 A.M. we had read the last week's Sunday edition of *The New York Times,* *The San Francisco Chronicle* and *Examiner.* By Sunday noon, all our usual chores were executed. At one o'clock all hell broke loose. The week's infractions were reviewed and punishment meted out accordingly. Tardiness, insolence, disobedience, slovenliness, forgetfulness. Definitions were looked up in the encyclopedia, in *Webster's Unabridged.* For our sins of omission or commission an appropriate passage from Emerson's *Essays* was copied one hundred times in Palmer method as we bent over the dining-room table. We were quite conscious of the fact that the bees were droning in the lavender bushes outside the windows and that the neighbors' children were playing baseball in the nearby orchard.

With penance completed, we then wrote out the weekly schedule. A chart of each fifteen minutes of our day from rising to bedtime was neatly drawn, very much like a calendar, and then submitted for inspection. At La Paloma Punctuality was next to Obedience, which in turn far surpassed Godliness.

Sports were taboo if they couldn't be fitted in during the hours allotted for recreation after school. The village pastor (we often found him sitting on the sofa beside flirtatious Mother when we returned home from school) attempted to give me the tennis lessons which I craved. When this crime was discovered by Mr. Fontaine, I was soundly punished and the parson's visits ceased.

In the spare time from homework and house-and-garden chores, we read. I must have gone through most of the books on the public-library shelves. At twelve, when asked to select the school play, I chose *Everyman.* The Brontës, Jane Austen, George Eliot, the Dumas', *père et fils,* Dickens, Scott—all of them found their way under my pillow at night, or were stashed in the honeysuckle hedge by the back door for furtive moments. Even two volumes on *Married*

Love by Marie Stopes discovered on the living-room bookshelves were treated to the same fate.

Olivia, who forbade me to speak to her in front of her friends during school recess, was now writing poetry. One day I had returned from school and the on-the-way-home library with a Zane Grey or Conan Doyle under my arm. She snatched it from me and hid it under a sofa cushion. Two members of her literary set were breaking the quarantinelike rules of our house and dropping by for a heady discussion of meter and syntax. She would not be disgraced by the mundane reading tastes of her younger sister. Mother was not the only snob under our roof!

The atmosphere of all-work-and-no-play at La Paloma became increasingly perilous. Mr. Fontaine must have been going through what is termed today the male menopause. His mercurial changes of attitude toward his two budding stepdaughters were obvious to us both: his blinding rages, his too lingering caresses.

Mr. Fontaine had already disowned his son, George, who while a brilliant student at Stanford had become engaged. Against his father's wishes George had begun a romance with beautiful, auburn-haired Lauren Wasson, of the real estate family. Cut off without a cent, George left Stanford and married his redhead. Of this marriage, there were two daughters, Barbara (named for Danny's daughter who died in infancy) and Suzanne. Only in later life did G.M. allow his granddaughters inside the fortress on La Paloma.

Forbidden to tarry or speak to anyone on the way home from school, one afternoon I was forced to disobey G.M.'s edict when an anxious mother of a classmate, who lived only a few houses away, inquired after her son's health as she stood clipping her rose hedge. Replying to her as politely and succinctly as I could, I continued on to our back gate. G.M., by then also known by us as The Iron Duke, interrogated me upon his return that evening. Had I spoken to anyone on my way home against his orders? Not knowing what information he had, I felt it safer to confess my conversation with my schoolmate's mother. Enraged, purple with fury at my disobedience, he charged at me like a bull; a blow to the face from the flat of his hand sent me hurtling through a glass door.

With Mother and Olivia stanching the blood flowing from a gash above my left eye, I heard Mother say, "I shall write their father about this."

I tucked this information away for future use: perhaps Father would get me out of this military camp.

Once we had run away. Olivia masterminded the plan. We were to sneak out just before dawn, our empty beds would be discovered by distraught parents in the morning. They would be desolate. Remorse would soften their hard hearts, so that upon our return we would be pampered and appreciated.

As the night sky grayed, we struggled silently into our blue jeans, out our bedroom french doors onto the balcony, over the garage roof with its glass-covered solar heating system. Down a drainpipe we shinnied until our Keds rested on the tops of the garbage cans in the utility yard. The rest was easy.

We struck out for the Goodriches'. My stalwart leader, with great sangfroid, detoured along the creek bed, waiting for daylight. We were to arrive there just in time for breakfast! The early-morning mist was rising in the fields. Color began to dapple the trees as the eastern sky turned pink. The first birdcalls sounded reveille to the dormant insects. My heart thumped against my ribs. The frosty air against my cheeks turned my breath to steam. The countryside at dawn was a new, exciting experience. So was running away.

Tapping at their bedroom window, we awoke our friends Margaret and Libby. At breakfast Olivia related the reasons for our jailbreak to their mother. "Aunt" Henriette Goodrich listened to the terms set out by my sister: we would return to our grieving parents on Olivia's conditions only. Mother was telephoned and she soon arrived. She and arbitrator Aunt Henriette retired to the library. When they emerged, a quiet, thoughtful Mother drove us home.

Peace reigned for several days at La Paloma. Danny addressed us in a patient tone. He said "please" and "thank you" after his requests. It didn't last long.

You may wonder why we didn't rebel before. Why we didn't go to the school principal or superintendent instead of tugging at our skirts to cover the weals made on our thighs by wooden coat hangers or the hearth broom. Though the principal took a belt strap to an unruly student, though knuckles were rapped with rulers by teachers in class, not one child would ever dare complain about treatment at home. We were all too proud. One didn't "let the family down." One never criticized one's parents to an outsider. Not only that it "wasn't done," but it was a reflection on the talebearer. No one wanted to be pitied.

8

FAREWELL TO SARATOGA

UPON OCCASION DURING THESE YEARS, WE WERE ALLOWED TO DO VARIOUS theatricals. Portia and Nerissa from *The Merchant of Venice* for five dollars each at drawing-room soirees. Restoration comedy skits at the local women's club and school plays *if* permission was granted.

My first lead was in the eighth-grade graduation play *Flyin' High*, a kitchen-sink drama suitable for the occasion and probably never again to see footlights. The pastor's wife was my drama coach and director, as well as makeup artist. As I was madly in love with the school football captain, I yearned to excel in the role: he would be in the audience that evening. After the performance, Mother strode backstage, where I was tremulously waiting in the wings for exuberant praise *and* my athletic hero. After looking contemptuously at my makeup, Mother's only comment was "You look just like Harpo Marx!"

With her huge brown eyes and long golden-brown hair, Olivia made an enchanting Alice in a local production of Lewis Carroll's *Wonderland*. Her beauty, as well as her talents, developed early. She also played the witch in *Hansel and Gretel* while I was a diaphanous specter with homemade wings in its Angel Chorus. That school production was the only time that the two of us would ever be under the same proscenium arch.

In high school Olivia was to play the lead in *Pride and Prejudice* at a special fund-raising production for new gym equipment. As extracurricular activities were forbidden, she sought permission from Mother, whose only comment was "I shall have nothing to do with it. You will have to ask your stepfather."

Olivia didn't ask him. After nights of studying her lines by flashlight under the bedcovers, the morning of the performance dawned. Coming downstairs with books under her arm, she was met by The Iron Duke, red-faced with fury. The ultimatum: if she left the house today, she left forever. He would not tolerate disobedience. Unable to let the school or her classmates down, she left forever.

After the play that evening, Olivia by habit took the bus back to Saratoga. Then realizing she no longer had a home to go to, she walked a mile up the hill to the picket-fenced house of "Topsy," our name for Eva Leigh Harriman, an adorable childless Ohio-born little old lady who had paid us pocket money in summer and on Saturdays for setting up and working her handlooms. (As her first name was Eva, we had dubbed her Topsy years before. Many happy hours had been spent in her cottage as she treated us to the Saturday opera broadcasts, and "alfresco" lunches, as she called them, on her front porch. These meals consisted of peanut butter and jelly sandwiches and milk, but were elegantly served on individual trays. Topsy had her own version of the manners of the *haut monde*. She also had warmth and tolerance toward us. In her house we were always happy.)

On this momentous midnight, Olivia threw pebbles at Topsy's bedroom window until Mrs. Harriman opened her front door and her heart to the homeless actress who was to share her house until she won a scholarship to Mills College. A group of kindly, interested friends provided my sister with board and pocket money for some time.

Refusing to stay under the same roof with Mr. Fontaine when my sister was unwelcome, I was sent back to the Lundblads. I soon found myself waiting on tables, stringing beans, and washing dishes afternoons after school and evenings. After months of living in a hall bedroom, partitioned off from the very corridor that Olivia and I had promenaded along in our borrowed costumes years earlier, the situation became intolerable. I was moved to the house of the editor of the Los Gatos newspaper, where I was to be baby-sitter for my board and room.

At my new home, lonely as I was, I first felt that I was a person in my own right. I adored the baby, but I almost killed her. On summer days Olivia and I were occasionally invited to the Goodriches' pool to swim. One July day in 1933, enraged by something I said or did, Olivia threw me down on the poolside flagstone border, jumped on top of me, and fractured my collarbone. That night I was tending the baby while her parents were away playing bridge, and I dropped her. Thank God she was made of foam rubber. I telephoned frantically for help, and the parents came at once. Though fortunately the baby was not injured, it turned out that I was. Next morning I awoke in agony, and after X rays were taken, I was told I needed a long recuperation.

Where to go, what to do? Next day I found myself in bed in a Saratoga nursing home, my left arm in a sling, school soon to start, no means of support of any kind. So with my right hand, I wrote my father.

In August, Father arrived, a total stranger to us. Since his bringing us to the United States, he had never written, never sent us cards, or Christmas or birthday gifts. We had seen him only once, for a few minutes at the railway station in Los Altos. Mother, always afraid of kidnapping, would not let him within ten feet of us.

Now, with Mother's consent, Father took Olivia and me on a two-week holiday to Carmel. The three of us stayed at La Playa Hotel while arrangements for our future were worked out. It was decided that he would provide Olivia with fifty dollars a month (quite a sum in those days) and I would return with him to Japan and Yoki-san, whom he had married at the British Embassy in Tokyo in 1927. Now Olivia could continue her education and I would have a home.

Though the Saratoga part of my life was thus to end when I was fifteen, I shall always bless Mother for choosing that foothill village as our nurturing ground. Spring brought yellow acacia, coral-colored Japanese quince, violets and daphne, thrashers and robins. To steal out on the bedroom balcony of a scented spring night made jade-green by the moon, to survey great stretches of orchard blossoms on all sides, was to anticipate paradise. Summer ripened the sun-drenched apricots and prunes. Autumn colored the sycamores and maple, and quail foraged for the last berries beneath the drooping pepper trees. Winter glazed the mud puddles, such fun to shatter with our rubber shoes on the mile walk to school. At ten, in my Keds and blue jeans, I took solitary hikes through fields and across brook-splashed stepping-stones, alert for the rattle of a coiled snake. And a great deal of my reading was done in the ferned bower of my secret hideaway on Bean Hill, opposite the vicarage. An occasional deer or fox darted out from the thickets of deadly nightshade and wild honeysuckle. The coyotes in the higher hills bayed to the moonlight when first we came. One coyote once moon-gazed tranquilly on our Green Cottage porch, a solemn sight to the five-year-old peeking through the curtains. Night sounds came from hooting owls in search of field mice, from the Lundblads' mongrel lovestruck with the moon.

The last time I drove Mother back for a visit, we got lost amid the cement tentacles of the freeways, in the jungle of billboards and road signs. Someone shouted an epithet from a passing car as I slowed down to read an exit sign.

9

MAID IN JAPAN

NOW IT WAS GOOD-BYE TO SARATOGA, TO BEAN HILL, TO MY CHILDHOOD.
The bustle of buying luggage and clothes in San Francisco, where
Father and I now prepared for the voyage, obscured any doubts that
I might have had of my future. A stranger to his fifteen-year-old
daughter, Father bought me suits and evening dresses at The White
House and I. Magnin's that were far too sophisticated. Naturally, I
did not restrain his extravagance or guide his masculine tastes. One
ensemble—a blue-and-gray mixed tweed with a large caracul collar, a
jaunty black-veiled pillbox hat—was selected for my departure on the
Tatsuta Maru.

Bearing a gardenia corsage and a bottle of champagne, Mother
and Olivia came to the ship to see me settled in my stateroom.
Mother kept an icy distance from Father, who was not asked to the
party. Olivia, at this time in her life, sided with Mother.

As the ship pulled away from the pier, I found my way forward on
deck, new high-heeled suede pumps wobbling under my thin legs. In
fur-collared suit, corsage and all, I struck a dramatic attitude against
a smokestack, stifling my tears and fears as best I could. From the
dock, Olivia and Mother roared hysterically, doubling over with

peals of laughter at the sight of the theatrical fifteen-year-old figure, posed like Miss Liberty, receding in the distance.

Twenty minutes beyond the Golden Gate, the sophisticated traveler found her head in her stateroom basin. Seasickness kept me in that bathroom for three days, sleeping on the floor between bouts of nausea, despite Father's insistent knocks on the locked cabin door. The scent of gardenia still recalls that none too Pacific voyage, homesickness, false courage, mal de mer, and the porthole I did not know could be opened.

Beyond Hawaii my spirits rose. Avoiding as often as possible the deck-chair lessons of Greek, Latin, and chess that Schoolmaster de Havilland insisted upon (he labeled me illiterate like all American-educated students), I found a friend. Fred Maytag of the washing-machine family was a solitary round-the-world traveler, his last freedom before the restraints of marriage that awaited his return to the Midwest.

To me, Fred Maytag was an older man, though he was actually only twenty-two. Our deck-rail talks, so like the imaginary ones I had had with H.R.H. the Prince of Wales, dances to the ship's orchestra in one of my super-elegant gowns, lashing ourselves to stanchions on deck during a typhoon, all made me feel a total sophisticate by the time the *Tatsuta Maru* docked at Yokohama.

But not for long. Yoki-san met us at the pier. I had expected a kimonoed, willowy, formally coiffed stepmother, rather like the doll Mother had brought from this land of cherry blossoms when she returned from her divorce. Instead, I was embraced by a waddling, double-chinned matron, sporting a beige-and-maroon crepe Parisian outfit, a matching beret tilted over one eye, her knees dimpling above her lizard-skin pumps. A long cigarette holder darted between chubby bejeweled hand and dark-rouged mouth. O-jo-san's stomach turned to ice. Oh, for Mother-with-the-laughing-voice. Even my barrack bedroom at La Paloma now seemed a sanctuary.

The taxi ride to Tokyo and the Imperial Hotel, where the de Havillands had lived since their marriage, was downright embarrassing. Overly demonstrative, Father's anticipation of the resumption of their marital bliss was unconcealed. Attempting to welcome her stepdaughter warmly, Yoki-san covered me with sticky kisses, patting me maternally and fluffing my hair while accepting the same treatment from her husband on her other side. It was Yoki-san's day. It certainly wasn't mine.

The Imperial was a low-ceilinged, rambling-corridored, beige-stone edifice that Frank Lloyd Wright had designed to withstand earthquakes, to house short Japanese travelers, and to ignore the comforts of taller European customers. Here I was unceremoniously plunked down. My small room with its midget-sized bed was to be my cell until arrangements could be made for my schooling. Father fished out pocket money, told me to ring for room service if I became hungry, and hastily shut me in. He'd see me in the morning . . . he and Yoki-san had urgent business to conduct in their adjoining suite.

The voyage was over, ties with America cut, the future obscure. Strange Oriental sounds drifted through my french windows. Stumbling through the clutter of luggage, I opened the windows wide to gaze onto the land of my birth. Smoke rose over the city as twilight descended. That red, red sun-on-white-sky, just like the national flag, had left pink fingers on the thatched rooftops.

A newsboy cried, "*Asahi, Asahi Shimbun,*" as he jingled the bells on his running feet, beating sticks of bamboo together with his hands, announcing the evening edition. The clatter of wooden getas on sidewalks, the plaintive notes of a distant samisen, a dog bark. I sensed I'd heard these sounds before.

My reverie was interrupted. From the adjoining room arose noises, too. Odd ones. They got odder and odder. Despite Marie Stopes's *Married Love* and the nocturnal sounds I occasionally heard from Danny and Mother's bedroom, I was thoroughly bewildered. Nothing I'd read in the romance of Milady and D'Artagnan in *The Three Musketeers* nor the sex-illumination talks with Topsy about the sacred-temple-within-me had prepared me for this onslaught of animal noises emanating from my father's bedroom.

Lonely, lost, confused, I got up the courage to telephone Fred Maytag's rooms. He had booked into the Imperial overnight before resuming his global journey. It was very late when I reached him, but he willingly agreed to be the confidant of my troubles.

Fred opened his sitting-room door to a very small, crying, country girl, far from the blasé companion he had known on board the *Tatsuta*. When I told him the cause of my alarm, he wrinkled his nose in laughter. He sat me down in an upholstered chair. With infinite gentleness and kindness, never touching me, he explained the facts of life. In detail, he described the anatomical differences between the sexes and their multiple uses. He briefly took off his robe. I had never seen a man's genitals before. Though in name only, when I returned to my room at midnight I was at last, I felt, a true sophisticate.

Thus prepared, I was a cinch at the American School in Kami-Meguro, a suburb of Tokyo, which was to be my home for the next year. Going on sixteen, with an American wardrobe and refurbished English accent (Father, like Mother, gave diction lessons), I found that the children of missionaries enrolled there were far too naïve for this cool cat from California. Only a few Embassy teen-agers or those from homes of American families in business in Tokyo could match my speed.

My roommate was Eleanor Child, later to become the mother of Gigi Perreau, a child movie actress of much talent. Eleanor and I were the self-appointed stars of the dorm. Dressed in kimonos after school hours, we shunned our earnest, plodding dorm mates. Eleanor's father, an American, was with Harley-Davidson. Her mother, English and hospitable, often invited me to their beach house at Kamakura for weekends.

These were happy days. Mother had written old friends in Tokyo and Yokohama who welcomed me, too. Against my father's orders the school principal allowed me weekend passes, as the deserted dorm was no place for this swinger on holidays. I found myself, now sixteen, dancing with ambassadors, such as America's Joseph Grew and Belgium's Baron de Bassompierre, at parties at the Grand Hotel, at the Yokohama Athletic and Cricket Club on Yokohama's "bluff," sipping sloe-gin fizzes and gimlets with British Standard Oil and Shell bachelors, and the language officers from the American Embassy. I felt like the belle of the ball in my white moiré evening gown with its White House label.

In love with love and my new freedom, overly sentimental and craving affection I never knew as a child, I soon acquired a series of beaux. I became engaged to most of them. The Kamakura weekends gave me ample opportunity to see them all.

Two suitors were especially adorable to me. Much older than I, possibly in their early thirties, Rupert Burne and A. E. "Copper" Hewitt shared a weekend beach house at Hayama, near Kamakura. Mrs. Child would give me permission to divide my weekends, so, thoroughly chaperoned, I spent idyllic days with the two bachelors from Shell Oil. Swimming by day, dining in the moonlight on Japanese fare on their veranda with their friends, I became a grown-up. I look back on those lazy days as the happiest of my life. Neither man ever made a pass at me. If only time could have stood still.

But my schoolgirl life was not all gimlets and galas. It was difficult to adjust to dormitory life, to live with other girls and teachers in such close proximity after my years in periodic solitary due to illness. My health took other forms of weakness: a great many visits were paid to the American Hospital for treatments for sinusitis. These were interspersed with exciting trips to Kabuki or No dramas. Five feet four inches, weighing less than a hundred pounds, I had to be on self-administered injections of insulin to increase my appetite.

Occasionally, a dreaded weekend with Father and Yoki-san could not be avoided. Then Father would stride down the Ginza, puffing away on his habitual cigar, loudly clearing his throat. O-jo-san walked a step behind him, Yoki-san brought up the rear. At a stoplight, out my stepmother would dart (now in more becoming Japanese garb, thank God), and taking her handkerchief from her kimono sleeve, she would flick an imaginary speck of dust from Dana-san's shoe. Back to the end of the line she would waddle.

Christmas was horrendous. Father rented a house in a compound for the occasion. Joan was to have a real Yuletide, tree and all. It is with chagrin that I recall pillow-dreaming most of Christmas Day, rather than brave those two new parents awaiting me below. Innocent of the cause of my procrastination, they blamed the need of so much sleep on my hard work at school.

When I appeared downstairs in midafternoon, Yoki-san presented me with a beautiful plum-colored kimono, obi, tabis, and all, which she most kindly and gently dressed me in, showing me how to wind and tie the brocade sash. I was grateful to her for this but not when she insisted that I sit in her lap and be her little girl. Father presented me with Galsworthy's *The Forsyte Saga* and W. W. Jacobs' *The Monkey's Paw*—both most appreciated.

Despite their zeal to give me a proper holiday, I was embarrassed and uncomfortable. Ashamed of my father's imperious manner, of my stepmother's pudginess (she reminded me of those Japanese toys, weighted at the bottom, that always right themselves), I longed for New Year's. I had been invited, unbeknownst to Father, to be a houseguest by friends of Mother, a delightful couple who took me on trips to Lake Hakone and Miyanoshita, showed me the exquisite Japanese countryside, entertained me with their university friends, and escorted me to Japanese theatre. Father bumped into the three of us one night at the Kabuki. The school principal got what for . . . so did I. I was *never* to see any of those dreadful friends of Mother whom he had chivied at social functions so long ago.

For Father's second marriage had ostracized him from the European colony. His days were spent at his chess and go clubs, where I watched him play in silence for hours on end, sitting cross-legged on the tatami-ed floor, the wooden playing board with its black and white stones, called *ishi*, before him. His nights were spent in his suite at the Imperial with Yoki-san, to whom he remained married until her death, and who was, he told me, the best kind of wife a man could have.

As he played the stock market with fervor and took frequent trips to the United States, he may well have been caching money away in bank accounts in anticipation of the coming war. In 1933 and '34, Korean refugees clogged Tokyo's railroad stations. It was obvious that Japan had expansionist ambitions. Japanese students of both sexes were dressed in uniform. An anti-European climate had sprung up. Curse words were hurled at white-skinned passersby along the Ginza and from moving trains. *Baka* is not a pretty word, yet I heard it often as a jingoistic youth shook his fist in my direction. Father, married to a Japanese, must have had a fairly good idea of what was to come.

Except for the time when Father found out about my extra-curricular activities with Mother's friends, the school year passed without crisis. Summer was spent partly with a school chum and her missionary parents. Here I spent most of the time in my room, reading. One book I devoured was Hervey Allen's *Anthony Adverse* (which my sister was to film for Warner Brothers only four or five years later), not missing a line as I periodically rose from my chair to stand under the nearest doorway. For an ominous rumble often started on one side of the city, followed by rattling windows and undulating floors, as frequent earthquakes shook the Shiba district. Nauseous smells rose from the canals or from the oxcarts where honey buckets of human waste were transported to the countryside, there to be dumped on lettuce and strawberry fields. No wonder the Japanese are a hardy race.

Another dreaded family vacation. This time Father had booked us into the seaside Keihin Hotel in Kamakura for the month of August, a room for himself and Yoki-san, one across the hall for me. Naturally I was delighted to be so near the Childs and my Shell Company bachelors at Hayama, but getting away from my sharp-eyed father was going to be a neat trick.

Usually I took my meals with Father and his wife in the dining room. In those days eight courses were nothing for lunch or dinner. Soup, fish, the inevitable curry course, all sandwiched between the first and the entrée, followed by salad, dessert, savory, and cheese. Potted palms waved over the string orchestra as the Japanese musicians sawed away on Strauss and Friml. An occasional breeze stirred the dwarf pines along the shore, ruffled the dusty, camera-laden tourists as they gazed up at the awesome Buddha in the park.

Meanwhile, I renewed my visits to friends, often slipping out of my room after dinner and returning by midnight. One of my particular beaux, Alfred Nipkow, frequently came to pay court. Father always raised his eyebrows and made ugly, suggestive references to my questionable virginity.

I was reminded of G.M. and those too intimate caresses: Father now found his stranger daughter growing attractive to him, especially in her bathing suit. Often he would walk along the beach with me, usually berating Mother, but always requesting that I appear in my one-piece blue "bathing costume." I was on guard.

One evening he announced that Yoki-san was ill, possibly pregnant, that he would have his bed moved into my room. I rejected his proposal with some degree of coolness. His masculine pride was wounded. Soon we were enemies.

Rightly suspecting that I preferred the company of my friends to his and Yoki-san's, he delivered his ultimatum: there would be no college for me. I could stay in Japan, be nursemaid for his future child for my board and room, or return in disgrace to my frivolous, immoral mother. (Hadn't she left him for a plebeian American?) I deserved to be condemned to that materialistic, illiterate country.

Angrily defending my mother, pointing out that she had met my stepfather long after Father had abandoned us in California, I readily chose the latter course. I was under age, not yet seventeen, and could not have married without his permission, though there was no lack of offers. By the first of September, my one-way tourist-class ticket was in my purse beside my British passport.

Of all my suitors, Alfred Nipkow, handsome, hazel-eyed, had always held the edge. His father, a Swiss businessman, had been a flutist with Mother's amateur musical group. Mrs. Nipkow looked very much like Merle Oberon, with the same sweet English voice. She had often had me as a weekend guest at their home in Yokohama, lending me her fur coat to put over my ball gown on chilly Saturday nights. Their chauffeur, driving Alfred and me back to school Sunday evenings, must have overheard much heavy breathing from the back seat. Saying sayonara to the Nipkows would be painful.

At their home, Mrs. Nipkow, warm, kindly, realizing this was the last time we would meet, gently took me by the hand and led me into the garden. "Now you must meet Alfred's grandmother." She guided me to a miniature teahouse at the back of the lawn which I had never noticed. There I was introduced to a tiny, shriveled Japanese lady, clad in a gray kimono. She sat squatting in front of a hibachi, smoking from a carved ivory tobacco holder.

The Nipkows' secret would have made no earthly difference to me. As both Father and Mother's brother had happily married Japanese women, I was not shocked to learn that my attractive beau was one-quarter Japanese. Eurasians at school had often been most personable and intelligent, despite the social difficulties they encountered.

I was doubly distressed. First, that the Nipkows thought that I would have minded Alfred's mixed blood; second, that I was too young to do anything but turn sadly from their door, never to pass through it again. As their daughter-in-law I might have been very happy.

In September 1934, with a few last-minute slurs about my being "no better than your mother," "good-bye and good riddance," Father placed me aboard the S.S. *President Hoover*. Fishing fifty dollars out of his dog-eared wallet, he announced that it was the last I'd ever get from him and he was cutting off Olivia's allowance, too. So there!

I was not to see him again for sixteen years.

10

RETURN OF THE PRODIGAL

IT WAS AUTUMN 1934. THE *President Hoover* DOCKED AT SAN FRAN-cisco's Embarcadero, disgorging its passengers, baggage, and freight. The afternoon mist swirled about the bustling figures as they speed-ily went their ways. On the pier, perched atop my steamer trunk containing its now faded, frayed finery, I pondered what to do, where to go, whom to call. The parting gift of fifty dollars from Fa-ther had dwindled to twenty-two. My newly blonded hair had taken care of that. Upon sailing out of Yokohama's harbor I had rushed to the ship's beauty shop, intent upon washing away my schoolgirlhood with peroxide and ammonia.

No one knew I was in San Francisco. Had Father cabled Mother? I doubted it. Olivia was on tour with Max Reinhardt's *Midsummer Night's Dream*. G.M. was hardly likely to fetch me. I had a brain-storm. From a pay telephone booth on the dock, I reached "Uncle" Hugh A. Studdart Kennedy at his San Francisco office. He was in, thank God and Mrs. Bruiner. Within half an hour, his chauffeured limousine was pointing south toward Saratoga and La Mirada, Uncle Hugh and his world-weary traveler in the back seat, my steamer trunk behind.

La Mirada, a white, red-tiled hacienda amid flourishing lawns and gardens abutting Montalvo, would be my home for the next several weeks. It had been the recipient of many of my floral arrangements in the past, the scene of the de Havilland sisters' skits and Shakespearean readings.

Under its Spanish roof resided Mrs. O. A. Hale, "Auntie Mame" to us long before Patrick Dennis had thought of his famous character. The now partially paralyzed, sweet-faced dowager was the widow of O. A. Hale, founder of the department stores of that name. With her lived her only child, Clarisse, and her son-in-law, Christian Scientist practitioner Uncle Hugh. So devout was the household that a visit to doctor or dentist was never for a moment considered. This tranquil, luxurious estate was as near a haven as I could have wished for. Mrs. Hale and the childless Kennedys opened their hearts as well as their home to me.

Mother was telephoned and she soon arrived. My Victorian father had evidently written her about my nocturnal truancy, about my secret weekends to which he attributed riotous orgies. Forgetting his own sexual indiscretions, he was preoccupied with the subject of immorality, constantly accusing Mother of it. Hadn't she been in the theatre? You can take a parson's son to Hokkaido, but you can't get the sermon out of the boy.

This pale, blond, fully grown stranger had no place in Mother's life as she now lived it. With Olivia declining her scholarship to Mills College in favor of her tour in the Shakespearean play, Mother had settled into making a solitary home for G.M. at La Paloma. She also assisted with drama classes at Stanford University, read plays professionally, and at last acquired a group of friends with whom she played bridge. Now the wayward fledgling was standing sheepishly before her, my very presence demanding that she assume a mother role again. She did what she could. With little personal income, there wasn't much she could do.

Mother and the Kennedys decided that I should continue to accept the hospitality of La Mirada, arranging flowers for its many rooms, helping with small secretarial tasks until a solution to my dilemma could be found. Olivia would soon be playing at San Francisco's Opera House in the Reinhardt production and could attend a family powwow.

The kindness of my hosts eventually healed my wounds. Their Scottish secretary restored my humor, the chauffeur taught me to drive. The Chinese cook prepared meals that added a pound or two to my wraithlike figure. Like G.M., "Auntie" Clare inspected my closet and its wilted wardrobe. In her religion, God would provide; I got out my sewing kit and started mending what was still mendable.

Olivia arrived on her day off from A *Midsummer Night's Dream* for a conference with Mother. They decided I would study French and ballet, and resume my drawing lessons. My elder sister could hardly afford to send me to college, and my uncertain health forbade my attempting to earn my way. It was Olivia's turn to provide me with a fifty-dollar-a-month allowance. G.M. was not expected to be heard from at all.

One incident at La Mirada was to mark me for life. A string quartet was playing Beethoven in the drawing room after dinner, attended by several guests as well as my mother and sister. Sitting on the floor by the musicians' feet, enthralled with the music, I reached out my hand spontaneously to a young man sitting beside me, a member of Olivia's cast, though not a suitor. As moved by the music as I was, he grasped my hand and held it with no attempt at concealment. Mother beckoned to me. I arose and went with her behind the lacquered Coromandel screen at the end of the room. "I saw you," she whispered. "You're nothing but a whore!"

Quietly I resumed my place on the floor, choking back my tears. If ever I had been innocent, it was in that overt gesture of rapture, that expression of emotion evoked by the music. Mother's remark was to ring in my ears, to mark my life forever, to cause me frustration, anguish, and despair.

Aboard the S.S. *President Hoover*, I had met a young American consular officer who looked very much like Fred Maytag. Edward Anderson was charming, attractive, and in search of a wife. Having no foreseeable future, no permanent home, I readily accepted his proposal of marriage. I promised to join him at his post in Toronto when I was eighteen and had my mother's permission. I was still only in love with love, longing to escape from parental supervision. Our ineffectual attempt to shatter my virginity in his cabin—a romance aborted by a knock on the door—seemed a pledge to him.

Mother agreed that Edward indeed seemed a suitable solution to my dilemma, that I could become the consul's wife when all the amenities were taken care of—if after she met him, he won her approval. Telephone calls were exchanged between the engaged couple, between his mother and me. I studied French at night school to speak the language I would need as his wife in Canada.

To be within walking distance of the Los Gatos High School,

where my French classes were held, I moved from La Mirada into one room of a cottage owned by a devout Bahai. My landlady abhorred the eating of meat, so I subsisted on whole-wheat bread, dairy products, fruits, and vegetables. The occasional smell of my broiling lamb chop would send her scurrying into the garden.

Any friends of my own age from earlier Saratoga days were off at college or following other pursuits. I was back in solitary. Continuing my French and painting lessons, I read copiously. My ballet classes led to a dance recital at San Jose State College. It was clear to me and the audience that I was not destined to be an Isadora Duncan or a Maria Tallchief. I still think I might have been a passable painter. In my Bahai cottage I pillow-dreamed and bided my eighteenth birthday and the arrival of my fiancé.

Destiny had other plans. Two other "uncles," George Dennison and Frank Ingerson, owned Cathedral Oaks, a rambling studio of many rooms at Alma, in the Santa Cruz Mountains. "The Boys," as these two bachelors were called by the community, were highly talented artists, had studied in Italy and England, and were the creators of the fabulous enameled Ark of the Covenant, which is a cherished possession of Temple Emanu-el in San Francisco. These uncles continued to give me drawing lessons as they had when I was a child, truly loved both Olivia and me, and were always ready to assist us in our search for roots and identity.

One day, early in 1935, Frank and George excitedly told me that they had just spoken on the phone to their dear old friend, the revered actress May Robson. In Los Angeles, Miss Robson was about to go into rehearsal with *Kind Lady*, a mystery drama by Edward Chodorov. She was looking for a young English ingenue, a scarce commodity in Hollywood. Would I audition? Would I!

Mother and Olivia were now sharing an apartment at the Château des Fleurs on Hollywood's Franklin Avenue, a pseudo-French edifice that Baron Haussmann would hardly have permitted in Paris, but one well suited to Tinseltown in the Thirties. Olivia, under contract to Warner Brothers, was filming Hermia in *A Midsummer Night's Dream* with Victor Jory, Evelyn Venable, and Anita Louise. Max Reinhardt, of course, was directing. Uncles Frank and George drove me down the coast to southern California to Hollywood for the audition.

My first impression of southern California was its blue, blue sky, its balmy flower-scented air, its gardens in perpetual bloom. As we drove down the coast highway, past Santa Barbara and Carpinteria, there was little to attract the eye: treeless beaches on one side, orchards and cultivated fields on the other. Then came Malibu, a long row of houses dotting the shore. The Malibu colony was made up of actors, writers, and producers who, with free periods between pictures, could retreat to their beach houses for several days or weeks at a time, temporarily deserting their Hollywood or Beverly Hills residences.

Farther south, at Santa Monica, the beach "cottages" were more formal. William Randolph Hearst's compound of two-storied white buildings, interspersed with lawns, and Irving Thalberg's place bordered the highway. On the street side, every house was enclosed by tall fences and gates; on the ocean side, a stroller on the beach could spy umbrella-shaded tables, canvas chairs, an occasional swimming pool or tennis court in front of huge plate-glass windows. I had seen photographs in film magazines of Douglas Fairbanks, Sr., immaculately dressed in white flannels, ascot, and blazer, entertaining William Powell, Jean Harlow, Cary Grant, and Virginia Cherrill as well as titled European guests on his beach-side patio.

As Uncle Frank turned our car inland along Sunset Boulevard, past sun- and wind-bleached houses clinging precariously to crumbling cliffs or hidden behind fields of greasewood and yucca, we came to well-ordered gardens framing houses of startling architectural dissimilarity—Spanish haciendas, French châteaus, Tudor or Cape Cod cottages. Rose-covered picket fence joined ivied stone wall, became a wrought-iron grille, turned into a chain of wooden wagon wheels with little embarrassment. We next came upon a carved wooden sign above a bridle path bisecting the boulevard which read, "WELCOME TO BEVERLY HILLS." On our left sprawled the Beverly Hills Hotel, a conglomerate of all the architectural styles we had just seen. Shaggy royal palms nodded their fronds overhead while red and yellow cannas fringed the stucco edifice.

Now splendor of the first magnitude dazzled our eyes: an Italian villa, a Colonial town house, a replica of a Rhenish castle. And so it went until a road sign told us we had reached Sunset Strip, an important demarcation: The Strip was a tax buffer between independent Beverly Hills and a Hollywood which had been annexed by money-hungry Los Angeles.

The Strip was a mishmash of houses converted into shops, restaurants, nightclubs, even a whorehouse. Opposite a palace of pleasure stood Utter McKinley's funeral parlor, its facade warning of the inevitability of death: a giant clock with no hands. Perhaps the morticians were in cahoots with the brothel, suggested Uncles Frank and George. "Have fun while you may!"

Next loomed Ciro's white-cake-of-a-nightclub and La Maze Restaurant, later to be renamed La Rue's. On the opposite side of the boulevard the Trocadero and Mocambo nightclubs nudged each other between one-story office buildings. Empty lots sported garish billboards and FOR SALE signs as we entered Hollywood.

Just inside the city border, the Château Marmont apartments, a builder's dream of Windsor Castle, towered over the Garden of Allah, a cluster of bungalows which would have been an Arabian nightmare in Marrakesh. Schwab's drugstore faced kosher delicatessen and Tyrolean chalet. Only the palm trees flanking the eyesores seemed majestic. Hollywood then was a one-street town. Hollywood Boulevard began with the Hollywood Hotel, on the corner of Highland Avenue. A white wooden structure, the hotel had the casual air one might find in Key West or Singapore. Surrounded by lawns and semitropical verdure, its wide verandas provided rocking chairs for the tourist trade. Almost opposite was the Roosevelt, a large "city hotel" looming over Duffy's Theatre and scattered parking lots. Soon came Grauman's Chinese theatre, an exotic opium dream. After a jagged skyline of dwarf shops and a few giant office buildings, we drove past the huge replica of a brown derby perched on the roof of the Brown Derby Restaurant. The Pantages Theatre, a 1920's rococo extravaganza, marked the south end of Hollywood's business district.

By the time we weary motorists reached the sanctuary of the Château des Fleurs, with its iron grille gates bearing a resplendent crest, I felt as though we'd toured the world.

11

THE ASPIRING NEOPHYTE

AT THEIR CHÂTEAU DES FLEURS APARTMENT, MOTHER AND OLIVIA greeted me and the two adopted uncles with warmth. An appointment with Miss Robson and the director, Henry C. Potter, was arranged. After reading my part with the star, I found that I had won the ingenue role. I was seventeen, I was an actress!

Rehearsals began at the Biltmore Theatre in Los Angeles, a long streetcar ride from Hollywood. My insecurity and fright were masked with feigned nonchalance until the day I discovered the director's notes in his chair after we had broken for lunch. With my name and a few corrections of line readings, Henry Potter had written "Blah, blah, blah!" I never slurred a speech again, never slouched, never gave him a chance to say anything about my appearance on stage that could be termed "blah."

With Ralph Forbes as the leading man, we opened at the Lobrero Theatre in Santa Barbara. I was to learn much from Miss Robson. The cast was rightly in awe of this *grande dame*, none more than I. Waiting in the wings on opening night, I tackled my stage fright by standing in a dark corner and shooting up a "Dear God and Mrs. Bruiner," as I still do. (The only analogy I can think of to the terror before one's first stage entrance is the feeling of having an attack of Montezuma's Revenge miles from a toilet.)

Briefly coming offstage, Miss Robson spotted me waiting for my cue, still enmeshed in my very long-distance call to Mrs. Bruiner. "You'll never make an actress if you're not nervous," she chided. "You've got to have the 'old firehorse' instinct." During the run, she called me into her dressing room to elaborate on her theory.

"It's not *yourself* you should be worried about," she instructed, "not if you know your lines." She continued by saying that an actor must be alert for any untoward moment onstage. Another actor may forget his dialogue, you must be ready to jump in. A prop may be missing, you must improvise. Any number of things may go wrong onstage. It is up to every actor to be aware at all times and adjust skillfully to the crisis . . . *the show must go on.*

That phrase has been used by many a heartless producer to cajole an ailing actor out of a sickbed, a grieving parent from the deathbed of his child. It has been used in every conceivable way to keep the box office open, the curtain rising at show time. Miss Robson's version, I believe, is the real meaning of the timeworn admonition.

Miss Robson also taught me backstage manners. It would not have occurred to any member of the cast to call this venerable star by her first name, or on arriving at the theatre to pass her dressing-room door without a formal greeting, or to leave the theatre after a performance without a suitable leave-taking.

I am continually stunned at the total lack of manners I find in dinner theatres or summer stock today. Not only the instant first-name familiarity, the trivial conversations before, during, and after rehearsals which are times for observation and concentration, but the vulgar and often obscene language used so casually. The directors can be just as guilty as the actors and stage personnel. How in the name of Kean, Henry Irving, or Ellen Terry do they think that such expressions aid, abet, or embellish the performance about to take shape under their direction? I shall forever worship director Stuart Bishop, who quietly turned to a foulmouthed actress during rehearsal. "The character you're playing doesn't use language like that." The so-called lady prided herself on her professionalism. It didn't occur to her that she should maintain that attitude backstage and at rehearsals, too.

While I am on the subject of the aspiring neophyte, one story told to me by Dame May Whitty may succinctly illustrate the point. During the shooting of *Mrs. Miniver*, she had a "two-shot" with young actor Richard Ney, who later married the star of the film,

Greer Garson. She asked the handsome new-to-Hollywood actor to react so that the next line would make more sense. Richard willingly replied, "Of course, Dame May, I shall do as you say, but I think my way is better." The titled English actress looked down her nose. "Young man, you haven't *got* a way!"

The reviews of *Kind Lady* were good. After Santa Barbara, we played San Francisco and finally the Biltmore in Los Angeles. While in San Francisco, I concluded a semi-truce with G.M., who was living alone at La Paloma, Mother having assumed the role of chaperone, secretary, and hostess to Olivia in Hollywood.

When the California tour was over, I used the money left from my salary to take dramatic lessons and to study at the Max Reinhardt Drama School. In the latter classes, we were taught Shakespeare and Goethe by reciting in musical terms . . . whole notes, half notes, quarter notes, to sustain, to bridge, to arch as in musical phrasing. As Herr Professor Reinhardt's English was almost nonexistent, this was an excellent way to teach us without linguistic difficulties. I learned to listen to the music of the words, the cadence of the lines, as well as to the speaking voice.

Yet for all my many dramatic lessons, I had to throw away much that I learned from them once I went into films. All was external, all was artificial, all stage technique too easily detected by the microscope eye of the camera. Sanford Meisner was holding classes, instructing in the Stanislavsky Method of realism. This technique was more adaptable to the screen.

The best and shortest drama lesson was given me by that great woman's director, George Cukor. In 1939, on the set of *The Women*, I asked him what gestures, what tonal qualities he wanted for the young wife I was playing. George simply said, "Forget all that. *Think* and *feel* and the rest will take care of itself."

Those few words are the greatest gift any director, any drama coach ever gave me. When I attended a lesson at The Actors Studio while playing *Tea and Sympathy* on Broadway, I watched the gifted director-critic Harold Clurman conduct an acting class. I saw him illustrate a scene from *Medea* for a bewildered student from the Midwest. He clutched a stage curtain, raised his head majestically, and said, "Be a pillar, feel like a pillar." Both the pimply girl and I turned to stone.

All those diction lessons of Mother and Father were invaluable.

Those music lessons when I was sent out of the room, out of sight of the piano, and asked to name each note the teacher struck. Those ballet lessons, those book-on-the-head recitations from Keats's "Ode on a Grecian Urn" with appropriate gestures, the "ma-may-me-mo-moo's," the pear-shaped sounds intoned to the scales. And try these exercises:

Asks an inquisitive lady of a boat-mender:

> Are you copper-bottoming 'em, my man?
> No, I'm aluminiuming 'em, mum.

or:

> Round and round the rugged rock
> the ragged rascal ran.

or, for vowel sounds:

> How now, brown cow.

No Hollywood class gave me half the training I'd had at home from my Royal Academy Mother. Her favorite, based on Latin declensions, was:

> Boy-i-bus kiss-i-bus
> Sweet girl-i-orum.
> Girl-i-bus like-i-bus,
> Want-um some-orum.

I thank God for all her efforts, yet I doubt if she was actually training us for the stage career Lilian Rusé was denied. If so, it was never mentioned, only that her offspring had to be cultivated English ladies. It was more the class system than ambition for her daughters. Had Mother brought us up in Italy or India, our schooling would have been the same.

Through training, an actor learns to move and feel from his toes up. His ear must be quick to detect intonation, emphasis, cadence, stress. It must also be able to twitch! The director guides, brings out, enlarges, controls. But the actor must come to the stage equipped with the technique, the talent, the ambition, the imagination, the patience. The theatre audience is the ultimate teacher, instructing the actor on the degree to which he has executed both the author's and the director's intent.

In our profession, there is no end to learning. Alfred Lunt and

Lynn Fontanne, that magical couple who lighted up Broadway for so many years, continued to polish their performances from a Broadway opening night through closing night. I was fortunate to see them in *The Guardsman, There Shall Be No Night, Amphitryon 38*, in Dürrenmatt's *The Visit*, and several of their other plays. I have made it a point to see most of the memorable actors on the stage— Katharine Cornell, Helen Hayes, Leslie Howard, Lee J. Cobb's haunting *Death of a Salesman*. One of the greatest plays, to me, was *A Man for All Seasons*, interpreted exquisitely by Paul Scofield.

The actor and director learn much from observing others on stage as well as off. In the final analysis, my greatest drama teachers were the great actors.

12

EIGHTEEN

On October 22, 1935, my eighteenth birthday, Mother and Olivia took me to dinner at a Hollywood Boulevard restaurant, Musso-Frank. There, in celebration, they ordered a bottle of champagne. As we raised our glasses in a toast, the head-waiter lifted mine from my hand. I was not twenty-one! Nineteen-year-old Olivia giggled and guzzled her bubbly.

Another incident at this restaurant gave me much-needed courage. At lunch one day, a courtly wild-haired gentleman wove through the maze of tables toward us. Bowing, he kissed my hand, saying, "Forgive the intrusion, but I must pay homage to your beauty." My admirer was the pianist Artur Rubinstein. Mother and Olivia were quizzical, and I was stunned! Nela, Artur's beautiful Polish wife, eyed me stonily from across the room. (Later the Rubinsteins were to entertain me frequently at dinners in their Beverly Hills home. Often Nela would spend hours in her kitchen, preparing intricate Polish dishes. She was an excellent cook, a delightful hostess. After a gourmet meal, Artur, Jascha Heifetz, and Gregor Piatigorsky would enthrall us with Bach, Beethoven, and Haydn trios.)

We were always enthusiastically greeted at Musso-Frank. The maître d'hôtel would ceremoniously escort Mother to a prominent table, all bows and smiles. Many months later we learned that there was a Hollywood madam also named Mrs. Fontaine; hence our preferential treatment. Mother and her girls never went back to that restaurant again.

My fiancé, Edward, duly arrived from his consular post in Canada to claim his bride. During the many months since I had seen him, he had figured largely in my pillow dreams. I was thrilled to have a beau, someone in my life that I'd met on my own. Yet I was beginning to have second thoughts about the impending marriage. Mother and Olivia offered no advice.

My decision was reached one morning on the beach in Santa Monica. Edward and I had taken a picnic lunch, beach towels, books, suntan lotion to the shore in order to be alone and get to know each other again. Lying on a beach towel, I began to read aloud from my volume of poems by Rupert Brooke. I wanted Edward to know how much I had dreamed about him during our separation, which the poet could express far better than I.

I read:

> Today I have been happy. All the day
>   I held the memory of you, and wove
> Its laughter with the dancing light o' the spray,
>   And sowed the sky with tiny clouds of love,
> And sent you following the white waves of sea,
>   And crowned your head with fancies, nothing worth,
> Stray buds from that old dust of misery,
>   Being glad with a new foolish quiet mirth.

Halfway through my reading, Edward gently closed my book. Taking my sandy hand in his, he made a monumental error. "You're not really an intellectual, you know. You're only a bit of fluff," he smilingly chided. I saw red. He'd missed the whole point of my reading. Long before Women's Liberation, neither my brains nor my gender could be put down by any male!

Brideless, Edward went back to Toronto. I consigned myself to the greasepaint and my shaky career, to the Château des Fleurs and my two female relatives.

Under this roof, Mother's bet was on her firstborn, her proven breadwinner with a long-term contract. All her efforts were on Olivia's behalf. Olivia was now the head of the household, to be nurtured, curried, obeyed. A surrogate G.M., Olivia now ruled with total autonomy. Joan made a passable cook, housekeeper, chauffeur for the rented Ford, a go-for. After all, Olivia was paying the rent.

One day, while I was waiting in the Ford outside the makeup department at Warner's to deliver lunch to my sister, Mervyn LeRoy, the producer-director, poked his head through my open window. After mutual introductions, he offered to put me under personal contract. At home, Mother agreed with Olivia that I simply could not accept this opportunity. Warner's was Olivia's studio, her domain. Its gates could not be opened to both of us.

What's more, I must change my name—"de Havilland" was Olivia's, she was the firstborn, and I was not to disgrace *her* name. Mother and I rode up and down the avenues of Hollywood and Beverly Hills in search of an adequate professional name. To use my first and middle names, Joan de Beauvoir, sounded right, but who could pronounce it? Burfield Street gave me my first theatrical name. After I did a small part with Joan Crawford and Franchot Tone in *No More Ladies*, my name was changed to St. John. Yet, with the English, this is pronounced "Sin-jin," and it became too confusing to agents and casting directors. One evening at the Trocadero nightclub, where I had been taken by a beau of Olivia's, a fortune-teller, flashlight in hand, wandered to our table.

"What is your wish?" she inquired, peering into my palm.

"For a stage name that will bring me luck," I pleaded.

"Think of a name with *e* on the end," she quickly replied. The only name with the proper ending I could think of on the spur of the moment was Fontaine. "Take that," she advised, "Joan Fontaine is a success name." So, not because of my stepfather, not because I particularly liked the combination, Joan Fontaine was born that night. Legally, Joan de Beauvoir de Havilland is still my name and I use it on all documents not related to my career. Given my druthers, neither Joan nor Fontaine would I have chosen.

The director George Stevens once asked me my real name. Hearing it, he burst into a roar of laughter, saying that when my sister's agent had proposed her for a part in one of his films, he had turned the suggestion down. "Any actress who'd assume as theatrical a name as Olivia de Havilland I can do without!"

Mother was in her element at the Château. No longer accountable to G.M., she could preside, elegantly coiffed and gowned, at tea. Olivia brought home aspiring actresses such as Jean Parker, Beverly Roberts, Jean Muir, and Julie Haydon, who later married critic

George Jean Nathan. Over the lapsang souchong, Mother would flirt with young actors and a journalist or two. Martini-making became my specialty after the tea things were cleared away. Three to one they were in those days, served in a chilled stem glass. Occasionally we danced the "Lambeth Walk" or the "Big Apple" to the phonograph. This constituted our entire social life at that time.

Weekdays at dawn, I drove Olivia up Highland and over the pass to her studio in Burbank, returned to the apartment to do her personal laundry, tidy the two-and-a-half rooms, pack her lunch, and have it ready in her dressing room when she broke from her set at noon. The trip was repeated in the evening, when the Ford and I would wait outside in the dark until my sister was good and ready to depart from her cronies in the makeup department. I did all the errands, most of the cooking. Mother answered Olivia's mail and remained in readiness should her position as hostess and chaperone be called upon. As for Olivia's and my relationship, she was the star and I was the servitor on probation.

The arrangement was untenable. Between lessons and occasional jobs, I was ruled by Mother and Olivia with an iron hand. I was once sent back to Saratoga and G.M. in disgrace. I'd had a dinner appointment to meet a dear old English actor I'd met through a newspaper correspondent. He was looking for a young actress, one who could assume a Japanese accent for his radio program. Suitably chaperoned by a mutual friend, we held the reading after dinner at the actor's house. Thanks to my year in Japan, my accent was accurate and I got the role. As it was still early when the audition ended, the gentlemen decided to take me to the Grauman's Chinese to see a movie. It happened to be an "owl show." As I'd never been to one, I didn't realize that it would go on until after midnight. Nor, in any event, could I very well have demurred with my new-found employer.

Two irate women were waiting up for me at the Château when I was escorted home. No radio show for me. I was being sent back to La Paloma. Mother, using her iciest voice, subsequently made telephone calls to the two gentlemen. I never heard from them again.

Now I was back in Saratoga under G.M.'s roof, the one I had fled from several years before. I was back with the archdisciplinarian, now to become his housekeeper and errand runner. There was no hope for a future, no way of extricating myself as I had almost no money in the bank. All my school friends had gone off to college. I

Lilian de Havilland
in *Kismet*

Tokyo rosy cheeks

Walter de Havilland
about the time he met
Lilian Rusé

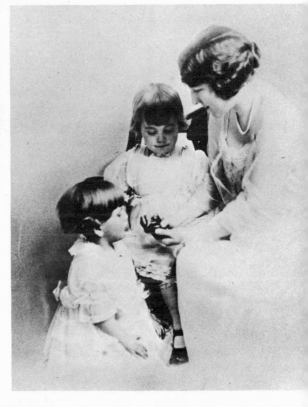

Lilian with her two girls

House in Japan

Father's second favorite game

"Hakone" in Saratoga

La Paloma

Belles of
the Prune Belt

Joan and Olivia in a Restoration comedy skit

The Iron Duke

A trying reunion with Pater, 1933

ol cat from California at Ameri-
School in Japan

No More Ladies: Franchot Tone, Joan Crawford,
Robert Montgomery and 18-year-old "Joan Burfield." Director George Cukor said I was so nervous he had to take away my one line!

O contract player at eighteen

ERNEST A. BACHRACH, RKO RADIO PICTURES

Gunga Din, with Douglas Fairbanks, Jr., Cary Grant, and Victor McLaglen

With Miss Hepburn, who saw promise in the starlet

ALEX KAHLE, RKO RADIO PICTURES

Damsel *really* in distress

Conrad Nagel, my girlhood film
crush . . .

. . . and at a premiere ten years later

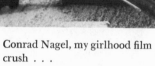

The Women: Norma Shearer, J.F.,
Rosalind Russell, Paulette Goddard,
Mary Boland

Hoop, hoop, awry! St. John's Chapel, August 20, 1939 (see page 106).

With Brian
in the Waco

Family tea at
Rodeo Drive

was painted into a corner and there seemed no escape. I would simply remain in this barracks for the rest of my life.

Soon, however, the phone rang. "Hollywood calling." No, it was not a great offer of stardom, or an agent with a Broadway play. It was from the Château des Fleurs. The chaffeur was needed again on Franklin Avenue.

13

CONTRACT PLAYER

BACK IN HOLLYWOOD, I ATTENDED WITH MY FAMILY A DINNER PARTY at the home of a British press correspondent. There I met a theatrical agent who soon placed me under contract with his agency. Then followed many an interview with casting directors at all the studios. In the rented Ford that I borrowed from Olivia, and in clothes often loaned by her, I made the rounds.

At Paramount, the drama coach gave me a scene from *Cradle Song* to memorize. One afternoon, after I had memorized the role, she led me into the casting office. The casting director was on the phone. Covering the mouthpiece with a hand that sported a star-sapphire ring, he whispered, "Go on, do your stuff, kid." He flicked his cigar ash onto the floor. As rehearsed by the coach, I knelt down beside the desk and began the scene, that of a young novice pleading with her Mother Superior. Appropriately, tears came as I progressed, commingling with the ashes on the carpet. The casting director kept saying, "Yeah, yeah, gotcha," into the phone. When both the scene and his telephone call ended simultaneously, he got up from his desk, gazed out of the window, and said, "How do you look in glad rags?" I looked down at my sweater and skirt and agreed to come back dressed in something more glamorous.

Rushing home, I changed into one of the two "after-five" dresses I owned, loosened my hair from its accustomed bun, and sped back in the Ford to the studio. "Well, that's more like it," the casting director beamed, his eyes caressing my ninety-eight-pound figure. "Whatcha doin' for dinner?" I thanked my stars that my dinner would be at the Château des Fleurs. (Paramount was one of the last studios to employ me; that casting director was then no longer there.)

I beat against studio gates to no avail. Irving Thalberg had hired me for *No More Ladies* because he wanted a "lady" for the role. The other Hollywood producers were looking for sex kittens, starlets they could put under contract who would be available, both night and day, to entertain their out-of-town business associates.

It was while we were living at the Château des Fleurs that I began to understand the rigors of film-making. I got broken in the hard way, or rather my head did. I was making a "quickie," a three- to five-day film with the champion shot-putter of the year. I was playing the usual role of "the girl rooting from the sidelines," just as I was to do again in *The Duke of West Point*.

Between takes on location, the handsome athlete would practice with a member of the crew, using for the shot anything at hand. Walking from the last camera setup on my way to my outdoor dressing room, I crossed a tennis court only to hear a shout of warning too late. A huge rock sailed through the air, felling me and splitting my scalp open.

A studio car was immediately requisitioned. A hefty gaffer (man in charge of lighting) picked me up in his arms, cradled me in the back seat. We hurtled toward Santa Monica and St. John's Hospital as he attempted to stanch the blood pouring from my gaping wound with a grimy handkerchief.

By the time we entered the hospital elevator I was too weak from loss of blood to stand on my feet. The gaffer crouched on the floor, making a lap for me to sit on, all the time murmuring, "I wish I could take it for you." He held my hand in the operating room as my blood-soaked hair was cut away and ten stitches closed the wound.

Though I never saw my Good Samaritan again, I have never forgotten his kindness. I have always had the greatest respect and admiration for the film crews I've worked with. They labor long hours, often under trying conditions. I have found them always amiable, obliging, and uncomplaining.

The night of the accident, I lay in my hospital bed, not even sure where I was. Eventually Mother arrived, then the film-unit manager. He bore a gift from the athlete . . . the large stone which had connected with my skull. It was now autographed by the Olympic champion!

After the proper condolences, the unit manager explained to Mother and me that the studio had thoughtfully rearranged the shooting schedule . . . I wouldn't have to report for work until five the next day! However, if I didn't appear, he regretted, I would be cut out of the picture.

A studio car took me directly from the hospital to the makeup department the next afternoon, where the hairdresser attempted to wash away the blood from my begrimed hair, to cover the bandage with stray locks. This procedure proved to be the most painful part of the whole experience. Weak and in pain, I somehow managed to get through the scene. Only when I heard the assistant director yell, "Wrap it up!" and the film was finished did I burst into tears. It was two in the morning.

Though my agent failed to catapult me over the studio walls, another chance for a career came, again from the theatre. I was given the ingenue role in Henry Duffy's *Call It a Day*, starring Violet Heming and Conway Tearle. After the opening-night performance at Duffy's Theatre on Hollywood Boulevard, the highly respected film producer Jesse Lasky was ushered backstage and into my dressing room. Mr. Lasky was noted for his good taste, the quality of his films such as *The Gay Deception* and *Here's to Romance*. I was extremely flattered that I had caught his attention.

Soon Mother and I found ourselves in Mr. Lasky's paneled office. I affixed "Joan Fontaine" to the bottom of a seven-year contract. No changing names now. Mr. Lasky shook our hands as we were about to leave and smilingly promised that Olivia's little sister would be a big star under his management.

After the run of *Call It a Day*, Little Sister found herself a run-of-the-mill player at R.K.O., for Jesse Lasky sold them my contract almost immediately. I had nothing to say about it. Lucille Ball and Anita Colby were also part of the studio stable, as it was called. Ginger Rogers was the queen of the lot while her mother was our designated drama coach. I went to only one lesson, as my mother could teach rings around any Hollywood acting instructor.

Before long I was given a small part in James Barrie's *Quality*

Street, starring Katharine Hepburn and Franchot Tone and directed by George Stevens. The most notable thing about the picture was the superb costuming by Walter Plunkett.

At dawn, on location, Miss Hepburn would streak on to the R.K.O. ranch in her station wagon, dressed in her habitual slacks, her auburn hair flying. At noon wicker baskets of lunch for the cast were brought from her car. To be invited to join the picnicking group was a singular honor for a struggling neophyte. (I found Miss Hepburn as fascinating then as I did in her most recent Broadway appearance, in Enid Bagnold's *A Matter of Gravity* in the spring of 1976. George Oppenheimer, the *Newsday* critic, took me to the opening-night performance. At Sardi's Restaurant later, he asked me what I thought of the play. I, feeling that the script had been overworked and was unworthy of her, said, "For me, Miss Hepburn can read the telephone book . . . and I wish she had!" George printed my remark in his review.)

During this film I came to respect and admire Miss Hepburn. In fact, I probably owe my motion-picture career to her intercession on my behalf. She went to the R.K.O. office of an old producer-friend of hers. "Put that girl in leads in 'B' pictures," she commanded. "She may go somewhere." The producer later told me of this visit. I made about sixteen "B's" before getting my first real break at another studio, when I was twenty-one. I am grateful to Miss Hepburn, and especially for the training those films gave me.

In 1937, Jesse Lasky borrowed me for *Music for Madame*, where I played "the girl on the piano bench" opposite Metropolitan Opera tenor Nino Martini. *You Can't Beat Love* with Preston Foster followed, then *The Man Who Found Himself* with John Beal. It was then that I first saw my name in lights. A friendly publicity girl whispered that a sneak preview would take place the next afternoon in Glendale. Mother and I set out in the Ford. Sure enough, when we located the theatre we saw on the marquee in bold flashing letters *The Man Who Found Himself*, starring *John Beal* and *June Fountain*. To this day close friends affectionately call me "Baby June Fountain."

Already disillusioned with Hollywood after Mr. Lasky had sold me to R.K.O., like so many pounds of meat, I had yet another eye-opener in store. The "press junket" was another name for accommodating theatre owners and press writers. A handful of starlets would be taken to a resort or hotel out of the city. Here male guests of the studios would be wined and dined, currycombed, backslapped, given their pick of the new crop with whom to spend their idle hours away from their wives. It was an accepted practice. I was ordered to go on one such jaunt to the Lake Arrowhead Springs Hotel. Mother, of course, went along.

During dinner at the hotel, with my mother sitting beside me, the publicity boys rubbed their hands together and whispered that we were all meeting in the bar after ten o'clock. I was to join them *if* I could get rid of "the old lady." Mother, overhearing, huffed, "Not my daughter. She's going to bed. She's being photographed in the morning." I saw raised eyebrows all around, frowns, winks. I dutifully marched with Mother to our suite and remained there until after breakfast, when a phony photographic layout had been scheduled.

That morning, Mother made numerous calls in vain. No photographers, no press representatives lifted hung-over heads from pillows until noon. A still photographer at last appeared begrudgingly. Shots of me were taken in a bathing suit by the pool, on the veranda, in the garden. Mother remained in close attendance. By midafternoon, with our luggage we were unceremoniously herded into a studio car and sent down the hill toward home and Hollywood.

When I returned to the studio the next day, all hell broke loose. I'd been snobbish, standoffish. Who did I think I was? If I didn't cooperate, I'd be fired. There was no room at the studio for a starlet who was "difficult." (How many sins this word covered for those who needed an alibi!) After I returned home in tears and Mother had heard the story, she was furious. We drove back to the studio. Mother marched into the publicity department, past the desks of mouth-gaping secretaries and flacks and into the office of the head mogul who had delivered the edict. She denounced him for an uncouth, conniving procurer and stormed out. My contract was dropped.

Now I found myself at Edward Small's studio in *The Duke of West Point,* cheering from the sidelines for football players Louis Hayward and Richard Carlson. At Republic, I played opposite Richard Dix in *Man of Conquest.*

Fred Astaire had been looking for a new partner, feeling that he had too long been teamed with Ginger Rogers. After trying me out in a couple of dance numbers in the R.K.O. rehearsal hall under the eye of his brilliant choreographer Hermes Pan, Fred nodded and gave his consent. Directed by George Stevens, I would play opposite

Fred in a musical based on the P. G. Wodehouse novel *A Damsel in Distress*. For me the title was appropriate.

Before the film began, I took tap-dancing lessons from Ruby Keeler's brother, who came to the house each day with a portable wooden dance floor. Why these tap lessons I never knew. I didn't have to do any tap steps in the film. I showed little promise. Obviously, I was not to give Ginger a run for her dancing shoes.

A great deal of the film was shot on location. The studio car would pick me up at dawn each morning. In the car would be various other players in the film as well as the distinguished English actress Constance Collier. I remember her being especially concerned about me, asking if I'd ever been in love. She looked wistfully out of the window and commented, "I was lucky. I had ten beautiful years with a man. That is almost more than one can expect."

On location at the R.K.O. ranch, in front of George Burns and Gracie Allen, Ray Noble, Reginald Gardiner, Monte Blue, I danced blisters on my size-four feet. The summer heat only added to my misery. All those ballet lessons I had taken in my early youth had not prepared me for duet dancing, for the leaps and lifts devised by Astaire and Pan. I tripped over fences and stepping stones to the tune of "Things Are Looking Up." George and Ira Gershwin also wrote the haunting "Foggy Day in London Town" for our film. I also fell on my face.

At the gala premiere at the Pantages Theatre in Hollywood, I was escorted by a borrowed beau of Olivia's. I was dressed in a long lilac chiffon gown and white fox cape, both borrowed from the wardrobe department. A purple orchid was pinned to the fur, as was the custom in those days, every swain being expected to produce a silver-beribboned corsage for his date. Klieg lights flashed over the theatre, brightening the skies for miles around. Microphones were shoved under well-fed faces all the way from the curb to the lobby.

My escort and I were ushered to the leather-chaired loge section amid the movie titans and their bejeweled wives. The theatre darkened, the film began. During my number with Mr. Astaire, the lady behind me loudly exclaimed, "Isn't she AWFUL!" I sank to the floor. I was consigned to "B" pictures once more.

There was either a scarcity of young English girls in Hollywood, or George Stevens took pity on me, for he signed me for *Gunga Din*, starring Cary Grant and Victor McLaglen. I played the fiancée of Douglas Fairbanks, Jr., a tiny role of little importance. But I lost a chance that might have furthered my stage career. Through the Reinhardt Drama School, I had been assigned to understudy the role of Marguerite in *Faust*. Margo, that enchanting actress in *Lost Horizon* who has been married to actor Eddie Albert for many years, was playing Marguerite. The title role was played by Conrad Nagel, Mephistopheles by Victor Jory. One night during rehearsals at the Pilgrimage Theatre, Margo was taken ill. I found myself on the stage balcony, reciting the casket scene. A voice thundered from the back of the outdoor theatre. "Who iss dat girrl?" shouted Reinhardt. "She iss vonderful!" The German director pressed forward to shower me with compliments, quite unlike his reputation for Teutonic rigidity. He wanted to place me under personal contract. How soon could it be arranged?

Returning home triumphant after this exciting, almost fictional evening, I heard the telephone ringing persistently. R.K.O.'s assistant director was sending a car for me early the next morning. I was wanted on location for my small part in *Gunga Din*. I remembered my seven-year film contract. My hopes of a stage career under the aegis of Max Reinhardt were dashed into the sands of India, simulated on the outdoor sets at Lone Pine, California.

There on location my days were lonely. Cary Grant was involved with Phyllis Brooks, who was with him on location, while in Hollywood Douglas Fairbanks, Jr., was squiring Marlene Dietrich. I remember being goggle-eyed as Doug, clad in caracul-collared evening coat, a red carnation pinned to the lapel, a black fedora framing his handsome face, awaited Miss Dietrich outside her dressing room at R.K.O. of an evening. I spent my time daydreaming about George Stevens, too infatuated to do anything but quake as he directed me on the set.

George Stevens, who was part American Indian, maintained a stoic mien, often keeping the cast and crew waiting for hours and even days while he sat in reverie or paced back and forth behind the set. It was Carole Lombard who solved the mystery of George's brown studies. "You know what that s.o.b. is thinking about when he's in one of his trances? NOT A F—ING THING!"

I was in love with George for many years, as were many of his other leading ladies. But I learned little or nothing from him as a director. His direction to me was simply "I don't know what's wrong. Let's shoot it again."

* * *

Out of the blue I heard indirectly from Father, who had apparently been following my fledgling career in the papers. From Japan he wrote R.K.O., informing the press department that his nineteen-year-old daughter was failing to support her aging father, had left him destitute. To back up his tale of woe, he came to the United States and called a press conference aboard his ship when it docked in San Pedro. He was photographed pointing to white strings that laced up his black boots, his idea of humiliating me into sharing my weekly paycheck with him. I didn't.

The photograph was duly published in the Los Angeles papers. No one paid any attention: In that town too many relatives had come out of the woodwork once someone had achieved the slightest success. It was yesterday's news.

Later, before the outbreak of World War II, Father and Yoki-san fled Japan for the United States. When Yoki-san was interned in Colorado, Father had sufficient money to install them both for the duration of the war at the Broadmoor, the luxurious resort in Colorado Springs. It certainly did not appear that he needed financial help from his struggling actress-daughter.

14

THE WAY OF A MAN
WITH A MAID

THE FIRST TIME I MET CONRAD NAGEL WAS NOT ON THE STAGE OF
Faust. I had met him many months earlier at a broadcast of "The
Hollywood Hotel," which he emceed. I was acting a role in "The
Play of the Week." He had been a crush of mine since those early
days when we saw his films at the Los Gatos movie theatre. After the
show was over, I was flattered when he asked me for a date . . . to
attend a football game. Conrad, divorced, with a daughter, Ruthie,
two years younger than I, quickly passed the test with Mother. Since
he was at least twice my age and a Christian Scientist, my body-
guards felt it was safe for me to accept his invitations to dinner with
his friends, to quail shoots, and to picnics at his house in Malibu.

We soon saw each other steadily, Conrad occasionally visiting me
on the set at R.K.O. One day, to my horror, the assistant director,
learning that Conrad had entered the gates, yelled to the guard at
the stage door, "Wheel him in!" The remark hit the newspapers and
was erroneously attributed to me. I was saddened that the studio
derided our friendship, for Conrad deserved much respect from the
industry. Not only had he been the king of the Paramount lot for

many years, but had been one of the few silent-film actors to adapt successfully to talking pictures. He had fought to keep Beverly Hills from being incorporated into Los Angeles, had been instrumental in its layout, in planting the trees on the drives and creating several parks. He was one of the founders of the Academy of Motion Picture Arts and Sciences, its early president, and involved in the creation of the Academy Awards. I was proud to be linked with the son of an Iowan minister and felt that he represented the best of Hollywood.

It was because of Conrad Nagel's receding hairline that wigmaker Westmore had been brought over from London years before. The father of the Westmore brothers started a flourishing career as toupee maker to balding Hollywood actors. I remember the shock of opening a closet at Conrad's beach house and seeing at least six wig stands, each bearing a wig of different hue and style—from boyish crew cut to pigtailed peruke. Not an extraordinary sight in an actor's house, but a bit of a jolt nevertheless.

Conrad had made a strong impression on me as a child of ten or eleven in the original film of *Quality Street* and in *Glorious Betsy*, opposite Dolores Costello. So had she. I often put myself to sleep at night replaying their scenes, weeping into my pillow at unrequited love, or clutching it passionately during imaginary embraces. He was a dashing, romantic figure and Miss Costello the epitome of blond femininity. And Mother would have approved, for they were both obviously "of breeding."

Conrad had beautiful diction and he dressed in quiet good taste. All his suits were made by the leading Beverly Hills tailor of the time, Eddie Schmitt. I had met handsome young eligible men, including Robert Stack and Jon Hall, yet after my Japan days with older men, they seemed far too immature for me. Conrad had solid roots. I doubt that I was aware then of a father-figure attachment. Conrad's appeal to me was that I appealed to him! He thought I was attractive and said so. Up to this time, by the time I was nineteen, no man in Hollywood had asked me for a date or dared crash the protective ring drawn around me by my two zealous watchdogs. Besides, I had little choice. It was either accept Conrad's invitations, since he'd been approved, or stay home.

Soon, in his shiny black Cadillac, Conrad was driving Mother and me for a weekend sight-seeing trip to the Furnace Creek Inn in the Mojave Desert. On the way, he proposed marriage. Mother, from the back seat, prodded, "Oh, go ahead. Be a sport." Sensing that the scene had been prearranged, remembering the story of Mother's impetuosity when Father proposed to her on the ship off New Orleans, I hesitated. Though Conrad was attractive, charming, a "safe" gentleman of comfortable means, he no longer fitted my pillow dreams. All my present-day fantasies were about director George Stevens, with whom I had never even had a date.

Even though I had refused to commit myself, Conrad continued as though we were an engaged couple. Mother and Olivia embarked for England shortly after H.R.H.'s famous radio abdication "woman I love" speech, leaving me in Conrad's charge. There were no questions asked . . . there might well have been!

A group of Conrad's friends were going duck hunting in northern California. With Austrian sportsman Count Kurt von Guntardt and his wife, we would be staying overnight at a French provincial manor in Montecito. Olivia and Mother would have smiled their approval.

After the dinner of game, served on "Pink Tower" Spode in the well-appointed dining room, the hunters soon retired in anticipation of an early breakfast and getaway. I was given a spacious corner bedroom overlooking the gardens. Red-and cream-colored French toile covered the walls and windows. A signed Sheraton double bed welcomed me.

At three in the morning I got up to use the bathroom. The toilet would not stop flowing. From the adjoining room, awakened by the sound of the jiggling handle, Conrad arose and came to my rescue. He speedily repaired the faulty plunger and escorted me back to my Sheraton bed.

Saying it was hopeless to try to sleep since the alarm clocks were set for five o'clock, Conrad drew up a chair and sat by my bed. I've now forgotten our conversation, but suddenly Conrad rose from his armchair, threw back my bedcovers, and before I could protest, the dire deed was done. One might say I was surprised out of my virginity. I was twenty.

When I had recovered my composure, I could only thank God and Mrs. Bruiner that the wretched hymen was no more. What anguish the protection of that tough little membrane had caused! What concern of my parents, of G.M., of Olivia. Whatever had all that fuss been about?

The whole experience had been no more than a quick surgical violation conducted with considerable modesty and no conversation. It reminded me of the time when I had to stand up in class as a child and be vaccinated. This just wasn't as neat . . . and hurt more. Yet I was smugly pleased that I could now consider myself an adult.

On the drive up the coast to the duck blinds, Conrad asserted that he was no rapist, that for the first year of his marriage he had slept with his bride in their double bed in total innocence. Only when they consulted a doctor about their childlessness were they enlightened on how to get the stork to visit them. Until that doctor's visit, neither the minister's son nor his wife had the slightest clue. Conrad had feared that our relationship might continue on a platonic basis for years had he not taken the initiative. I readily forgave him, for I saw distinct possibilities in this newfound indoor sport. That night at the local inn, he crept into my room, put the twin beds together, laid the mattresses crosswise on the frames, and began to teach me some of the intricacies of the game.

Many years later I told my Montecito hosts of the deflowering in their Sheraton bed. They promised to leave it to me in their will. Alas, they didn't. Being sentimental, I wish they had.

On long lazy afternoons at his beach house, after a picnic of Reuben sandwiches picked up at the Brown Derby on the way, Conrad instructed me carefully and thoroughly. He was a kind, sophisticated lover. The irony, for me, was it was all-pain-and-no-pleasure. It was two years before a cyst was removed with my left ovary. The pain from it had denied me that ecstasy that Marie Stopes and Topsy had promised I could expect. And always Mother's "You're nothing but a whore" rang in my ears whenever the bedroom doors closed behind us. I simply could not forget her words.

Despite tales of wild Hollywood parties, Conrad's friends, all many years my senior, were most circumspect. His group included actor Rod La Rocque and his beautiful wife, Vilma Banky, who was known as "The Hungarian Rhapsody," Bill and Leatrice Joy Hook. By then retired, once married to Jack Gilbert, Leatrice Joy was the only member of her profession allowed to join the staid Los Angeles Country Club. I often watched Conrad play eighteen holes with them there. It was a special roguish pleasure for actors to get around the club rules. A later exception at the club was Randolph Scott. When Randy told the admissions committee that they only had to look at some of his films to know he was not an actor, he was given his membership . . . but by then he was married to a du Pont.

Conrad and I continued our relationship until, in the spring of 1939, he took his daughter for a month's motor trip to New York. He felt that Ruthie was going through a difficult period and needed closer contact with her father. I was hurt, felt abandoned, if not jealous, and when he telephoned me only once during the four-week absence, I resolved to end our friendship. I was neither emotionally secure nor mature enough to share my man's life with a daughter almost my own age.

I saw Conrad once more after I broke our "engagement." In New York, many years later, he drove me out to his golf club on Long Island for lunch. As amiable as the reunion was, I realized that had I married him, my life would have been spent playing golf with an older generation. My career would never have materialized, as he would not have encouraged a working wife.

At Conrad's funeral in New York in 1970, I hesitated over which name to use in the memorial book. Did he first know me as Joan de Havilland? Burfield? St. John? After a pause, I wrote "Joan Fontaine" and gently closed the book.

15

NELLA VISTA

IN 1937 WE MOVED TO NORTH HOLLYWOOD, TO A THREE-BEDROOM, GRAY stucco house on Nella Vista, off Los Feliz Boulevard. Olivia, now possessing a driver's license, could motor through Griffith Park to Warner Brothers. I was not far from the other studios and my drama classes. With the earnings from my R.K.O. salary, I bought myself a secondhand Mercury convertible and a fairly decent wardrobe.

We furnished the house in English antiques, white chintz embossed in huge pink roses and beribboned in blue. One day Mother returned from shopping with a handsome set of books under her arm. Having just decorated her bedroom in turquoise and white, she set her purchase on her desk, declaring, "There now, the gold and red of the bindings is just the touch of color the room needs!" Looking closely, I observed the title of the four volumes. It was the Krafft-Ebing *Psychopathia Sexualis*.

At Nella Vista, Mother presided at tea and dinner. I continued to be housekeeper: planning the meals, buying the wines, and planting the garden. A Scandinavian "daily" did the cooking and housework. If Olivia had special guests to dinner, I was served a tray upstairs in my bedroom. Such is the law of primogeniture. Olivia was the principal breadwinner, and I was a paying guest.

Mother started lessons with Mme. Maria Ouspenskaya, acted at
the Pasadena Playhouse, and had several small parts in movies. Just
what her stage name was I can't recall. She changed it several times,
as I had done. Ironically, "Fontaine" had already been usurped by
her younger daughter! I do remember that she wished to be called
"Tim" or "Kit" by our suitors. As secretary to Olivia, she signed her
correspondence "Delicia Bracegirdle."

In the spring of 1939, M.G.M. signed me to play in *The Women*,
Clare Boothe Luce's successful stage play, to be directed by George
Cukor. The cast was impressive: Norma Shearer, Joan Crawford,
Mary Boland, Rosalind Russell, Ilka Chase, Paulette Goddard. Oddly
enough, my small part in the picture brought me my first critical ac-
claim. I'd had a good director.

Once my hairdresser Betty, who also coiffed Paulette Goddard,
told me that Paulette had looked up at her from the makeup table,
turned around, and said, "You're pretty, why are you a hairdresser?"
Paulette then told Betty that she, too, had had to work as a young
girl, picking strawberries in the fields. One day, she straightened up
and said to herself, "I'm pretty, why am I doing this?" She never
picked a strawberry again.

The differences in the stars made my mind boggle. Miss Shearer,
not only because of her beauty and talent, but also because her husband, Irving Thalberg, was the most important producer at M.G.M.,
had long been the queen of the lot. Hers was a dignified, delightfully
warm demeanor. A maid, dressed in black uniform, with frilly cap
and apron, attended her before each take, handing the star a mirror
and powder puff from a makeup tray. Joan Crawford, on the other
hand, had the democratic touch, knowing every grip and electrician
by name. She was costumed, as we all were, by that master couturier
Adrian. My particular remembrance is of Joan in a gold lamé halter
top and slit evening skirt. Joan kept a ball of yarn tucked in her
midriff as she knitted away between setups. Roz Russell was a tom-
boy, hearty, frolicsome, highly popular with the cast and crew. But
best of all was our director, George Cukor. He handled all the
women in the star-studded cast with tact and gallantry, so that what
might have been a highly charged assignment for any other director
turned out to be a happy association all around. We adored George,
as do all actresses who work with him.

I had known Joan Crawford since my small part in *No More Ladies*. She, like Mother, had also bought a copy of Krafft-Ebing's mag-

num opus. Since Miss Shearer was the gracious lady of the lot, Miss Crawford decided to be the cultured one. I often heard Joan's operatic vocalizing emanating from her studio bungalow at lunch hour. She wore huge horn-rimmed spectacles between takes or in her sound-stage dressing room, where an immaculately uniformed chauffeur, complete to puttees, placed a portable phonograph each morning. Strains of *Manon* or *Tosca* would seep onto the nearby set during rehearsals, much to the annoyance of our director.

One afternoon, Russian actor Ivan Lebedeff paid a call on Miss Crawford and was invited into her stage dressing room. In ten minutes Ivan came pelting out, white of face. As I happened to be close by and knew him, he rushed over to me. In shock, he blurted out, "Poor Joan! She's just told me that after her tragic life with men, she can no longer find sexual satisfaction unless she is tied to a bedpost and whipped!" He staggered away, hands against his ashen face. I could only chuckle. I had read the same chapter in *Psychopathia Sexualis*, too! Joan's imagination was on the dramatic side . . . and she obviously was an inspired conversationalist.

As Norma Shearer was number-one star of the M.G.M. lot, it meant that her name had first billing over the title of all her films. Since there was no leading man in our all-woman cast to share the credits, Norma agreed to allow Joan Crawford's name to appear opposite hers on the same line. Waiting until halfway through the shooting schedule, Rosalind Russell's agent telephoned the studio to announce that his client was ill. No, he had no idea when she would be well enough to finish the picture. The studio was frantic. The wily agent then suggested that Miss Russell might have a miraculous recovery if her name was permitted to appear above the title of *The Women* along with Norma's and Joan's. Realizing there was little alternative if the film was to be completed on time, the studio was forced to agree. The agent then telephoned Roz to tell her of her new star billing and to inquire when she would be well enough to return to work. The gleeful coconspirator exclaimed, "Right this minute!"

It was at the Thalbergs' house that I saw the rough cut of *The Women*. George Cukor and the cast were invited, as well as the inimitable Mrs. Patrick Campbell. The aging British actress, who had once been an intimate of Bernard Shaw's, was having a rocky time making ends meet and had come to Hollywood to try her luck. Her caustic tongue had caused her grief in the past and she was now, supposedly, on her good behavior. After the film was over and the lights came on, Irving Thalberg asked Mrs. Pat how she liked his wife on the screen. "Oh, charming, charming," lilted the tactless one. "Such tiny little eyes!"

It was Miss Shearer who, as the story goes, complained to her husband after seeing the rushes that she was not being photographed well. Irving questioned the cinematographer, reminding him that he had been shooting Norma for the past ten years. Unlike Mrs. Patrick Campbell, the photographer was the height of tact. "You see, Mr. Thalberg," he apologized, "since I began filming Miss Shearer, I've grown ten years older."

I had met Paulette Goddard one night at Charlie Chaplin's the year before . . . a night that was to change the course of my career. At dinner, where Paulette presided, though it remained a mystery whether she was Mrs. Chaplin or not, I found myself seated next to a heavyset, bespectacled gentleman who seemed particularly knowledgeable and pleasant. Soon we were chattering about the current best sellers. I mentioned that I had just read *Rebecca* by Daphne du Maurier and thought it would make an excellent movie. My dinner partner gazed at me through his lenses. "I just bought the novel today. My name is David Selznick." Who was I and would I like to test for the part of "I" de Winter? Would I!

During the fall of 1938 and the spring of 1939, I tested many times, first with John Cromwell directing, finally with Alfred Hitchcock. So did every eligible actress in Hollywood, including Virginia Mayo, Vivien Leigh, Loretta Young, Susan Hayward, Lana Turner, Anne Baxter, and Geraldine Fitzgerald.

Against such competition, winning the coveted role looked hopeless. My agent advised me to forget it. Anyway, by August 1939 I was getting married to Brian Aherne, moving out of Nella Vista, starting a new life. A week before my wedding, David Selznick called me on the telephone. Would I delay my plans and test once again? I declined.

16

LOVE AND MARRIAGE

IT WAS ON A WARM FLOWER-SCENTED EVENING IN THE LAST WEEK OF June 1939 that I met Brian Aherne. He was giving a cocktail party in his white colonial two-story house on Rodeo Drive in Beverly Hills. Brian had made *The Great Garrick* with Olivia in 1937, but had never asked her for a date. They had met again when Mother and Olivia were on shipboard during their trip to England, when I had been left in the all-too-tender loving care of Conrad Nagel. Still, despite later reports of columnists, there was no particular attraction between Olivia and Brian.

Brian had been born in King's Norton, England, in 1902. He was six feet two, extremely handsome, and a well-established actor on both stage and screen. His great triumph had been playing Robert Browning to Katharine Cornell's Elizabeth Barrett in Guthrie McClintic's Broadway production of *The Barretts of Wimpole Street* in 1931. Coming to Hollywood for *Song of Songs* with Marlene Dietrich, he later decided to make California his home. He was excellent in *What Every Woman Knows* with Helen Hayes as well as in *Beloved Enemy* with Merle Oberon, both of which I had seen.

Little sister Joan and Mother had been invited to his party as well as Olivia. I found myself in the garden behind his house among many members of the British colony, all with drinks in hand. Brian introduced us to his guests, leaving me to chat with an old friend, Mrs. Joseph Levy. When I explained why my name was no longer de Havilland, that I had changed it on the advice of a fortune-teller, Mrs. Levy, declaring that she had psychic talents, too, proceeded to read my palm. "You. are going to marry your host," she foretold, "and soon!" Hearing my laughter, my tall, handsome host threaded his way through his guests to hear my friend's prognostication. Since Fate had so decreed, perhaps we'd better have a date . . . he was free Wednesday or Friday evening . . . which was convenient for me? I said I'd take both. Within a week we were engaged. Within seven weeks we were married. He fitted my pillow dreams.

My fantasies were not simply romantic ones, involving me with a Prince Charming. They were far deeper than that. They envisioned a home, haven of rescue, a sanctuary. My earliest nightmare at age five, which I still remember vividly, was of being lost in a giant cabbage patch. Suddenly, in my dream, all the cabbages rose like Jack-in-the-boxes. As I tried to run out of the field, the ghoulish heads towered over me, waving their outsized arms, like bare tree branches in a storm. The gardener, on his horse, raced through the field, scooped me up, placed me before him on the saddle, and rode out of the cabbage patch to safety!

At twenty-one, I still wanted so much to be safe, with a protector's arms around me. How many temporary homes had I had? How many temporary jobs? How many contracts signed and dropped? By the time I met Brian I felt like a ball being bounced about by Destiny. To me, a career was mainly a means of survival, a method to pay my own way, a search for identity and self-expression. I longed for stability, permanency, a place to belong, someone to belong to. When Brian proposed, aged thirty-seven and looking not unlike my own father, I felt I had come home.

Meanwhile, I had met Howard Hughes. One afternoon, dismissed from the set of *The Women* earlier than usual, I stopped at the M.G.M. studio gates on my way home. There, at the flower stand, I spied Olivia's favorite pink-tinged 'Ophelia' roses, which she liked to keep in a silver Jensen vase in the living room. Buying an armful, I drove home, still in studio makeup and in my work slacks and sweater.

I breezed into the living room, bouquet in hand, to present the flowers to my sister. Mother, hostess-gowned, was presiding at the tea table. In one corner of the room, pressed against the wall, was a tall string bean of a man, dressed in white shirt, white dungarees, snap-on black tie, and tennis shoes. When he stopped trying to iron the wall in his timidity, we were introduced. It was Howard Hughes, come to pass inspection before being allowed to take out my older sister.

Olivia was less than pleased with my intrusion: this dutiful, thoughtful baby sister bearing roses had obviously planned her entrance. What absolute rot! I hadn't known anything about the tea party, much less that she had met Hollywood's most eligible bachelor. Nor did I have any control over the supply of 'Ophelia' roses at the stand, or my shooting schedule that day. After Howard left, Mother became a frustrated referee—as she had many times before. Rumors of the "feuding sisters" being circulated by the Warner Brothers' publicity department were not without foundation, yet hardly for print. Both of us led such circumspect lives that our studios were at a loss to make the two sisters exciting. Warner's took the initiative.

There has always been great curiosity about the relationship between Olivia and me. From birth we were not encouraged by our parents or nurses to be anything but rivals, and our careers only emphasized the situation. As both Olivia and I can be classified as achievers, our impetus may well be the sibling rivalry that still exists. Perhaps, without it we might never have striven to excel, might have been quite content to be housewives or schoolteachers. I doubt it, however. I felt "different" from my first conscious moments. I think Olivia did, too. As very young children we didn't conform or wish to conform to the usual behavior patterns. We didn't want to be like everyone else. We strove to be individuals, to make our personal mark on whatever we were doing. Only in our clothes did we try to be inconspicuous, wearing the same saddle shoes, the same-length dresses as our classmates. To this day we have maintained our own individuality.

I forgot about the still handsome, shy millionaire Hughes and continued seeing Brian, meeting his friends, dancing at the Cocoanut Grove. We flew in his open-cockpit, two-seater Waco biplane to Del Monte in northern California to arrange for our August wedding at St. John's Episcopalian Chapel, then opposite the Del Monte Hotel, where Danny had often taken us on weekends in our childhood.

One evening before the wedding date, Olivia said that there was to be a surprise party for me at the Trocadero. I was to come unescorted. It was all very mysterious. Going to the assigned table at the Sunset Boulevard nightclub, I was startled to see not Brian, but Howard Hughes and a few of his friends. Howard was the host. After a dinner of caviar blinis and sour cream and much champagne, Howard led me onto the dance floor. Scarcely moving his feet to the music, he towered over me as he cocked his head to listen to my nervous chatter. It was obvious that Howard was going deaf. Paying no attention to my conversation, he told me that my impending marriage was a huge mistake. That I was not marrying Brian, I was marrying him. He alleged that he had been in love me ever since our chance meeting over the 'Ophelia' roses.

I was shocked. Olivia had been seeing him steadily. I knew her feelings for him were intense, that the relative tranquillity at Nella Vista now rested upon the frequency of his telephone calls. No one two-timed my sister, whatever our domestic quarrels might be. Not if I could help it. I had heard rumors that Howard saw girls in shifts (no pun intended). Olivia was on the early shift, while actresses such as Hepburn and Rogers were rumored to have later dates with him. Howard evidently needed very little sleep.

As I was leaving the nightclub with Olivia, Hughes slipped me his private telephone number, whispering that I was to call him as soon as possible. The next day I phoned him and arranged to meet him that afternoon. I had to find out whether he was serious or indulging in some ghoulish jest. He chose as our rendezvous the garden of a Polynesian restaurant in Hollywood. We both had a lemonade. I listened to his proposal. He seemed in deadly earnest and had not changed his mind from the previous evening. I, seething inside at his disloyalty to Olivia, said nothing.

Upon returning to Nella Vista, I showed Olivia the slip of paper with Howard's private number written in his own handwriting and told her about my afternoon's encounter. I gently tried to explain that her heart belonged to a heel. In addition to the rumors in newspaper columns, the warnings from her friends, now she had real proof. Sparks flew. Hell hath no fury like a woman scorned . . . especially in favor of her sister. This, plus my engagement to Brian, was very hard for her to take.

Preparations for my wedding to Brian began. Engraved invitations were in the mail. Olivia was to be a bridesmaid, Mother the matron of honor. At I. Magnin on Wilshire Boulevard there were daily fittings for all three of us. There was trousseau shopping. Bits and pieces of furniture I'd acquired at Nella Vista were moved to Rodeo Drive for my return from the honeymoon. Evenings were spent with Brian's friends, mostly British, welcoming a new member into their close-knit society.

My account at the bank totaled $21,000. Not bad for a twenty-one-year-old to have saved from her earnings. Out of this, I gave Olivia $3000 to even our score for the allowance she had given me before I got my first job. I set aside $5000 for the trousseau, the pre-wedding party, and the breakfast following. I left $2000 in the bank for emergencies. The remaining $11,000 I mailed by check to G.M. Fontaine. Though he cashed it, he was never to mention my gesture. I wanted to start my married life beholden to no one. I felt I owed my own father nothing except for my unplanned creation.

At his Rodeo Drive house one afternoon, sitting on a couch in the bar, Brian presented me with my engagement ring, saying, "These things are awfully expensive. This cost two hundred and fifty dollars, you know." It sounded like something my father would have said. Looking at my ring finger thoughtfully, secretly wishing I had a microscope, I wondered what husbands did about pocket money for their wives. After all, if I was giving up my career . . . but the subject never came up—then or ever during our marriage.

On August 19, 1939, Brian and I, Olivia, the Buddy Leightons (he was the M.G.M. producer of *Captains Courageous* and *Lives of a Bengal Lancer*, and the best man), ushers actor Alan Napier, painter-director Jean Negulesco, and sportsman Tim Durant boarded a plane at Los Angeles Airport for Monterey, California. There we were greeted by more ushers and friends from San Francisco.

After leaving our luggage at the Del Monte Hotel, we proceeded to St. John's Chapel for the wedding rehearsal. All went well and the rector took the betrothed couple into his study. After we'd signed necessary documents, he asked of us two things. First, that I be baptized. I promised that I would, but didn't say when. His second request was that we kneel down and pray before consummating our marriage, and every time subsequently that we indulged in marital relations. Embarrassed, scarcely knowing each other, Brian and I got the giggles.

Returning to the hotel suite I shared with Olivia, I heard the phone ring. It was Mother in Saratoga. No, she couldn't join us for the pre-wedding dinner-dance. Danny was not coming at all, fearful that the excitement would give him a heart attack. She would join us in the morning. Uncle Hugh Kennedy would have to give me away. Mother had already taken care of the menus, the seating. The flowers were being flown down in a special plane from San Francisco's Podesta Florists. She had arranged for the photographers, the police cordon, the limousines, the organist. As staging was her forte, I was justly confident that she had done a magnificent job.

That evening Brian and I met our guests in the hotel's private dining room. The two empty chairs were removed and the party progressed, despite the fact that Brian was suffering from acute sinusitis and my face was swollen from a recent wisdom-tooth extraction. Dinner and toasts over, the dance music began.

Olivia spied an old friend from Hollywood, Pat diCicco, across the dance floor. They both slipped out into the gardens. Brian whispered that his sinuses were bothering him, and, taking Jean Negulesco with him, he soon retired to the cottage they were sharing. Left with our guests, I was grateful as they trickled away to their rooms. By midnight I was alone in mine, spreading out my bridal gown and veil for the noon wedding. The phone rang. This time it was Jean, saying that Brian had cold feet and wanted to cancel the wedding. Jean, in his Rumanian accent, said no, Brian wouldn't talk to me, he was too agitated.

Having no parents with whom to discuss this shattering development, not knowing when Olivia would return from her tryst, I could only say to Jean that I would be at the church at noon and Brian could take it from there. If he wanted to divorce me the next day, he could, but I did not know how to stop the preparations Mother had set in motion.

Olivia came in at three in the morning, sat on the edge of my bed to tell me about her nocturnal exploits with diCicco. I was too numb from the effects of Jean's call to do anything but listen. I never told her or Mother about the incident. I was too humiliated.

At ten that morning, I woke Olivia to get her ready for the photographic sitting. Mother breezed in, gay with excitement about her "production" to follow. She went off to check the arrangements and to dress. I donned my wedding dress, unfortunately putting the petticoat under instead of over the hoop of my satin gown. The photographs of us coming out of the church, published in a spread of the wedding by *Life* magazine, clearly show my error. My wedding day had not started well.

At eleven-thirty, Uncle Hugh fetched Olivia and me from our rooms. The great moment was approaching. Outside the hotel, roped off from the crowd of spectators, we waited in the broiling sun beside the limousines. No Mother. Uncle Hugh and the police captain frantically called her room, searched the lobby, while Olivia and I listened to the strains of organ music emanating from the church across the way. Mother finally appeared through the hotel revolving door. She'd misplaced a brooch which she considered essential for her gray lace Schiaparelli gown. The claret-colored plumes atop her velvet hat waved in exasperation. Brian was standing with his best man, Buddy Leighton, in front of the altar at this very moment. No, things were not going well.

Persuading Brian's broochless mother-in-law-to-be to enter the car, we finally arrived at the church steps. The organ struck up Wagner's "Wedding March." Down the white rose-tree-lined aisle Uncle Hugh and I slowly walked with measured pace. Next came Mother and Olivia. My sister was dressed in sea-green tulle, topped by a velvet-ribboned hat of the same color and carrying a bouquet of apricot and yellow tuberous begonias. I clutched a satin muff, and white stephanotis ornamented my veil. Mother nodded her plumes and waved left and right to the pews as she swept along behind us.

Brian had been waiting at the altar. The organist had repeated his repertoire over and over. The reluctant bridegroom had not been confident, after the midnight call, that he would not be stood up. As I reached his side, he muttered out of the corner of his mouth, "That's the last time you'll ever keep me waiting." Kneeling in front of the altar, we promised to love, honor, and cherish each other until death did us part.

17

MAN AND WIFE

THE CEREMONY WAS OVER. OUTSIDE THE CHAPEL, WAITING LIMOUSINES drove the guests to the wedding breakfast. Brian and I rode alone through the cheering, rice-throwing crowds to the hotel entrance. The bridal couple exchanged cool pleasantries.

Even taking into consideration the elegance of the flowering trees, the white satin ribbons lining the church aisle, the all-white bouquets on the altar, Mother had now outdone herself. The wedding breakfast tables were covered in chartreuse satin, cascades of pink, yellow, and orange begonias flowing down them. The entrée of chicken, ham, and mushrooms under glass was followed by flaming cherries jubilee, ladled out of carved ice figures. Obviously Mother had charmed the chef as well as the maître d'hôtel. Champagne corks popped, toasts were drunk to the happiness of the newlyweds. More toasts to the mother of the bride, reveling in the success of her production (not me, but the *mise en scène*).

I slipped away to change while the white-ribboned boxes of wedding cake were distributed to the guests. My going-away outfit was a two-piece, hunter-green light wool suit by Nettie Rosenstein, stone-marten furs, new brown suede pumps and gloves. I left my bridal clothes in my room for Olivia to pack and return to Rodeo Drive.

This she did, but not the veil. (Years later I learned from Mrs. Albert Lasker, the room's next occupant, that it had been left on the bed; not knowing to whom it belonged, she had turned it in to the hotel housekeeper. I never saw the veil again, much to my distress, for I had wanted to save the whole ensemble for a future daughter and her wedding.)

In a shower of good wishes, confetti, and rice, we departed in Brian's light-blue Packard convertible, driven up from Beverly Hills by his houseboy. On the road to San Francisco, Brian stopped the car: the rice would hurt the motor. I got down on my hands and knees, and with my new gloves flicked the white grains from the car floor while he checked under the hood.

Both of us were exhausted. After driving the seventy-five miles to San Francisco's Fairmont Hotel, we were grateful when the door of our suite shut out the last departing bellboy. Brian's sinusitis was no better. My swollen jaw was throbbing. My psyche was still numb from the midnight telephone call which neither of us mentioned.

After ordering champagne and dinner, we both changed our clothes, I into a white lace-trimmed negligee, Brian into a navy-blue-and-red-patterned dressing gown. He hoped I'd excuse the worn elbows; he'd ordered a new robe from his tailor in London, but it would take months to deliver. After a knock on the door, our dinner was served in our suite by a bevy of unctuous waiters. The door finally closed on the embarrassed newlyweds, the thirty-seven-year-old groom, the twenty-one-year-old bride.

During dinner, perhaps to conceal his apprehensions, Brian recounted his previous romance with Marlene Dietrich, his affection for her daughter, Maria. He got up from the table to illustrate ballet steps he had taught the child, having learned them while going to the Italia Conti Drama School in London. He asked me if I would object if he took Maria out one night a week. Pulling myself together, I replied, "No, not if I can go out with Conrad Nagel on those nights." He never mentioned it again, though Marlene called him several times during our marriage to ask his advice about her daughter.

With Brian pirouetting about the room, his dressing gown flapping, its tassels waving in the air, I grew increasingly numb. The foghorns in the bay hooted their melancholy warning, the plaintive sounds I remembered from my childhood.

Finally, closing the bedroom door behind us, Brian said he wished he'd remembered to pack a hot-water bottle for his sinuses. I could have used an ice bag on my aching cheek. The lights were turned out. Somewhere, from the cornice of the hotel room, I felt, Mother was watching.

During the night, I rose quietly, slipped on my negligee, and went into the adjoining room. I huddled on a marble window ledge and watched the fog whirl past our Nob Hill aerie. Brian found me asleep there in the early morning. Mrs. Aherne had a wedding night not to remember!

After breakfast we set off in the convertible for the lodge at Benbow Lake, a charming resort a hundred miles north of San Francisco. Unfortunately, photographs of our wedding had been in all the Bay papers that morning. As we registered at the desk, necks craned in our direction. The Ahernes from Hollywood were not as sophisticated as they appeared.

That evening, still at table in the dining room, Brian suggested that he go up the stairs to our bedroom first. After his pseudo-nonchalant departure, I tarried in the lounge, pretending to be engrossed in an old magazine. All eyes were riveted on the bride. Wristwatches were surreptitiously consulted, conversations lagged. After ten minutes spent in a constant blush, I tossed down the magazine, bolted up the staircase, and, to the great amusement of the guests, tripped and fell flat on my face.

Never had I slept a night beside a male before, but now yet another unaccustomed familiarity: Brian and I shared a bathroom. I just couldn't. Supposedly in search of a lost handkerchief, I braved the curious guests again. Back in the lounge I finally located the door that read "Women." I used that downstairs john throughout our stay.

Then I got the curse. Brian was indignant. In Father's voice, he accused, "Did you know this would happen?" Although I never knew in advance when this unmentionable would occur, I apologized profusely.

Next afternoon we were in a canoe on the lake, attempting to fish. Brian, his sinus condition improved, was singing, "I am Chou Chin Chow from China, Shanghai, China." I was basking in the quiet of the forest-edged lake, the chance to be away from the curious guests. A bellboy waved a towel at us from the bank. "Hollywood calling for Miss Fontaine!" Oops! We paddled to shore. I got out and took the call in the lakeside telephone booth.

It was my agent. "You've got it, you've got it!" he crowed. "*Rebecca*. You've got the part and Selznick wants you to hurry back and sign a long-term contract!" Stunned, I could only murmur that I wasn't sure I still wanted a career. I hung up and got into the canoe as Brian rowed toward the middle of the lake.

After another refrain of "Chou Chin Chow" and nary a nibble from a trout, I hesitantly relayed my agent's offer. Brian looked up into the sky, rebaited his hook, and said, "Why not? You're going to a new house, new friends. I shall be away all day filming *Vigil in the Night* . . . with Carole Lombard. You'll be lonely." Dropping his line into the water, he added, "Do it for hat money." There! Mrs. Bruiner and God had put their heads together. I wouldn't have to ask my husband for an allowance. Thus, despite his subsequent protestations that he did not want an actress for a wife, Brian sanctioned my making *Rebecca* and signing the seven-year contract which was contingent upon getting the coveted role.

As for me, continuing my career was based solely on economics. I had spent too many precarious years not to want my own security, derived from my own efforts. No man was ever going to hand me fifty dollars and a tourist ticket home. Not again.

The honeymoon was over.

On our drive south to Beverly Hills, to my new home, new life, new career, we arranged to stop off for a picnic with "Tim," as Mother wished to be called by her handsome, famous son-in-law. No "Mother" business from him! Generally good at arithmetic, she pointed out that he was nearer her age than mine. Since she had never divulged the year of her birth, or even the day, I had to take her word for it.

On a wooded knoll we sat around a checked cloth spread on the grass. Upon it stood a bottle of wine from the nearby Almadén vineyard, a hamper of delicacies brought by Mother. About us, the wild asters wore purple, in mourning for summer. The sad autumnal sun filtered down through the branches of the sycamores. A leaf would fall, to mingle with the foie gras sandwiches.

Mother was at her delicious best, flushed from the success of her production at Del Monte. She said just everyone had telephoned to tell her it had been a triumph. Her lilting laughter rang through the quiet air as she flirted outrageously with her new son-in-law. The actor flirted back. Ah, yes, Violet Kemble Cooper, oh, Sybil Thorndike. Don't tell me you know Edith Evans, too! They were having a great time: Sir Henry Irving, Ellen Terry, Sir Gerald du Maurier. They all got dusted off, as did Bernard Shaw, Oscar Wilde, Max Beerbohm, James Barrie.

I sat, sucking a blade of grass, wondering whether *Rebecca* was too modern to mention . . . Daphne's father was Sir Gerald du Maurier. That should help.

I broke into the animated conversation to say I had some news Tim might like to hear. There was a moment of silence while Brian poured Pinot Chardonnay into our paper cups. I plunged ahead, rattling off the fact that I was going to film *Rebecca,* and, to toss some names around, I added that Laurence Olivier and Judith Anderson would be in it, too.

"Very nice, Joan." Tim smiled and patted my knee. Turning to my new husband, she went on, "Now, Brian dear, did you ever know Mrs. Patrick Campbell?"

Brian related one after another of the actress's famous *bons mots, faux pas,* quick retorts. Tim giggled with her whole body, raising her paper cup to the raconteur. Brian clunked cardboard rims. I plucked another stalk of wild oats and wondered who had sown it.

Continuing our journey down the coast to Santa Maria, where we planned to stop overnight, I realized Mother had not asked me one question about my marriage, my state of mind, whether I was happy. So that's why, at the picnic, I had felt rejected, left out. Mother had let go. I was no longer her charge.

That night, in our double bed at the Santa Maria Inn, the bell in that "sacred temple" rang for the first time.

18

RODEO DRIVE

AND SO THE HAPPY BRIDAL COUPLE ARRIVED AT THEIR WHITE, ROSE-covered cottage, brick path, picket fence, and all. The fan magazines were delirious. As the Prince Charming carried the blond princess over the threshold, all those fairy-story characters stood on the lawn and applauded. Cinderella, Snow White, Elaine of Astolat. Lancelot, Prince Igor, Ivanhoe. And there was another figure who could well have been out of fiction, looming from the shadows, by the name of Adolf Schicklgruber.

From August 20 to September 3 was a short time to live a storybook romance. That autumn morning when Britain declared war on Adolf Hitler's Germany, and France speedily followed, the Ahernes' tranquillity was abruptly shattered. So it was with all the British in manicured Beverly Hills.

Calls to the British consul were placed from every bedside phone before the morning tea could steep. Should every male and female born under the British flag take the next plane home? Were we needed, expected, commanded? Eric Cleugh's advice was to carry on as usual, he'd get word to us all. No, women wouldn't be needed. Married men? Unlikely. Several actors such as David Niven and Leslie Howard packed and returned home anyway.

Eric advised that we'd be better off in America, raising money, making speeches. Bundles for Britain and Thumbs Up were formed. Brian became a flight instructor. I joined a group of women mobilized into sewing units, making endless shirts, mufflers, and mittens.

A room was given to us adjacent to the Trocadero. Here, any day of the week, bending over donated sewing machines, could be found Mrs. Ronald Colman, Mrs. Charles Boyer, Mrs. Nigel Bruce, Dame May Whitty, Heather Angel, Heather Thatcher with her monocle, Mrs. Herbert Marshall. Miles of pale-blue flannel were cut and sewn into pajamas for "our poor boys." As Dame May had been through the First World War, she and her daughter, Broadway director Margaret Webster, were the organizers. The pajamas I sewed would have crippled the wearers long before they ever walked through a mine field.

Simultaneously, I was called on the Selznick lot to rehearse. Photographic tests with dear genius cameraman George Barnes, with whom I was to work for many years. The makeup was done by Monty Westmore, one of five Westmore sons of the London wigmaker. Buddy, Ernest, Wally, and Percy all made me up during my Hollywood film days. The brothers founded the cosmetic line that bears their family name.

By mid-September, the film was under way. The cast was exceptional. David O. Selznick, meticulous in every detail from publicity to dialogue, from sets to location sites, combed the casting directory. Every player must be exactly right. Reginald Denny, George Sanders, Nigel Bruce, Gladys Cooper, Florence Bates, the Pasadena lawyer who played Mrs. Van Hopper. D.O.S. was a perfectionist, as shown by his already completed chef d'oeuvre *Gone With the Wind*.

In the preceding fall of 1938, I'd been sent by D.O.S. to the office of George Cukor. He was preparing the Margaret Mitchell epic and already had cast Vivien Leigh, Clark Gable, and Leslie Howard. He needed a Melanie. I made a grave error. I had just come from a Junior League luncheon, was dressed in a gray faille coatdress, a Burgundy velvet toque, silver-fox furs around my shoulders, all of which I had worn in an R.K.O. "B" picture and purchased after the film was completed. "Too chic, too chic!" George threw his hands into the air. "Melanie must be a plain simple southern girl."

"What about my sister?" I parried.

"Who's she?" Over the intercom George asked his secretary to arrange an interview with the Warner Brothers actress. Olivia de Havilland was to make a superb Melanie.

With my sister acting in the longest, most important film to come out of Hollywood to date, with me at Selznick's playing in *Rebecca*, with Brian co-starring with Carole Lombard, the family was riding the crest of the wave. Asking Olivia and Mother to drop by for dinner one work night—"Come just as you are"—I drove home to Rodeo Drive in my makeup and slacks as Olivia arrived, similarly attired. Brian, behind the bar, mixed the two work-weary sisters a welcome drink. We'd all been up before six.

The doorbell rang. Mother swept in in full sail with importance. "Get me a martini immediately," she commanded. "I'm utterly exhausted." She announced that she'd come straight from her lesson with Mme. Ouspenskaya and had been "going through an imaginary revolving door all day!" Mother was not impressed by movie actors. *She* was involved in stage technique, with the Stanislavsky Method.

To my knowledge, Mother saw only one film of mine. She acted as my substitute when I was in the hospital for the removal of an ovarian cyst. Brian escorted her to the premiere of *Rebecca*. Meeting the powerful columnist Louella Parsons at the postpremiere press party at Ciro's, Mother was fawned over. "This must be a golden moment for you, Mrs. Fontaine . . . your daughter catapulted to stardom by this film." Mother looked coolly down her aquiline nose and replied, "Joan has always seemed rather phony to me in real life, but she's quite believable on the screen."

Never, ever, did Mother acknowledge that she had seen me on the screen during my entire Hollywood career. She never admitted viewing any of Olivia's films either. At least, not to me.

In 1963 she watched me rehearse with Macdonald Carey in *Marriage-Go-Round* at the Music Tent south of San Francisco. When I was dismissed for the day, she chided, "Joan, I couldn't understand one word you were saying. It's not my ears, it's your diction!" She absently patted the hearing aid on her left bosom.

19

REBECCA

MAKING *Rebecca* WITH ALFRED HITCHCOCK WAS A LEARNING TIME. HE combined two attributes of a great cinema director—he knew acting, he knew visual mood. He would sketch on an oversized drawing pad exactly the effects he wanted. He'd then show the model to his cinematographer George Barnes, the head gaffer, and to me. One such drawing was of "I" de Winter, the character I played, cringing in an oversized wing chair, light just crossing her face so only the terrified eyes peered out. The rest was in darkness. We all could see precisely what he wished to photograph.

Joan Harrison, who with Robert Sherwood adapted the script from Daphne du Maurier's novel, was constantly on the set lest an *if, and,* or *but* be questioned. Hitch's petite wife, Alma, had been a cutter, so her advice was invaluable. I am sure that the film was a three-way collaboration, with Selznick as the devil's advocate.

Before George Cukor, I'd never worked with an "actor's director" and have worked with few since. Most of them, like George Stevens, knew the camera well, but once George said "Action," the actor was supposed to know his lines and make the best of them on his own. On the other hand, Hitch had a good ear. He had patience, authority. He had taste. Most of all, he had imagination. We liked each other and I knew he was rooting for me. He had a strange way of going about it, as actors who have worked with him have verified. His technique was "Divide and conquer." He wanted total loyalty, but only to him.

The very first week of shooting, he confided to me that Olivier really wanted his fiancée, Vivien Leigh, in my role. Again, Hitch said that Larry had just come to him, saying Fontaine was awful and that Vivien was the only one who should play opposite him. As was Hitch's intention, I believe, I could hardly be friends with Laurence Olivier after that, though I hope I didn't show it.

Olivier did show it. One morning when I'd been married less than six weeks, Larry used a four-letter word as he blew a take. Though I'd seen it, in those pre-*From Here to Eternity* days, written on walls and fences, I'd never heard it spoken aloud. Hitchcock must have seen my shocked expression, for he cautioned, "I say, Larry old boy, do be careful. Joan is just a new bride."

Turning to me, Larry countered, "Who's the chap you married?"

Proudly I boasted, "Brian Aherne."

Mr. Olivier strode off, hurling over his shoulder, "Couldn't you do better than that?" I was shattered. Arriving home that evening, I gazed upon my Prince Charming with new eyes. Try as I would to forget his remark, Larry had rudely awakened me from my pillow dream. I never told Brian.

Vivien got her revenge, too. One Saturday evening she and Larry had asked us to a cocktail party at their rented house on Crescent Drive. The maid showed us to the pool, where Brian and I waited alone in the garden for an hour. Eventually, Vivien and Larry sauntered, arm in arm, across the lawn from the house. They offered no apology. I don't know whether they'd deliberately given us the wrong hour; we left without finding out. Vivien and I were to cross swords again in 1965.

The British are a cliquey lot. Not only on the set did Gladys Cooper, Judith Anderson, Nigel Bruce, George Sanders, and Olivier hang together, but they would sit in one another's dressing rooms, swapping theatre stories, recalling old chums from their Mayfair days.

On my twenty-second birthday, my one day off in the two-month shooting schedule, the assistant director called our house at noon, saying Hitchcock wanted me on the set at four that afternoon to rehearse a scene for the next day. No, I didn't need to be in costume and makeup. Begrudgingly, I drove to the studio, where I was told to wait on the set in my green canvas cubicle until called. When I could have been home, working in the garden, enjoying my day of leisure!

Suddenly I heard "Happy Birthday to You" being sung by many voices. Emerging from my dressing room, I was surrounded by the entire crew, Monty Westmore, George Barnes and his assistant, Jack Warren, my hairdresser, the wardrobe girl, and Hitchcock. On a tea table, the gift of one of the carpenters, who had made it himself, stood a lighted birthday cake. An afghan crocheted by the wardrobe girl. Assorted presents from the crew. The only actor present was Reginald Denny, who told me that the hour's delay was caused by the fact that numerous telephone calls had been placed to Judith Anderson's dressing room, where the other actors had congregated. The British brigade couldn't be bothered to attend my surprise party.

The Beverly Hills British colony was a tight little island, too. Brian's group consisted of the Ronald Colmans, he the self-appointed King-of-the-colony, while the self-appointed queen was Basil Rathbone's wife. She reputedly changed her name from Ida Berger to Ouida Bergere. Then there were Sir Cedric and "Pixie" Hardwicke, Herbert Marshall and his American wife, Lee Russell, the Aldous Huxleys, Christopher Isherwood, Maureen O'Sullivan and John Farrow, Mr. and Mrs. C. Aubrey Smith. Also David Niven, Merle Oberon, Sylvia Ashley, married to Douglas Fairbanks, Sr., the Walter Pidgeons, Claude Rains, Ray and Mal Milland, Boris Karloff, Madeleine Carroll, Ida Lupino, Cary Grant. The list goes on and on. All these British were working in Hollywood as the Forties began, when the studios were making so many films from such English novels as *Mrs. Miniver, Pride and Prejudice, Waterloo Bridge, Ladies in Retirement,* and *Random Harvest.*

This tight-knit set occasionally opened its door to non-British such as Clifton Webb, Cole and Linda Porter, Rosalind Russell and her husband, Freddie Brisson, Clark and Ria Gable, Tyrone and Annabella Power, Constance Bennett and Gilbert Roland, Gene Tierney, Oleg Cassini, the Gary Coopers, Joan Bennett and husband Walter Wanger, the Artur Rubinsteins, Ethel Barrymore, and her son Sammy, the Fred Astaires, Humphrey and Betty Bacall Bogart.

To be asked to the Colmans' "house on the hill" was considered the stamp of approval. They honored us by giving us our first dinner party when we returned from our honeymoon. Ouida Rathbone's parties were command performances. Spending money like a Hollywood producer, Ouida would give lavish dinners, champagne flowing like the conversation of the illustrious guests. Greer Garson told me that when she was making *Mrs. Miniver*, she telephoned Ouida from her set to say she was exhausted and had to be in the makeup department at six the next morning. Might she beg off? Ouida imperiously replied, "You will come. You will sit at the table through the soup course, then you may leave. I've had your name embroidered in pink satin ribbon on the lace cloth at your place."

Greer went.

We were all obliged to attend one particular pre-Christmas party of Ouida's. For British War Relief, she, as the reigning hostess of Hollywood, had decided that this time people would have to pay to come . . . at one hundred dollars a plate. Naturally, we could not refuse to buy tickets for such a worthy cause. It would be a white-tie affair. Snow machines would provide cover for the lawn outside the Beverly Hills hotel. (That lawn is now the parking lot.) Sonja Henie would skate on man-made ice. All the guests would pull up to the hotel's canopied entrance in sleds hired for the occasion.

It was obvious the British War Relief would see very little revenue from the spectacle, but the papers would extol Mrs. Rathbone's showmanship. It was with dread that five hundred of the loyal and true began to dress for the soiree.

At six, it began to rain. By seven the drives of Beverly Hills were coursing with water. The manufactured snow on the hotel lawn was reduced to slush. A few loyal-to-Basil friends arrived at the ballroom promptly at eight o'clock, finding it difficult to conceal our Cheshire-cat smiles.

But Ouida had the final word. Taken with a sudden attack of flu, she was home in bed. Devoted Basil put every guest on the phone to Ouida. We all lied that the party was brilliant. It had been, undeniably, a washout.

20

TROUBLE IN PARADISE

BORN MAY 2, 1902, BRIAN WAS A TRUE TAURUS. SHORTLY AFTER OUR marriage, when we gave an intimate dinner at 703 North Rodeo Drive, Brian started on a conversation that could only be embarrassing to one of our guests. Surreptitiously putting my foot out, I managed to nudge his ankle. Without pausing in his monologue, he eyed me coldly and demanded, "What are you kicking me under the table for?" Brian was indeed a bull in a china shop.

Another instance of insensitivity occurred when, with Katharine Cornell, Gertrude Macy, and Nancy Hamilton, we'd all gone to see actress Margalo Gillmore replace Dorothy Stickney in her husband's Broadway play, *Life with Father*. Waiting for Margalo to join us at "21" after the performance, Brian asked us all what we thought of Miss Gillmore in the part. We all concurred, good actress that she was, physically she was not as petite as Dorothy, thereby lacking the Billie Burke quality demanded in the mother role. Just then Margalo, flushed from her first-night success, the praise from admirers in her dressing room, dashed into the restaurant. Brian, rising from our table, put his outstretched arm over her head and announced, "See, girls, Margalo's not all *that* big!"

But it was at our Christmas party in 1939 that I realized that I'd better not look for empathy, not to mention sympathy, in my marriage partner. As a surprise for Brian, I wanted our first Christmas to be a very special English one: holly and ivy, partridges on pear trees, suckling pig, roast beef, flaming plum pudding with hard sauce, a huge bowl of trifle sprinkled with almonds, citron, candied cherries.

A dear, highly talented friend, set designer John Hambleton, whom I'd met at R.K.O. and who would do sets for several films of mine in the future, agreed to have canvas flats painted to resemble an English tavern, to rent taproom chairs, to encase our stone terrace and so transform it into a pub, dart board and all.

By seven-thirty on the night of the party, most of the British colony had arrived, plus Rosalind Russell and her escort and the critic John McClain. Sixty guests milled about the newly created tavern, drinking eggnog, Pimm's cups, gimlets, rum punch, or just plain whisky-soda. I introduced, ladled, carved, served, went back for seconds, replaced the carols on the phonograph, wiped up spills, took out used plates to the pantry, emptied ashtrays. By 3 A.M. the happy guests had gone, the catering vans departed, the shambles left for cleaning up later.

As I was about to go up to fling my exhausted body into our double bed, Brian stopped me at the bottom of the stairs. Pleased as Christmas punch with my surprise present to him, he threw out his chest. "I say, I do think people like coming to *my* house!" Not even a pat on the head for me?

Before he awoke at noon, I packed and left for my Sheraton bed at Montecito and a respite from marriage. Furious at his lack of concern for me, and hurt by his lack of appreciation of my efforts, I most of all resented the first person singular for what I had thought was *our* house. Most of the redecoration I had paid for myself out of my salary from Selznick Studios. But after Brian's remark I realized that it wasn't my house. Then I must be a guest?

In London, before he came to the United States to give his brilliant interpretation of Robert Browning opposite Katharine Cornell in *The Barretts of Wimpole Street,* Brian had been desperately in love with actress Clare Eames, wife of playwright Sidney Howard. After a serious illness, Clare died in Brian's arms. He later told me that even during his great success on Broadway in 1931, he would find tears running down his face as he walked home from the theatre.

Our first trip east in 1940 was to stay in Hartford, Connecticut, where Clare's aunt, Helen Chapman, was dying of cancer. At best, it was not a happy experience for the new bride and I was particularly shaken at seeing Brian's and Clare's photographs on the living-room piano. During our days there, Brian played golf with his host while I roamed alone about the Hartford Museum, lunching on sandwiches in the rose garden.

On this trip I fortunately met an enchanting neighbor, Mrs. Walter Allen, mother of four. Leslie's heart was enormous. So was her body. Weighing two hundred pounds, Leslie had great energy, many friends, a lust for life. Though she was twice my age, we became fast friends and future traveling companions.

It was Leslie who first took Brian and me to the *cordon-bleu* in New York for cooking lessons. Here, under the fierce scrutiny of Dione Lucas, I made all kinds of gourmet delights, among them a whole napoleon. Thrilled by my masterpiece, I took it back to my hotel on its wooden board, maneuvering it through the revolving doors of the St. Regis, and past the desk for all eyes to admire. Only when it completely decomposed did I take it off the mantelpiece in my sitting room. Leslie also took me to Lucie Newman's needlework shop on Madison Avenue, where I was introduced to the delightful hobby of needlepoint.

Leslie took me to all the leading couturiers. To Hattie Carnegie, to Mainbocher, to Sophie. To hat designers Lilly Daché, John Frederics, Sally Victor. I'd order my seasonal wardrobe, have the first fitting, and scoot off to meet Leslie in the Maine woods. (On my return I would have the final fittings and take my chic clothes back to Hollywood, where they were often copied for films I was making.) Leslie would meet me in a cabin at Rangeley Lake. Our Maine guide would have already located the best sites for grouse or duck shooting, the best part of the lake for trout fishing. Autumn, we'd meet in Vermont for hayrides through the apple orchards. Sometimes Brian and Leslie's family would come along.

And it was Leslie who introduced me to Suffield, Connecticut, and the Philip Schwartz family. My first Thanksgiving in New England was spent at "Brookside," with this delightful, horse-breeding and -racing family in the rolling hills of that benign tobacco-raising countryside. At Brookside dogs padded underfoot. A duck blind nestled by the pond. As I'd longed for a brother, the Schwartz sons were instantly claimed by me. "Bunny" was the younger, tall, artistic. His older brother, "Phibby," was a few months younger than I, making him a mere child to my Hollywood eyes, but our Huckleberry Finn–Tom Sawyer relationship was strong. We'd beagle, shoot blackbirds molesting cornfields, tramp through the woods for pheasant or grouse, fish for shad in the Connecticut River. We would drive his Stutz Bearcat through Suffield, waving at the postman or the local banker. Later I was to rent houses in this jewel of a New England village, to which I gratefully escaped from Hollywood.

21

NO FEAR OF FLYING

BRIAN OWNED A PLANE AND I LEARNED HOW TO FLY. TOMMY OSTER-meyer was my instructor. Knowing that I had spent considerable time as navigator while Brian piloted, and came from an airplane family, Tommy lost little time in preliminary instruction. My first lesson was in a Taylorcraft. Tommy showed me how to execute spins, stalls, Immelmann turns. Then I took the stick and went through each maneuver.

After my fourth hour lesson, Tommy climbed out of his seat, threw the stick over his shoulder onto the tarmac, and waved me up! I was too astonished to do anything but obey. With one eye on the airspeed indicator, I pushed the throttle forward. Easing back the stick at 55 m.p.h., I climbed to a thousand feet, circled the field, and came in for a three-point landing. I walked into the hangar at Mines Field, helmet in hand, as coolly as though I were Amelia Earhart. I had earned my student pilot's license.

Ten years later, Tommy, out of the blue and probably in his cups, telephoned me to say that I was the best pupil he had ever had. I was to hear this again from my riding master in the hunting field in Ireland in 1957. G.M. and his rigid discipline weren't all bad—I'd learned to obey instructions.

Now Brian ordered a Warner-engine 145 Fairchild. We picked up the plane at the manufacturers' in Hagerstown, Maryland. Now we were to spend long hours in the air, crossing the United States several times, spending weekends flying to Del Monte, Hoover Dam, Palm Springs, wherever there was an airport. A trip across the country under the aegis of a British War Relief campaign called Thumbs Up was particularly notable. On one of our stops we were speaking at the Mormon Temple in Salt Lake City. It happened to be the anniversary of a college sorority and all the girls celebrated by coming to the Temple to meet the handsome actor. Microphones were thrust in front of us. Brian was to deliver a message to the R.A.F. pilots who would be listening to a shortwave rebroadcast. Did he have anything in particular to say to these brave airmen? Brian said yes, indeed, he did. "Chaps, keep your peckers up!" Silence enveloped the Temple. The girls fled in embarrassment. The presiding minister blanched. Only when I got my English husband back to our hotel did I inform him that in America "pecker" did not mean "chin."

With flying friends we would take off from Philadelphia in a seaplane to fish from the pontoons in out-of-the-way Maine lakes. One Indian guide told me that he hadn't been into such terrain since he was a boy. I loved the life. Often we would troll for bass or landlocked salmon in Moosehead Lake or paddle canoes down the Penobscot or the Allagash.

We would have idyllic days in late spring or early fall, stopping with our catch on sandy beaches. Our picnic lunches were my idea of heaven: ears of corn roasted in their husks over the campfire; potatoes covered with mud and cooked in the embers; "camp coffee" made from water right out of the lake; often lobsters, kept alive in salt water in the pontoons during the flight from Gloucester on the Massachusetts coast.

One late afternoon as I was trolling from a canoe, listening to the call of the loons, I heard the sound of a distant flute. It came from a cabin in the pine forest where flautist Kincaid of the Philadelphia Symphony spent his summer holidays.

Once we were flying over Millinocket, near the Canadian border, and were low on gas. Looking down, I spied a dock, a farmhouse, a gas pump. We landed the plane and knocked at the farmhouse door. The Dean Chase family and workhands were having their noontime dinner around the laden kitchen table. The sturdy white serving bowls contained produce from the farm, cooked with loving care by jovial Mrs. Chase: succotash, kale cooked with pork rind, mashed potatoes and country gravy, wax beans, corn bread, pork chops, apple pie. They insisted that we join them. Meal first, gas later. After stuffing us with the best of American cooking, Mrs. Chase cut huge wedges of pie for us to take to our fishing companions, awaiting us on the next lake. She included plates and forks. We protested that paper plates and plastic forks would be quite adequate. "Not for *my* pie," she proudly protested. I loved "Ma" Chase for her hospitality, but most of all for her honoring of her own handiwork.

For years thereafter, on each Christmas in Beverly Hills, I would receive boxes from the Chase farm: jams, honey, pickles, preserves, fruitcake. One year a double wedding-ring quilt arrived, made by Ma's sewing circle during the winter snows. Only in America could one find such generosity of spirit.

One fishing trip to Oregon brought us a fantastic catch. At sundown on the Deschutes River, Brian and I struck a school of whitefish. In half an hour we'd pulled in fifty-three of the silver beauties. What to do with them? We couldn't eat them all. We packed them in dry ice and shipped them off to friends. Alfred and Alma Hitchcock received theirs—the ice melted, the fish a rotting stink. Sensitive Hitch thought there was a hidden meaning behind my gesture! And when, on one of our trips to Williamsburg, I sent him a Virginia ham, he said with vengeful relish that he knew who'd sent it without looking at the sender's name on the package! Dear Hitch, what a love he was always!

22

HUMAN BONDAGE

MOST OF MY TIME WAS SPENT AT RODEO DRIVE IN BEVERLY HILLS, getting up at dawn six days a week, filming long hours at the studio, returning exhausted each night to study the lines for the next day's scenes. During my marriage to Brian, I made *Rebecca, Suspicion, This Above All, The Constant Nymph, Jane Eyre,* and *Frenchman's Creek.* With the exception of the last one, for which I was given the *Harvard Lampoon*'s award for the worst actress of the year, I can be reasonably proud of them all. They were made under the terms of my contract with David O. Selznick.

Once one is established, being under long-term contract has dubious merit. The studio is supposed to build the player, buying properties, issuing press releases, creating a star of the first magnitude. That is the way it is supposed to work. In the case of David Selznick, he never made another film with me, after *Rebecca,* but loaned me out to other studios. He loaned out his other contract players, too, including Ingrid Bergman, Jennifer Jones, Joseph Cotten, and Dorothy McGuire.

Ingrid and Joe, thinking they might embarrass David into being more generous, one evening disguised themselves as maid and butler, waited on table at the Selznicks' all through the dinner party until a guest spotted the hoax. I doubt if their charade softened the businesslike heart of D.O.S.

An actor pays 10 percent of his salary to his agent. There was a time when an agent had only two or three special clients. He advised them, kept in touch with the latest films on the production agenda, schemed, pushed, planned, haggled. The agent himself often bought suitable scripts for the actor, or he located them and brought them to the attention of producers. The agent, much like the impresario, designed a career, and his best interests were to keep his client alive and well and working in Hollywood. Eventually the system changed. Obviously, 10 percent of the salary of many actors is more than the increment from a few. So agents soon became a switchboard answering service, relaying to the actor any offers that might come in; accepting or declining them according to the wishes of the client; bargaining for the salary; drawing up any special details attached to the standard Screen Actors Guild contract. Agenting thus became a big wholesale business run by the 10-percenters, otherwise known as flesh peddlers.

I can't remember a film agent trying to get a role for me or finding a suitable assignment and going after it. I've had many agents during the course of my career. As affable as they may have been, wining and dining me, sending lavish presents on Christmases and birthdays, to my knowledge not one of them has ever suggested me for a specific role.

David O. Selznick was 90 percent brighter than the 10-percenters. He gave his contract players a percentage of the salary he got for them on loan-out to other studios, and pocketed the rest. Ingenious. I was under a seven-year, exclusive, fifty-two-week contract to him. As I remember, at the beginning my salary was $250 a week. If it took eight weeks to shoot Rebecca, I was then paid only $2,000—regardless of the fact that the film was a financial bonanza for Selznick. My yearly salary of $13,000 was increased only slightly by semiannual raises during the seven years.

Although I made no other films for him personally, D.O.S. made huge profits by loaning me to other studios. For example, my last film under the Selznick contract was The Emperor Waltz for Paramount. D.O.S. received $225,000 for my services. I received $75,000—minus my agent's commission.

If a contract player refused an assignment given him by his studio, he was "suspended," which meant that he was placed in a vacuum, a no-man's-land, until he came to his senses or another role was found for him. He drew no salary nor could he work at any other film company or go on the stage. An actor sitting at home, gazing at unpaid bills, waiting for the phone to ring, is hardly a most happy fella.

Jean Arthur, that delightful comedienne of *Mr. Deeds Goes to Town* and *You Can't Take It with You*, told me recently of a time when she had been under suspension by Harry Cohn and Columbia Studios for two years until her contract ran out. In 1937 she was given notice to appear at Warner's on loan-out at a certain date. Her inquiries drew no satisfactory response. She was not even told the title of the proposed film, the director, or the cast. As the time to report at Warner's grew near, Jean and her husband, Frank Ross, got into their car and drove up the coast of California to the northern shores of the Pacific. She was out of work, without an income for twenty-four months. It was on this layoff that they found and bought the house in Carmel where until recently she lived.

Studios also encouraged the actor to buy a large house, several cars, and to hire servants—perhaps to purchase a yacht or racehorses. This was considered necessary for the star's "image." It also brought him to heel very quickly when the studio applied pressure. If it did not, the trick was to submit a horrendous script which the actor would be forced to turn down, thereby putting himself on layoff. Many a dreadful part has been played by an actor whose financial affairs were such that he dared not refuse. Many an actor has ruined his career by taking such assignments.

Time spent on suspension was tacked onto the end of one's contract. I believe I would have had three more years of servitude to D.O.S. had it not been for Olivia.

After her triumph in *Gone With the Wind*, Olivia was handed a series of mediocre scripts when she returned to her home studio, Warner Brothers. Her employers felt she was now great "box office" and her name could sell any piece of tripe. She rebelled and was automatically suspended. Bravely, she took her fight all the way to the Supreme Court of California. In 1944, that august body handed down what is known as the de Havilland decision. It released all of us from having to serve the time extended on our contracts through suspensions. Every contract player owed Olivia a great debt of gratitude. The decision also contributed to the demise of the studio system and of Hollywood.

When Olivia's Warner Brothers contract expired, she was free to select her own scripts, including *The Heiress, The Snake Pit,* and *To Each His Own,* and win two Academy Awards. During the first half of the Forties, however, my career was under total control of David O. Selznick. I had several wonderful offers from Broadway, several great possibilities at other studios. Unless D.O.S. was willing and could get the price he demanded for me, I idly sat at home. I was told that I was ungrateful, arbitrary, and temperamental if I refused a role he arranged for me at another studio. Telegrams as long as a roll of bathroom tissue would be thrust by Western Union messenger through the mail slot at 703 North Rodeo Drive, all berating me in tyrannical language. It was part of his psychological warfare to keep his players in line.

Studios used the press for their own ends. The recalcitrant actor would read that he was misbehaving, perhaps even that there was marital trouble at home, that he was "slipping." Sooner or later, he capitulated. The barrage from Selznick when I refused to make the Technicolor spectacle *Frenchman's Creek* was so great that I eventually weakened and gave in. I think that was the turning point of my career. Had I had a more secure financial position, a more solid marriage, I might have held out. I should have retired from films until my contract ran out or D.O.S. offered me something better.

2

ON STAGE AND OFF

During 1940, I returned to the stage. A British War Relief production of Noël Coward's *Tonight at Eight-Thirty* was presented in Los Angeles and San Francisco. Noël came from London to see us. The illustriousness of the cast was staggering. No producer could have hired a more star-studded one. Imagine *Brief Encounter* played by Herbert Marshall and Rosalind Russell, *Ways and Means* with Brian Aherne and Greer Garson, *Red Peppers* with Reginald Gardiner and Binnie Barnes, *Fumed Oak* with Heather Angel, *Family Album* with Gladys Cooper (later to be replaced by Claire Trevor), Philip Merivale, C. Aubrey Smith, and Olivia's little sister. We played the entire run to sold-out audiences, and the British War Relief's coffers overflowed.

It was also the year I learned to fly and made my hole in one at Cypress Point. I was also nominated for an Academy Award. Though *Rebecca* earned the best film award for the year, I lost out to my friend Ginger Rogers in *Kitty Foyle*. I wasn't surprised or sorry. Ginger, always in dancing roles with Fred Astaire, now proved that she was a talented actress as well. She won over me in *Rebecca*, Katharine Hepburn in *Philadelphia Story*, Martha Scott in *Our Town*, and Bette Davis in *The Letter*. For me to have won it with my first good role would have been precipitous. The voters might well have thought Hitch was my Svengali, that after so many undistinguished performances in the past, surely it was Hitchcock who had mesmerized me into the performance I was nominated for. However, I did receive the New York Critics Award, as well as the Canadian.

The Motion Picture Academy was formed in 1927 by a body of film people who wished to raise the standard of production, to give the cinema a more serious place among the arts, to reward outstanding achievement. It was in no way a publicity stunt for Hollywood. It is not possible to influence the votes of Academy members. The voters may have their own studio loyalties, their own personal biases, but the Academy itself is comprised of members who have gained recognition in their film-making categories, and therefore are qualified to join the Academy upon invitation.

The most amusing Academy Awards went to the 1934 film *It Happened One Night*. Both its stars had been reluctant to film this comedy: Claudette Colbert was about to sail for Europe, Clark Gable was being "punished" by his studio for turning down another script and was ordered to make what was expected to be a "turkey." The rest is motion-picture history.

The first Academy dinner I had attended, held at the Los Angeles Biltmore Hotel, was in the spring of 1938. Bette Davis had already won for *Dangerous*, in 1935. I overheard a Warner Brothers publicity woman say with a chortle, "This is the last time Davis will win if I have anything to say." An employee of Bette's own studio! I was horrified. Evidently the woman felt unappreciated by Bette. Perhaps Miss Davis had failed to send her a Christmas present that year, had not waved to her across the set with enough warmth. After my experience with the R.K.O. publicity department, I was not surprised, only sad that studio politics even encompassed, though only in a minor way, the Academy. That night, Bette did win her second Oscar, for *Jezebel*, but it was her last, as the publicity woman had predicted.

Looking back on Hollywood, looking at it even today, I realize that one outstanding quality it possesses is not the lavishness, the perpetual sunshine, the golden opportunities, but *fear*. Fear stalks the sound stages, the publicity departments, the executive offices. Since careers often begin by chance, by the hunch of a producer or casting director, a casual meeting with an agent or publicist, they can evaporate just as quixotically.

It was and is necessary to play the game, don an artificial facade of amiability, to appear as though one has an independent income and a Hollywood career is just a lark that will continue forever. The truth behind this lie is that most of us actors, writers, directors, even those in the publicity and makeup departments knew that the industry was a day-by-day business, that layoffs, suspensions, idle weeks and even months were part of the pattern. Studios one day might be grinding to capacity while next month only one film would be scheduled. This meant feverish activity followed by anxious weeks with no paychecks for workmen, carpenters, electricians, all the way up to the producers. Those lucky enough to be under contract never knew whether their options would be renewed. One dyspeptic studio head, without a second thought, could pick up the phone and say, "Get rid of so-and-so." Then it was left to the artist's agent to break the news, "Your services are no longer required."

The client was then, in Hollywood parlance, "between assignments." Fear clutches the abdomen at every ring of the phone. So does hope. Is the caller a bill collector, an income tax examiner, a producer with a script, an agent with a contract offer, an invitation to a premiere . . . or a friend, also "between assignments," asking for a loan?

At Hollywood dinner parties I've heard actors, directors, and writers crucified as producers and their wives would loudly "thumbs down" a hapless artist to the merriment of the other guests . . . an Edsel car could not have come out worse. But the Hollywood philosophy was that if one studio could fire an artist, the other studios wouldn't want him either, no matter what good performances were in his record. *The Hollywood Reporter* and *Variety* revealed with alacrity just who was now off the payroll.

To stay and brave it out . . . or slink away into obscurity? Some simply committed suicide.

Often success was harder to take than failure. The actor or director with a sudden hit or the latest Academy Award was in great demand, being invited to serve on various committees, to attend all the industry functions. On the lot there would be much backslapping and fawning buddyship. Much "I knew it all the time," "We must get together," "How about lunch and golf at my club on Saturday?" The actor has a good memory. It's part of his job. He thinks of yesterday, ponders tomorrow. He returns home from the studio, wondering if he has any real friends at all.

By 1941 I realized that my marriage was in danger. Since I was away at the studios so much of the time, I knew that in my absence there was plenty of opportunity for marital dalliance. Brian was handsome. Hollywood was a mecca of beautiful women. An affair with a famous actor is a bangle on the charm bracelet of any marauding, ambitious female. And it is more fun to steal a successful woman's spouse than just any male.

Midnight telephone calls, oddly phrased telegrams, letters with feminine handwriting on the envelopes, even matchbooks with recognizable initials came to Rodeo Drive. I soon wore myself into a nervous, jealous, suspicious, unsatisfied neurotic.

My only escape was in taking trips by myself, meeting Leslie Allen, renting a house in Suffield. I had to get away from Rodeo Drive, from David Selznick and his telegrams, from the Hollywood columnists who daily predicted dire happenings to one's professional and personal life. From the Hollywood parties where box-office ratings, the latest motion-picture reviews, and studio intrigue were the only allowable conversation. Where producers, sucking expensive cigars, would sum up their stable of actors with remarks like "Errol Flynn? He can't act his way out of a paper bag." "Ann Sheridan? She's got the best pair of knockers on the lot." If you'd read a book, traveled, could discuss anything other than movies, it was best to keep quiet.

So I traveled. My first ocean voyage since returning from Japan was to the South Seas. But not before I made *Suspicion* at R.K.O., opposite Cary Grant, with Alfred Hitchcock once again directing.

The scenario, taken from Francis Iles's novel *Before the Fact*, was one that Cary felt would give him a serious acting role—unlike the comedies he'd been making, such as *The Awful Truth* and *Bringing Up Baby*. With his consent, I was assigned to the feminine lead of Lina, a dowdy, gawky heiress, married against her family's wishes, to Johnny, played by Cary, a scheming, N.O.C.D. ("Not our class, dear") adventurer bent on getting his wife's money. Originally, in the novel, he did this by killing her. For the sake of the fans, it was shot two ways, the alternative being a happy ending. The fans at the previews won out.

To a friend I wrote in May 1941: "I have just finished my first picture since *Rebecca*. We've worked on it for six months at the cost of a million and a quarter and *still* haven't finished the retakes. It *must* be good!

"P.S. Mother has given up her oil painting. Olivia and I have given her a grand piano—let's hope it keeps her out of mischief."

Cary was fascinating to work with. He took his career very seriously. He knew exactly where each light was, rightly insisted that his key and eye lights were positioned as he knew they should be. Actors who have made many films and watched their rushes after each day's work know more about their camera angles and lighting than anyone else. Loretta Young was as knowledgeable and instructive as was Cary.

(Years later, when I once corrected a still photographer who was taking me from an unflattering angle, he curtly informed me that he'd been in the business for eighteen years and needed no advice from me. He had no comeback when I retorted that I'd been in it for thirty-five!)

Cary had reputedly been a stilt walker in Bristol when his name was Archie Leach. His timing, his body movements were superb. Everything he did was in balance. The only mistake he made on *Suspicion* was not realizing that the part of Lina was the major role. It was through her eyes that the story unfolded. She had all the sympathy. He was the villain. Cary found this out halfway through the shooting schedule. That, plus Hitchcock's "divide and conquer" technique created a temporary distance between us by the end of the film.

After the film I was exhausted, thanks to a long shooting schedule, tension on the set, no comforting arms at Rodeo Drive to ease my fatigue after a day's grueling work. An ocean voyage was needed.

Alone, I boarded the S.S. *Mariposa* at San Pedro, bound for Hawaii, Samoa, and Tahiti. Brian flew the Fairchild overhead, circling the ship until we were well out to sea. My cabin was filled with fruit and flowers. A birdcage of yellow orchids from David O. Selznick hung from the ceiling. The record player sobbed out Kostelanetz's "Our Love," lifted from Tchaikovsky's *Romeo and Juliet*, over and over again as I luxuriated in the late breakfasts in bed and endless hours of sleep all the way to Honolulu. Emerging from my stateroom at last, I found there were several people aboard I knew or would like to, such as writer Gene Fowler (*Goodnight, Sweet Prince*) and his family, Charles Nordhoff and James Norman Hall (*Mutiny on the Bounty*), Mr. and Mrs. George Cameron of *The San Francisco*

Chronicle. There was also a slight, blond gentleman from Pasadena, Tom Wanamaker, of the department store family. We soon were dining together and prowling the ship. Both of us were camera buffs, liked rum drinks and our own company. We giggled our way across the Pacific, which was just what I needed to take my mind off my problems with Selznick and Rodeo Drive.

Having tea at the U. S. consul's house in Pago Pago, in Samoa, was delightful. Browsing in Tahiti through the fruit and flower markets in Papeete at dawn, swimming in the sea at Moorea, photographing native girls scrubbing their sarongs on riverside stones brought back impressions of Gauguin's paintings. James Hall took me to meet his native family in their green-and-white seaside cottage, the ducks and chickens flapping a welcome as we ascended the rickety steps.

Aboard the *Mariposa* were Mrs. Lurline Matson Roth and her two daughters, Lurline and Bernice. After our stop at Tahiti, the homebound passengers transferred to the S.S. *Monterey*, as I did. The boat was about to weigh anchor. Tom and I lingered on the dock, snapping our last rolls of film. Glancing up at the stern, I spotted the Roth twins looking over the rail at the bustle and hubbub below. My last pictures of Papeete show the twins on deck with, just under them, in bold letters painted on the hull, "TWIN SCREWS. KEEP OFF."

I returned from my travels in time for Olivia's twenty-fifth birthday. I invited her and her current escort, Jimmy Stewart, to dinner, planning a menu with her favorite dishes, even baking the cake myself. Two hours after the time they were asked for, Olivia and Jimmy rang our doorbell. When I remonstrated that the dinner was hardly palatable any longer, Olivia announced, "It's my birthday. I can arrive whenever I like!" Brian and I did not make a habit of inviting her to our dinner parties after that, for it was a sure way of losing the cook.

24

HOLLYWOOD GOES TO WAR

DECEMBER 7, 1941. PEARL HARBOR. ROOSEVELT'S VOICE OVER THE RADIO telling the American people that this day would "live in infamy." Hollywood was stunned but soon rallied: there might be a buck to make out of the war at that. A series of war films were rushed into production.

Actors William Holden, Robert Young, James Stewart, Robert Montgomery, Wayne Morris, Bob Cummings, and many others left the sound stages for training camps. Actresses toured with the U.S.O. and attended bond rallies. Many of our writers, actors, and directors, assigned to the special film unit of the Signal Corps, returned to the California sound stages to make technical war films. Directors John Ford, George Stevens, John Farrow, Anatole Litvak, John Huston, Frank Capra, and many others were attached to film units here and abroad.

During the war studio players were expected to do their patriotic duty by serving coffee and doughnuts at the Hollywood Canteen to the many soldiers and sailors passing through Los Angeles or to those who came from army and naval bases nearby. We even had a few Russian servicemen, as it was the time of *rapprochement* between their country and ours.

One evening in the smoky, ill-lit canteen a tiny gob was jitterbugging with a tall, glamorous lady. Chewing gum voraciously in time to "Cow Cow Boogie," the sailor looked up at his partner and exclaimed, "Say you look just like Joan Crawford. Whatever happened to her?"

With a dignified smile, the elegant star replied, "I *am* Joan Crawford."

"Yeah?" replied the gum-chewer without missing a beat. "Whatever happened to ya?"

I became a nurses' aide, working long shifts at the Good Samaritan Hospital, the Los Angeles County Hospital, and St. John's in Santa Monica. Our training with the Red Cross was thorough and intense. We students saw a film on brain surgery, a live birth, and a major abdominal operation during the course in nursing technique. I was staggered to hear the surgeons discussing their golf games as they performed a stomach resection. We nurses' aides got the bedpans, bed making, bed baths, the serving of meals, pulse and respiration charting to perform. In a ward at the County Hospital I was bathing a man with a severe case of diabetes; his circulation was so poor that his toe came off in my washcloth. Often I would come home to Rodeo Drive dazed by the suffering I'd seen that day.

When our Fairchild was grounded, as was virtually all private aviation, and Brian became a flight instructor at Thunderbird Field in Phoenix, Arizona, I trudged the hard floors at St. Joseph's Hospital in Phoenix as a nurses' aide. Whenever I'd take a house in Suffield, I would nurse at the Hartford Hospital. After a duck shoot at dawn in the blind at Brookside, Phibby would deposit me at the hospital on his way to the Colt factory, where he was employed, picking me up in his car on his return after a ten-hour shift.

Because of my Red Cross affiliation, I found myself for the second time at the White House. Many of us, including Lily Pons, the Walter Pidgeons, Sir Cedric and Lady Hardwicke, had been there previously in connection with war relief efforts. During this visit F.D.R., who had been a polished, amusing host on the previous occasion, was absent from the White House. In the Red Room, Mrs. Roosevelt, all politics and serious conversation, allowed Harry Hopkins and his wife, Louise Macy, the only other guests, and me to have one daiquiri, served in silver stemmed goblets before dinner. At table, for the first course, oysters on the half shell were put before us. Knowing that I was allergic to uncooked shellfish, I politely downed one of the little live gray creatures and camouflaged the rest with lashings of cocktail sauce.

That oyster was a five-thousand-dollar mistake. By midnight I was in agony. Somehow I got myself by train to New York and the Hampshire House. Instead of doing a U. S. Steel radio program as intended, I vomited steadily for three days. David O. Selznick, with his friend Bill Paley of C.B.S. and then-wife Dorothy, sat by my bed each day, offering useless advice.

The conversation that evening at the White House swung around to taxes. Boldly, I told Mr. Hopkins, then adviser to the President, that I felt the tax structure was most unfair to those in a profession whose years of prosperity were uncertain. This would apply especially to athletes, actors, writers, and musicians. I pointed out that Margaret Mitchell had spent many hungry years writing Gone With the Wind. When the book was sold, she found herself in a very high bracket. Saving for the uncertain and perhaps lean years ahead was virtually impossible under this system. I suggested that a percentage of high earnings received all in one year should be allowed to go into tax-free savings. Mr. Hopkins did not agree. "Those boys in Hollywood are getting away with murder. This administration is out to fix them." He was referring to the corporations, to the theatre chain-studio combines which were later broken up. Mr. Hopkins remained unconcerned with the individual's problem.

Later on, in California, I was invited to join the Hollywood Committee for Arts, Sciences, and Professions, sponsored by Mrs. Roosevelt and sculptor Jo Davidson, and known more succinctly as H.C.A.S.P. My close friend John Houseman and Olivia had already joined. Artur Rubinstein, Danny Kaye, Lewis Milestone, Artie Shaw, Dore Schary, and hundreds of other artists and writers across the nation belonged to branches of the same organization. I had attended three meetings when a columnist for the Los Angeles Examiner telephoned me. He said that the F.B.I. looked upon the group with skepticism, that it might well have Communist affiliations, and he advised me to resign. Though the accusation was never proved, I felt that as a new citizen I should withdraw, and did so.

In 1951, without a trial, without any accusations, and ironically just after I had returned from a South American tour under State Department auspices, my passport was revoked. Fortunately, on the trip I had met Edward Miller, then Undersecretary of State for South American Affairs. When I telephoned him, Eddie immediately called on Mrs. Shipley, head of the Passport Office in Washington. My passport was reissued, but on a six-months basis only. Evidently, my brief association with H.C.A.S.P. had been sufficient to brand me a danger to the country!

25

THE CONSTANT NYMPH

Shortly before the Fairchild was put into mothballs, Brian and I stopped off for a quick dinner at Romanoff's one Sunday evening after flying back to Beverly Hills from our grape ranch in Indio, which Brian had bought on the advice of G.M. A group of friends, including columnist Harry Crocker and David Niven, had backed the charming, suave Harry Gerguson, alias Prince Michael Romanoff. His restaurant on Rodeo Drive became a profitable, fashionable enterprise. Here the members of the movie colony would congregate for lunch or dinner over red-and-white-checked tablecloths.

On that Sunday evening, Brian was in his blazer and gray flannels, I in my habitual flying suit of gabardine jacket and slacks, my hair in pigtails. As we sat scanning the menu, Edmund Goulding, the director of *Grand Hotel* and *Dark Victory*, approached our table and shook hands with my husband. "Sit down and join us, old boy . . . and, er, this is my wife." Nodding to me, Edmund drew up a chair and began a tale of woe. He was about to film the classic by Margaret Kennedy, *The Constant Nymph*, which Brian and Edna Best had made in England many years before. It was being produced at Warner Brothers by Henry Blanke. Eddie had cast Charles Boyer in the male lead, Alexis Smith as the wife, and all the parts but the feminine lead.

"It's impossible," Goulding groaned. "Jack Warner wants a star, but she has to be consumptive, flat-chested, anemic, and fourteen!"

"How about me?" I chimed in.

"Who are you?" Eddie stared at me, the freckled, no-makeup face, the pigtails, the underweight body. Fortunately, I'd had the Academy nomination for *Rebecca* and had finished filming *Suspicion*, so my name was not entirely unfamiliar to him. "You're perfect!" he said, beaming.

The following morning, negotiations began with Selznick and Warner's. Playing the part of Tessa in *The Constant Nymph* was the happiest motion-picture assignment of my career. Not only was Edmund Goulding a skillful film director, but he had also been a successful stage director. The combination was an actor's dream. Each morning the cast would arrive at the studio at 8 A.M., an unheard-of luxury, and go immediately to the closed set. Here we'd sit around a table, just like the first rehearsals of a stage play. The first day we read through the entire script, which Eddie proposed to shoot as much in sequence as possible. Each day he and the scriptwriter would adjust difficult lines, iron out dialogue problems, discuss characterization and mood with the actors. Before noon, with only the cameraman, head gaffer, and property man allowed on the sound stage, we'd "put it on its feet" and walk the scene. Before breaking for lunch, every detail of the afternoon's work would be worked out, including camera angles, props, and lighting effects.

After lunch, the actors returned in costume and makeup, now thoroughly familiar with their lines, ready for the first take, the master shot. Instead of the fifty or sixty takes indulged in by directors such as William Wyler or George Stevens, Eddie, because of meticulous preparation, could call "Print" after the first or second. After the master shot would come the medium shots, two-shots, and finally the individual close-ups. No delays were caused by actors blowing their lines, by questions about inner meanings or motivations. All that had been thrashed out that morning around the rehearsal table.

By four o'clock the assistant director would yell "Wrap it up!" and the happy cast and crew would streak for home or the golf course, returning at eight the next morning. No early-morning makeup call for the actors. No sleepy crew wrestling with light cables at dawn: they didn't have to report until noon! The savings to the studio must have been enormous. Not only was the film precut, brought in ahead of time, but not one moment of indecision, dissension, or unpleasantness found its way onto the Goulding set. Tony Gaudio, the cameraman, did some of his finest work. Too bad the film wasn't a financial success.

Charles Boyer remains my favorite leading man. Charles, a brilliant actor in English and French, in theatre or on the screen, was a kind, gentle, helpful actor. Brian and I often saw him and his beautiful English wife, Pat Patterson, socially. I found him a man of intellect, taste, and discernment. He was unselfish, dedicated to his work. Above all, he cared about the quality of the film he was making, and, unlike most leading men I have worked with, the single exception being Fred Astaire, his first concern was the film, not himself.

26

OSCAR TIME

It was during the making of *The Constant Nymph* that I read in *The Hollywood Reporter* on the set one morning that I was one of five actresses nominated for an Academy Award under the category of leading lady. As *Suspicion* was not the classic that *Rebecca* was, I felt my chances of winning this time were negligible. Another of the five candidates was Olivia de Havilland!

Jean Hersholt, that gentle Danish actor who was best known for playing the *Dr. Christian* film series, was at that time president of the Academy. He telephoned me at the studio the day of the award dinner. Surely, I was attending the banquet? I told him it wasn't possible. Being in the middle of a film, I didn't want to have a late night only to get up at six-thirty next morning for the drive from Beverly Hills across the Hollywood Hills to the studio in Burbank in time for the eight o'clock session.

The next phone call to the set came from Olivia. I *had* to attend the dinner. My absence would look odd. The contestants in all categories were expected to be there, and, moreover, I was an Academy member. "But I haven't anything to wear!" I wailed.

Within an hour, Olivia arrived with our usual saleslady from I. Magnin. They deposited in my dressing room tan-and-white-striped boxes containing all the size sixes the store possessed. Between takes, I tried on the dresses, finally selecting a ballet-length black number with a lace skirt and mantilla, which was hastily basted to fit me. The studio hairdresser and makeup man obligingly stayed after work to do away with my pigtails and hide my freckles.

At the Biltmore Hotel that evening we sat at David Selznick's table through the usual fruit cocktail-to-parfait dinner. Hardly anyone touched the meal. Excitement mounted steadily as the presentation time grew near. Finally, the program began with categories such as special effects and shorts. At last came the principal awards: the best film of the year, best producer, best director, best actor, and best actress.

The award, that year of 1941, for the best picture, went to *How Green Was My Valley*, the best director to John Ford for the same film, and the Thalberg award to Walt Disney. The award for best actor went to Gary Cooper for *Sergeant York*. "Coop's" competitors were Cary Grant for *Penny Serenade*, Walter Huston for *All That Money Can Buy*, Robert Montgomery for *Here Comes Mr. Jordan*, and Orson Welles for *Citizen Kane*.

From the dais, Ginger Rogers, to whom I had lost the previous year, slowly read the list of nominees for the best-actress award:

1. Bette Davis for *The Little Foxes*
2. Greer Garson for *Blossom in the Dust*
3. Barbara Stanwyck for *Ball of Fire*
4. Olivia de Havilland for *Hold Back the Dawn*
5. Joan Fontaine for *Suspicion*

And then she said, "The envelope, please." The banquet room was silent. The gentleman from Price, Waterhouse slithered onto the stage. With trembling hand he presented Ginger with the sealed document. The mike amplified the sound of the ripping of paper. Ginger cleared her throat. "The winner is . . . Joan Fontaine for *Sus—*" The last syllables were drowned in gasps, whistles, applause.

I froze. I stared across the table, where Olivia was sitting directly opposite me. "Get up there, get up there," she whispered commandingly. Now what had I done! All the animus we'd felt toward each other as children, the hair-pullings, the savage wrestling matches, the time Olivia fractured my collarbone, all came rushing back in kaleidoscopic imagery. My paralysis was total. I felt Olivia would spring across the table and grab me by the hair. I felt age four, being confronted by my older sister. Damn it, I'd incurred her wrath again!

Actually, Olivia took the situation very graciously. I am sure it was not a pleasant moment for her, as she'd lost the previous year for Melanie in *Gone With the Wind* in the supporting-actress category. (She's made it up with two Oscars since, for *To Each His Own* in 1946, and for *The Heiress* in 1949, so the evening was only a temporary setback.)

There was nothing for it but that I get up, shakily make my way to the rostrum, and accept the award. Cries of "Speak, speak!" echoed through the room as I tried to find my voice. I haven't the faintest idea what I said in my acceptance speech. God knows I hadn't rehearsed anything.

It was a bittersweet moment. I was appalled that I'd won over my sister. At twenty-three I may have been the youngest leading lady to receive an Oscar. My actor-husband had never been an Oscar contender. A picture taken after the banquet of Brian sitting alone in the empty ballroom, feet up on a chair, my fur coat over his arm, waiting patiently for the photographers to finish with the winners, graphically illustrates the plight of a marriage when the wife is more successful than the husband.

That Oscar can be a jinx. Winning an Academy Award is undoubtedly a great accolade, supreme praise from one's peers, a recognition to be accepted gratefully and graciously. It can also damage irreparably one's relations with family, friends, co-workers, the press. In those days, winners of the Oscar seemed like minor members of royalty suddenly elevated to the throne. All eyes watched to see the slightest sign of arrogance, inflated ego, disdain. The press clamored for home sittings, still photos, any scrap or tidbit to fill the endless gossip columns, fan magazines, Sunday supplements. One suddenly had international recognition, the best table in restaurants, preferential treatment whenever one traveled. It was a fishbowl existence until the next year's awards, when a new winner would occupy the throne. Naturally, there was many a doubter, many a detractor, many an ill-wisher. It's an uneasy head that wears the crown.

The morning after I received the award, I took my Oscar onto *The Constant Nymph* set, cradling it like a doll in my arms. The crew applauded as I entered. Now I was out of my black lace gown and back into pigtails and the fourteen-year-old's wardrobe, consisting of tattered dress and tennis shoes. Kisses, hugs, congratulations from the actors, smiles and pats from the makeup man, the hairdresser, the wardrobe girl, and then . . . "On the set, everyone . . . ready for rehearsal!" Back to business as usual.

27

PLAYTIME, WORKTIME

DESPITE THE WAR, HOLLYWOOD DID NOT PULL IN ITS SOCIAL HORNS.
Premieres, tent parties, galas, many under the auspices of bond
drives, continued to be given. Mocambo, Ciro's, and the Trocadero
on the Sunset Strip continued to attract their quota of actors, out-
of-towners, socialites, publicity seekers, and tourists. The brawls of
Humphrey Bogart and his wife were often more entertaining than
the floor show.

The Ahernes did their share of entertaining, too. Food rationing
began and coupons were saved for special occasions. On the hall
table we kept a leather-bound guest book, a habit of members of the
motion-picture industry who felt that entertaining furthered their
careers. Besides, the I.R.S. allowed tax deductions for business parties.
As a guest entered a Beverly Hills house, he was obliged to sign in
before having the first cocktail. Flame-haired Greer Garson, never
without her mother, Nina, always courageously wore scarlet or cycla-
men. She also carried her own thick red pencil in her evening bag.
Her signature in the guest book was as much of a standout as she was.
Artur Rubinstein's was so modest it had to be read with a microscope.

Among the guests who crossed the welcome mat at Rodeo Drive

was Lenore Coffee, who had collaborated with her husband, Bill Cowan, on the highly successful play No Room at the Inn and who was enjoying the proceeds. The Cowans built a large house in Mandeville Canyon, with pleasant gardens and a Victorian interior. Brian and I were invited to their housewarming. After dinner, bored with the tedious conversation over liqueurs and cigars, I slipped away into the sitting room with a few of my close pals. Charles Bennett, our flying friend and an accomplished screenwriter, questioned me about David Selznick's reputation as a "chaser." I explained that I had first met Ingrid Bergman in D.O.S.'s office balcony, where I saw her wince under his embrace. "All right, Charles, you be David and here I come through your office door. See how fast you can catch me." I circled the room at high speed. Charles, pretending to pant, followed close at my heels. Our friends roared with laughter. I brushed a Victorian column upon which stood an ornate lamp. Crash! From the adjoining room charged my hostess, followed by Mrs. Edward G. Robinson and a bevy of anxious guests. Lenore shrieked, and rushed to the bathroom and locked herself in. Gladys Robinson pounded on the door. Was she afraid the hostess was attempting suicide? Thanks to Charles's and my caper, the evening was a disaster. The guests evaporated into the night.

Next morning I sent Lenore a coffin of flowers in case she had actually done away with herself. At noon, I telephoned her to offer my abject apologies and suggest that I find a lamp to match the remaining one of the pair. Lenore was brave. She rallied from the ordeal. At the end of the week I received a sizable bill for not one but two lamps, plus the cost of rewiring and mounting them.

Another frequent guest at the Ahernes' was Spanish pianist José Iturbi, who had given Brian and me a unique wedding present. Shortly after our honeymoon, he phoned one morning to Rodeo Drive and asked us to get on separate extensions. He then played the piano: El Amor Brujo was a wedding gift that no one could ever take away from us.

The Pierre Monteux were also close friends. Doris Monteux gave me another kind of present, one which made her marriage endure for over thirty years. At a rehearsal of the Los Angeles Orchestra in the Hollywood Bowl, with roly-poly Pierre on the conductor's stand, white-haired Doris chortled that her husband was irresistible to her, just as physically exciting as the first day they had met. Marking my incredulity, she said that she had an ironclad system: Whenever the marriage showed signs of inertia, she would announce to Pierre that she would be out to dinner that evening. She would have her hair carefully done, dress in her daintiest lingerie, her newest dress, smartest hat, and repair to the foyer of the St. Francis Hotel in San Francisco, close to the Huntington, where they lived for many years. Soon a handsome stranger would appear and, spotting the well-groomed lady sitting alone, ask her to dine. Over caviar and champagne, they would flirt outrageously, confiding as one can only to a stranger. She would lead her willing admirer back to her suite at her hotel for more flirtation, more champagne. Slowly, she would divest herself of her dress, her seductive lace teddies. Passionate lovemaking would fill the hours of the night. "Of course, in the morning, I'd find my lover had been Pierre all the time!" Love from a stranger is sometimes better than from a marriage partner, she believed, but best if he happens to be both. Pierre must have agreed with her.

The Ahernes did not spend all their time at parties, however. After a day's shooting, Brian and I spent many an evening at home. Remembering Mme. Monteux's recipe for a successful marriage, I would speed home from the studio and try to make myself as attractive as possible. After removing the panchromatic makeup I would bathe and change into a hostess gown. Brian would wear a smoking jacket. A cocktail in the bar preceded a hasty dinner.

After the meal, correspondence had to be answered, business and household details seen to. Lines had to be memorized for the next day's shooting, the alarm set for dawn. Lights were out by ten. Our double bed was scarcely rumpled when the occupants arose in the morning.

The next film I made after *The Constant Nymph* was at Twentieth Century–Fox. The Russian Anatole Litvak directed Tyrone Power and me in Eric Knight's sensitive novel *This Above All*, the story of a war correspondent and a W.A.A.F. (Women's Auxiliary Air Force). My turn for a war story! The film had its usual quota of English character actors and was very successful at the box office. It received tremendous word-of-mouth publicity because of an incident that occurred one evening at Ciro's between Paulette Goddard and Litvak. The morning after their rendezvous *The Hollywood Reporter* and *Variety* were being passed from cast to crew and back again on every studio lot. Hollywood was abuzz.

The gossip columns had printed that "Tola" Litvak had disappeared for a suspicious length of time under the table at which Paulette sat serenely. "Litvak" was altered into a crude pun, graphic enough to describe what the onlookers imagined was going on under the white tablecloth. Tola's version was that Paulette had simply dropped her evening bag, and, on his hands and knees, he'd had difficulty retrieving it in the dark. As with most gossip, the readers preferred to believe the lurid version.

Ty Power was very much under the thumb of his wife, French actress Annabella, several years older than he. Like Fred Astaire, I gather, he got a bit of flack over his leading lady each night when he arrived home from work. Therefore, he was circumspect, fairly distant, but would play endless games of gin rummy with me in my stage dressing room.

This was the time that Hollywood was deluged with Allied soldiers, sailors, and airmen of all ranks en route to the Pacific war zone. Brian and I took in many an R.A.F. pilot. And Cousin Geoffrey de Havilland appeared, literally out of the blue. The daring test pilot was to die over the Thames Estuary on September 27, 1946, while trying out a D. H. 108 research aircraft on a final check flight before attempting to break the world speed record of 616 m.p.h. He was thirty-six.

Of Geoffrey's death, our mutual friend Phillip Gordon Marshall wrote me: "One evening, just before he was killed, I was drinking with him in a quiet country pub near Hatfield, when Geoffrey quoted these lines from Swinburne's 'Laus Veneris':

'Ah yet would God this flesh of mine might be
Where air might wash and long leaves cover me,
Where tides of grass break into foam of flowers
Or where the wind's feet shine along the sea.'"

His body was found amid tall marsh grass, lapped by the sea, on the desolate coast east of the Isle of Sheppey.

Geoffrey spent several tumultuous days at Rodeo Drive. He was goggle-eyed over the feminine stars he met, especially his two cousins. He was alternately in love with Olivia or me, depending on which of us was in the Aherne bar at the time and from which bottle he was drinking. After an ossifying evening, he'd buzz our house at dawn, indicating to all of sleepy Beverly Hills that he was none the worse for the Ahernes' hospitality, that he was clear-eyed and intrepid.

Gala parties were given for those in high command. The Darryl

Zanucks entertained for General Mark Clark, the Samuel Goldwyns
for Leslie Hore-Belisha, Jack Warner for the Alfred Duff Coopers.
Visitors in uniform were a common sight in studio lots, Hollywood
nightclubs, and Beverly Hills restaurants. And to the Paradise of
Palm Trees flocked many displaced socialites. The European playground, now overrun by Nazi and Allied armies, was no longer available to Sir Charles Mendl and his chic decorator wife, the former
Elsie de Wolfe, or to Ludwig Bemelmans, Barbara Hutton, Erich
Remarque, Elsa Maxwell. Making their temporary residences in Beverly Hills were Baron Eric Rothschild, Baroness Renée de Becker,
the American-born Countess di Frasso. Hollywood became a stimu-
lating haven for those lucky enough to have incomes in America or
those who had managed to bring money with them from abroad.

Elsa Maxwell took a house with heiress Evelyn Walsh McLean,
who often wore her unlucky Hope diamond when she was introduced to Hollywood society. Elsa, the hostess with the mostest at
that time, knew how to give an amusing party. At one of their dinners, owing to a shortage of kitchen help, Elsa passed out colored
crayons to those on her star-studded guest list and gave a prize for
the most originally decorated paper plate. The guests then ate their
dinner from plates of their own design.

At a party in William Randolph Hearst's beach house, his hostess,
adorable Marion Davies, was greeting their guests from the top of
the marble staircase when her fabulous necklace broke. Plop, plop.
Down the stairs, one by one, bounced her priceless pearls. "Jesus, me
beads!" exclaimed Marion. Undaunted, she waved gaily to the
stunned guests below.

A story, which is probably apocryphal, concerns a visit to Hollywood by the Earl of Warwick. Hearing that there was a famous call
house run by a Madam Francis, he was given the address of Warner
Brothers actress Kay Francis by mistake. It happened to be the wedding night of tall, slim, dark-haired Kay and her groom, producer
Kenneth McKenna, when the Earl went to the wrong door.

Ringing Miss Francis' doorbell, announcing his distinguished
name to the flustered maid, his lordship was shown into the drawing
room. Upstairs, Kay, *en negligée*, was sipping champagne with her
new husband. Learning of the presence of her guest below, touched
that he would call upon her on such a memorable night, Kay bestowed a kiss on the bridegroom's forehead, promising to hurry back
as soon as possible.

Downstairs, Kay was graciousness itself. The Earl, always gallant, admired Kay's gown, her paintings on the walls, but soon tired of her overstimulated chatter. "You're delightful, Madam Francis," he admitted, "but would you mind bringing in the girls?"

28

GIVE AND TAKE

WITH WAR TEARING THE WORLD APART, HOLLYWOOD REACHED ITS ZE-nith. Not only was seeing films and film stars, who entertained them through the U.S.O., an escape for our boys overseas, but movies were also a respite between bombings for the English, as well as a source of relaxation for Americans working swing shifts in factories that were providing matériel for the Allied armies.

Despite gas rationing, going to the movies became a necessary di-version for millions at home and abroad. Hollywood boomed. Money poured in at the box office. Those fortunate enough to be part of Tinseltown had never seen such largesse. They spent their salaries as soon as they could cash their paychecks. Who knew what the future might bring? Hollywood was indeed the biblical land of milk and honey, with a little Sodom and Gomorrah mixed in for good measure.

Christmas in Hollywood was unreal. Presents were doled out like popcorn at a circus. At the studios, stars were expected to give every member of the crew a respectable gift, not only at Christmas, but at the end of shooting as well. A double indemnity for those unlucky stars who were filming in December.

Countless personalized pen-and-pencil sets, bottles of Scotch or bourbon, boxes of cigars, handkerchiefs and scarves were dispatched

Rebecca: J.F. with Laurence Olivier, Gladys Cooper, Reginald Denny

I have a *Suspicion* the milk is poisoned.

A Pyrrhic victory, April 1942

One sister wins, the
other loses

Weekend work after the
Academy Award—wash-
ing Nicky

RICHARD A. HOUGH

My favorite uniform—
my red fishing sweater

Directed by Alfred Hitchcock in *Rebecca*

My turn for a war film: *This Above All* with Tyrone Power

Charles Boyer, my favorite leading man

Charles Boyer and J.F. listen to Erich Korngold play his score for *The Constant Nymph* as director Edmund Goulding (extreme right) looks on. Cellist Jean Muir is on the left.

Jane Eyre and Edward Rochester
COLLECTION OF
R. BOWERS

J.F. with Basil Rathbone and Nigel Bruce in *Frenchman's Creek*

PARAMOUNT PI

J.F., Roland Young, Lady Hardwicke,
and Brian Aherne with FDR at the White House

As a nurse's aide, with
Louise Floyd SPRAGUE TALBOT,
AMERICAN
RED CROSS

Ivy with Herbert Marshall

UNIVERSAL PICTURES

One winner tries to congratulate another.

Letter from an Unknown Woman: I communicated intuitively with director Max Ophuls (far right); with Mady Christians and cinematographer Frank Planer, "Lisa" as a 15-year-old . . .

. . . and as the mature woman, with Louis Jourdan.

Threesome: Jimmy Stewart, J.F.,
and my daughter-to-be

Debbie in her nursery

Publicity photo of
"happy Dozier family"

ALEXANDER KAHLE

Publicity pose—wings courtesy of artist John Falter

Forbidden fruits are sweetest.

to the crew. Bath sets and perfume, blouses, handbags went to the women in the wardrobe and makeup departments. One year I gave bouclé sweaters to them all, wrapping each box in colored paper that matched the contents. Lunch hours in my studio dressing room were busy ones. Just before that Christmas, a faulty heater caused a fire and the presents were ruined by acrid smoke. Next day, I reordered over fifty sweaters from the same store, more wrappings, and began again.

Louella Parsons, the syndicated columnist for the powerful Hearst press, was a lady to be feared, to be pampered and cosseted by studios and stars alike. Flowers, cases of champagne, assorted lavish gifts arrived at the door of her house on Maple Drive whenever a birthday, anniversary, or Christmas came around. Her secretary would alert the studio publicity departments and the publicity-aware producers. A skillful line in Miss Parsons' column in *The Los Angeles Examiner* would remind the ambitious actor.

One afternoon before Christmas, Louella went the rounds of all the studios in her chauffeur-driven station wagon. Dropping into each publicity department in turn and imbibing a cup of cheer at the office parties, Louella would wait until her car was loaded with presents. Next studio, another libation, another armload of loot. Evidently the chauffeur was also celebrating the Yuletide season, for as Louella emerged from the last stop, now leaning heavily on the arm of the tipsy driver, they found that the station wagon had been rifled. Thousands of dollars' worth of perfume, wine, silver frames, alligator handbags, monogrammed lingerie had been spirited away.

The morning after Christmas, Miss Parsons' secretary dutifully telephoned all the studios. The station wagon would be calling at the studio gates again. The Queen of the Columnists expected it to be refilled with duplicate gifts. It was.

One Christmas, David O. Selznick's present to me was a set of imported Lowestoft, a two-hundred-and-fifty piece set from Carole Stupell in New York. In disfavor the next year, I received a five-dollar geranium plant. The price tag was still on it.

The *Los Angeles Times'* Hedda Hopper was another formidable Hollywood columnist. A Quaker, once married to actor DeWolf Hopper, she had been a friend of mine since the R.K.O. contract days when she played the part of my mother in one of my many "B" films.

Hedda had a mania for hats. Mountains of beribboned hatboxes were delivered each month to her Beverly Hills house on Tropical Drive. A studio anxious to publicize a new film would include the pertinent data for its film and advance publicity material in the box with a new chapeau created for her by John Frederics or Kenneth. The gifts cost the studios very little in the long run, flattered the *grande dame*, and got the desired space in her column.

When I was visiting her for tea one afternoon, Hedda pointed to quart-sized bottles of Arpège, Chanel No. 5, L'Heure Bleu, Je Reviens, and Shalimar, all gifts from producers or actors. "I make my own personal perfume," she confided. "I just mix 'em all together."

Edith Gwynne, who wrote a gossip column for *The Hollywood Reporter*, was a powerful figure, too. One morning on the set of *This Above All*, I read in her column that "the Aherne marriage is cooling. Watch for a split-up there." I was furious that our life at Rodeo Drive should ever hit the columns. I telephoned her immediately, demanding an explanation and retraction.

"I haven't seen you together anywhere in public," she retorted. Inasmuch as her boss, Bill Wilkerson, had an interest in Ciro's, where Brian and I seldom went, it was easy to piece together . . . we were expected to go there often in the future.

"How could you see us anywhere?" I protested. "I'm working at Fox thirteen hours a day, six days a week!" Edie Gwynne coolly explained that if we were still together in six months, she *might* print a retraction. At least she was giving us time to get ourselves to Wilkerson's nightclub.

Not all the columnists were of the same stripe as Louella and Hedda. Harrison Carroll of *The Los Angeles Examiner* was always fair, always checked his facts first and usually directly with the person he was writing about. Bob Thomas of the Associated Press did the same, as did Armand Archer of *Variety*.

My dear friend Harry Crocker was too much of a gentleman to be anything but innocuous in his daily column for the *Examiner*, entitled "Behind the Make-up." One day, a prankish typesetter reversed it and printed "Make Up the Behind." Harry's column was widely read that day.

Sheilah Graham, the close friend of Scott Fitzgerald, was also a formidable newspaperwoman. English Cockney, seemingly bland, and innocently wide-eyed, Sheilah could elicit confidences from a stone. She had no scruples about the intimacy of the questions she asked or about printing anything that made a good story.

I had a difficult time balancing my friendship with Hedda and rival columnists. She gave me an ultimatum: "It is either Louella or me. You can't be friends with both of us." When all eyes were focused on Hollywood one could not afford to have enemies in the press. I walked a narrow tightrope with both ladies, inviting Louella to one party and Hedda to the next.

Joan Bennett was not so cautious. Because Hedda had printed something grossly unkind about Miss Bennett in her column, Joan sent a live skunk, neatly caged in an elaborate hatbox, to Miss Hopper's house. Hedda had the last word. In her column the next day she profusely thanked the actress for her generosity and said that she would name the odoriferous varmint "Joan," after the donor.

For a time Hedda turned against me and maintained an on-and-off vendetta, using her column to spread her venom. Sir Charles Mendl, friend of us both, tried to patch things up. Asking us both for tea at his Benedict Canyon house, he escorted Hedda and me into the garden and left us alone to air our differences. Hedda, under an olive tree, wheeled on me. "The trouble with you, Joan, is that you've no humility!"

I stood my ground, and for the first time in my life I used the only explicit word that suited such an occasion. "Fuck you, Hedda!" She didn't give me much trouble after that.

Joseph Cotten (*Citizen Kane, Duel in the Sun*) went one step further. After reading a slanderous paragraph about himself in Hedda's column, he went up to her at a social function and delivered a swift kick to her rear. I should like to have been there to witness her surprised expression, her flowered hat askew, her dignity smarting as well as her behind.

In the spring of 1943 I discovered that I was nominated for an Academy Award for *The Constant Nymph*. Three nominations in four years? Unheard of. Brian and I, accompanied by another Academy contender, Jean Arthur, and her producer-husband, Frank Ross, attended the Academy evening, held, in deference to wartime economy, at the Melrose Theatre in Hollywood.

Jean hated public appearances, and especially to see herself on the screen. As we sat there, waiting for the ceremonies to begin, she told me of the time she sat in this same theatre watching one of her films. Behind her was a restless woman who got up and left after announcing loudly to the rest of the audience, "I can't stand that

Arthur's voice." Shortly afterward, Jean slunk out. She confided that that was the last time she saw herself on the screen in front of a public audience.

We both knew we hadn't a chance of winning. Our competition was stiff: Ingrid Bergman in *For Whom the Bell Tolls*, Greer Garson in *Madame Curie*. When last year's winner, Greer Garson, announced that Jennifer Jones would be taking home the Oscar for *The Song of Bernadette*, the four of us repaired to the bar at Rodeo Drive.

Jean had been magnificent in *The More the Merrier*. As often on suspension as I was, harassed by Harry Cohn at Columbia, she had become fatalistic about her career, reclusive in her private life. Over stiff drinks, she professed admiration that I was able to indulge in activities which helped to take my mind off my own career troubles with Selznick. That I flew a plane, golfed, fished, did needlepoint, gardened, took French lessons, cooked, and entertained, amazed her.

"Jean, how would you like to learn to cook?" I volunteered, with a recklessness induced by my third drink. "I'll teach you!" Forgetting our defeat at the Academy, we planned the menu for our first lesson. As Jean was artistic and liked to paint, we agreed that glazing and decorating a whole salmon might give her the enthusiasm to pursue her new hobby. We arranged to meet in my kitchen at ten o'clock, on what was now the same morning.

Not even bothering to read the morning paper's account of the Academy Awards, I arose early and sped to the Farmer's Market to purchase the supplies I needed for my first pupil.

At home, I poached the salmon, laid out the implements and ingredients Jean would need . . . and waited. By ten-thirty I was on the phone to her house. "Mrs. Ross is still asleep," answered the maid. At eleven-thirty . . . "Mrs. Ross hasn't rung down yet." At noon . . . "Mrs. Ross is still in her bedroom."

That was the end of L'Ecole de Cordon Bleu on rue Rodeo. Jean never rang back. The Ahernes ate salmon for weeks.

29

FOOTLOOSE AND FANCY-FREE

DURING THE FORTIES I FLEW TO NEW YORK ON BUSINESS. OFTEN I took the train. It was a luxury to board the Super Chief at Los Angeles or Pasadena, knowing that for three days I would be rid of outside pressures, of interviews and telephone calls from producers and agents, of David Selznick's chivying, of the petty problems presented by the morning mail, of the never-ending details of running a house.

In the days of transcontinental train service, smiling porters were as solicitous as mothers. They guarded one's privacy, acted as alarm clocks upon request, conjured up icy-cold martinis as though from a spigot outside the stateroom door. They presented the conductor and the menu-bearing dining-car steward as though they were Eastern potentates and you were the Aga Khan.

As the long black train snaked eastward over the Rockies, fresh Colorado trout would be boarded, then crisp Utah celery, next grouse and pheasant from the western plains. The uniformed dining-car steward would tip you off in advance—stowing away the best of the delicacies, so he implied, until you appeared in the dining car. Here silver cutlery danced on starched white linen tablecloths. Napkins as large as newspapers would slip off your lap at each bump in the roadbed. Bud vases containing a rose or two stood sentry on each table. Genial waiters balanced laden trays on outstretched palms. Wineglasses tinkled against the silver as you looked out of the steamy window. Lights from tank towns flashed by during the meal, then sudden darkness until moonlight revealed a snow-capped mountain or a shining desert floor.

Often on the Super Chief friends would be discovered. This meant cocktail visits in staterooms perhaps ten cars away; then a return visit with all the guests to your stateroom seemed essential. In cramped staterooms casual acquaintances became lifelong friends. Camaraderie and good cheer would follow as porters passed frosty glasses to eager hands over the heads of the sardine pack. Soon it was like New Year's Eve.

After idle days reading, writing letters, playing cards, or simply staring out of the now grime-stained windows, contemplating the vastness of our country from desert pueblos, impoverished railway towns, sprawling industrial towns, undulating fields, arrival in Chicago suddenly became exciting. While our cars were switched over from the Wabash Station to the Twentieth Century Limited at Dearborn Station, we would always head for the Chicago Art Institute to gaze at the Chester Dale collection of Impressionists until it was time to taxi to the Ambassador Hotel and its Pump Room. Here proprietor Ernest Byfield would have reserved the first banquette for his Hollywood guests, would proffer the exotic menu and extol that day's catch of whitefish from Lake Superior or the quality of the salmon just flown in from Scotland. His famous remark about the shashlik served on flaming swords by fancifully costumed waiters—"The customers like it and it doesn't hurt the beef much"—was typical. Byfield was the Florenz Ziegfeld of restaurateurs.

In New York during those years I usually stopped at the Hampshire House on Central Park South or at the St. Regis at Fifty-fifth and Fifth Avenue. Upon my arrival I would find the suite massed with fruit and flowers, a chilled bottle of champagne, courtesy of the management. Bouquets of long-stemmed roses and colorful floral arrangements bore cards from the studio currently employing me, from my agents, from fans. Friends would have left messages and invitations, publicists their long schedules of interviews to be held as soon as possible. Autograph seekers collected outside on the pavement. A studio limousine waited on the street to whisk me to appointments.

In the Forties, no chic woman appeared on the street in New York without hat or gloves. We wore real silk stockings, high heels, occasionally a bunch of violets or a fresh camellia on the lapel. On a warm day a scarf of mink or sable was carelessly thrown about a pearl-necklaced throat. Diamonds were worn only at night. At the theatre, hats or velvet ribbons, flowers or feathers were quite appropriate, while I cannot remember anyone not dressing for a performance at the Metropolitan Opera.

And these were the war years and immediately after. We felt deprived as we lunched at Henri Soulé's Le Pavillon, the Edwardian Room at the Plaza, at "21." Materials for clothes were rationed, hence the shorter skirts for women, the cuffless trousers for men. Shoes were also rationed.

One evening, returning in the studio limousine from the theatre with a charming Russian-born major, I slipped off my tight left shoe. The major took one look at my silk-stocking-clad foot and asked, "Where do you buy your shoes?"

"I did buy them at Bergdorf's," I replied, "but not this time . . . I've used up my coupons."

As I bade him good-night at the hotel door, the major commanded, "Meet me at Bergdorf's tomorrow at eleven sharp."

Promptly at eleven I turned up in the shoe department to find the major waiting for me with four shoe coupons he had obtained from friends. He sat on the stool in front of my chair, trying on my foot one pair after another. Salesmen gathered around, as did many customers. Finally the major was content with my selection, handed over the coupons, paid for the shoes, and had them wrapped. He would deliver them to my hotel himself.

Once outside the revolving doors of Bergdorf's I extended my hand to thank my generous friend. "Oh, no, you don't," he cautioned. "There is a price for my present!" My heart sank. I should have known. "All you have to do is promise that I may polish your shoes whenever you're in New York . . . I don't even need to see you."

Thereafter, every time I came to Manhattan, I would leave instructions at the hotel desk that a key could be given to the major in my absence. Often I would return to find my shoes neatly lined up like soldiers, shiny with newly applied wax. The major had been by.

It was in the Forties that I dined one evening in New York at the Pavillon with Sir Alexander Korda. He had just been divorced from exotic film star Merle Oberon. Over an excellent glass of Château-

Lafite he warned me, "No matter what, Joan, aim for the impossible. If you accomplish all your ambitions, there is nothing left." Puzzled, I asked the silver-haired producer what he meant. Holding his glass up to the light, he sighed. "I was a poor boy in Hungary when I conceived my dream . . . I wanted to belong to the most important nation, to become rich, respected, marry the most beautiful woman, be world-famous." He sipped thoughtfully from his goblet. "I've done all those things. I became a British subject, I founded my own film company, I owned a yacht, Winston Churchill is my close friend, I married Merle, I was knighted." Alex sadly contemplated the dark-red drop at the bottom of his wineglass. "Now . . . now I've no more dreams left." He signaled for the check. That was the last time I ever saw him.

30

LEND-LEASE, SELZNICK STYLE

ORSON WELLES WAS A HUGE MAN IN 1943. EVERYTHING ABOUT HIM WAS oversized, including his ego. Unlike Charles Boyer and Fred Astaire, Orson's concern was entirely for Orson: *Jane Eyre* was simply a medium to show off his talents.

The first day on the Twentieth Century–Fox lot, the director, slight, timid, gentlemanly Robert Stevenson, the cameraman, the script girl, and the cast assembled at 1 P.M. for rehearsal, an hour continuously changed by Orson but finally settled upon. The propman had already printed our names on the backs of the folding canvas chairs. We sat in a circle hour after hour, waiting for the arrival of the leading man, whose empty chair loomed large on the half-lighted set. At four that afternoon the stage door burst open. Orson whirled in, accompanied by his doctor, his manager, his secretary, and his valet, "Shorty." (Shorty was rightly named, being less than four feet tall.)

Orson strode up to a lectern, which we had not noticed before. Placing his script upon it and standing before our astonished group, he announced to director and cast, "Now we'll begin on page four!"

Bob Stevenson, suddenly demoted to director-in-name-only, knew he was in for a rough time. So did we all. However, Orson couldn't keep up to the position he had assumed. He was undisciplined, always late, indulged in melodrama on and off the set. He was also seeing Lena Horne, who was singing at a nightclub on the Strip. (Shorty would confide to me that Orson would have a tray in bed every night, which didn't jibe at all with Orson's version of his nocturnal exploits.)

Oddly enough, Orson wanted very much to be liked. We could only think of him as someone to handle carefully, to avoid as much as possible. Slowly, Bob Stevenson, with the expert help of William Pereira, regained the directorial reins. (Bill was the producer William Goetz's assistant, coordinating the sets, costumes, and casting in a masterful manner. He now is a most successful architect.)

One morning, as Orson was about to make an entrance in a scene, "Jane" following close behind him, I whispered in his ear, "Stand up straight. Your coat gapes at the neck if you don't."

"Stop the camera!" roared "Mr. Rochester." "Miss Fontaine says my costume doesn't fit. Get the wardrobe man, get the tailor, get the producer!" Anything to stall. "I'm not shooting this scene until my jacket's fixed!"

The wardrobe man scurried onto the set, the tailor at his heels. Bob Stevenson gave me a withering look. The jacket went to the wardrobe department to sit for an hour, then was returned just as it was. Orson was satisfied, the scene began again. That was the last time I ever made a suggestion to the boy genius.

At the completion of the film, we had the usual photographs to take. We were called into the still gallery at ten in the morning. I'd booked a four o'clock flight to Mexico City, where I was to meet Leslie Allen. When I entered the makeup department, the assistant director looked sheepish. No Orson. As he was never on time, we began to call his house. Shorty gave us a number of excuses. "Mr. Welles is on his way." "Mr. Welles says his alarm didn't go off." "Mr. Welles is still having breakfast."

Arriving at one o'clock, Orson confessed that he'd been lying in his tub all morning, sulking because I hadn't trusted him to be on time! I made my plane with only seconds to spare.

The false nose Orson wore in *Jane Eyre*, the contact lenses for the blind scene, the flowing cape—these were his main concern. He overlooked three little actresses in the film, who one day would command as much attention as he. They were Peggy Ann Garner, Margaret O'Brien, and violet-eyed Elizabeth Taylor.

* * *

Pasadena and Santa Barbara, Pebble Beach and Hillsborough. During the war and for many years after, these delightful California meccas of the rich were often the playground of the motion-picture colony. One sunny morning Francis Robinson of the Metropolitan Opera, Guthrie McClintic and his wife, Katharine Cornell, stopped at Rodeo Drive. We drove to Pasadena, where lawyer Alfred Wright and his warm and adorable wife, Marie, were giving a luncheon in honor of Miss Cornell, then playing in *The Doctor's Dilemma* at the Biltmore Theatre in Los Angeles.

The Wrights were old friends of Brian and the McClintics. I had known Mr. Wright, for we'd tangled over some contractual matters with D.O.S. when I was working at Twentieth Century–Fox. Alfred senior represented the interests of Darryl Zanuck.

And I knew young Alfred, too. A correspondent for *Life* magazine, he had asked for an interview with Olivia and me. We agreed, stressing one condition: we didn't want any emphasis put on the fact that we were sisters. Not only were we rivals at that time for the Academy Award, but we were always getting the same scripts submitted to us, being confused in the columns and in public. Alfred agreed and came to Rodeo Drive, where he interviewed us separately. When the magazine article appeared, it was entitled "Sister Act"!

In the Wrights' hall, my eyes lit upon the traitor, now in his Navy uniform. Alfred's younger sister was peeking down through the banisters. Later, she gleefully told me that I gave him a sound tongue-lashing and that he speedily retreated to take his first flying lesson with director Hank Potter. Obviously, going through a few barrel rolls and Immelmanns was much safer than facing another tirade from me. Neither of us could have foreseen that in 1964 I would become Mrs. Alfred Wright, Jr. So I got even with him for his treachery! But that's a story to come later.

David Selznick was hounding me to play in Daphne du Maurier's *Frenchman's Creek* on loan-out. The successful novel, laid in the time of Charles II, concerned a French pirate who pillaged the coastal towns of Cornwall where Lord Godolphin and his beautiful young wife occasionally entertained the court in their seaside mansion.

The film would have been less flamboyant had it been shot in black and white, a mood movie about a hopeless, daring romance, but Paramount planned to do it in glorious Technicolor, to make a garish spectacle and co-star a Mexican actor unknown to American audiences, Arturo de Cordova. My name would have to carry the film. Director Mitchell Leisen, known for his musicals, would lavish attention on the sets, costumes, location shots, but little on the acting. I rebelled, said I wouldn't play the part, and went on suspension.

Immediately Selznick barraged me with sheaves of telegrams. Hourly telephone calls from lawyers and agents would harass me. Columnists were coerced into printing that I was difficult, ungrateful, temperamental, uncooperative, swelled-headed. The pressure became intolerable. Brian was not amused. Home life at Rodeo Drive deteriorated under the psychological warfare subtly executed by Paramount and D.O.S.

After weeks of such treatment, I weakened, as D.O.S. and his lawyers knew I would. D.O.S. promised contractual changes, more money: "Oh, I can't even tell you all the things I'll do for you when you report to Paramount." I did report. He didn't remember his promises. Nothing was changed.

The day I was to report to Paramount, I finished my eight-hour shift as a nurses' aide at the County Hospital and stopped off at the wardrobe department to have my measurements taken for the costumes. Here I was met by designer Raoul Pène duBois, director Mitch Leisen, producer David Lewis, and Mme. Karinska, who was to oversee the costumes.

Mme. Karinska took one look at me in my blue-and-white uniform, my white cotton stockings, my serviceable rubber-soled shoes, and threw up her hands. "Vat! You promise me a be-ootiful voman and vat I get . . . a mouzze!" But the nurses' aide didn't remain a mouse for long. With red wigs, hoop skirts, sables and satins, laces and velvets, jewels and tiaras, I was turned into a glamour puss that "I" de Winter from *Rebecca* would never have recognized.

My co-star, Arturo de Cordova, was not a tall man. Lifts were put in his boots so that he might top my five feet four inches. He teetered as he walked. His wigs were as elaborate as mine. His accent was hardly that of a Frenchman.

The costumes, sets, and props all swamped the actors. Our acting was stilted, often melodramatic. The Technicolor spectacle drew laughter at the Radio City Music Hall premiere that I was forced to attend. Halfway through I sneaked out during a particularly raucous audience reaction.

During the filming, Arturo, whom I liked, and I were standing in our marks, waiting for a two-shot. Knowing that the film would be a disaster for us both, I asked him why he'd accepted the role. As a most popular star in Mexico, he'd certainly taken quite a risk to make his American film debut in *Frenchman's Creek.*

Overhearing me, Nigel Bruce and Basil Rathbone, both gossip lovers, twisted my remark. The trade papers next day made the most of it. I'd supposedly told my leading man to "go back to Mexico where he came from." The film was an unhappy one in every way.

Brian and I saw the first rough cut with producer David Lewis in the Paramount projection room. It was a final confirmation that David Selznick was more interested in money than the future of his contract players.

And I was not the only one to suffer. Ingrid Bergman, under contract to David, had made *Intermezzo* for him in 1938. After two years of idleness, she was finally loaned out in one disaster after another until she was fortunate enough to get *Casablanca* with Bogart. Ernest Hemingway himself had to intervene before she was given *For Whom the Bell Tolls* with Gary Cooper at Paramount. Another of D.O.S.'s contract players, Jennifer Jones, unlike Ingrid and me, was not going to sit around doing nothing—she married the boss!

31

DIVORCE

I KNEW THAT MY MARRIAGE TO BRIAN WAS DOOMED. NOT EVEN LOVERS, we were scarcely friends. We filled our lives, as so many married people do, by simply playing house. Both Hollywood and marriage had lost their glamour for me.

Brian's film career was declining. I was frustrated by my Selznick contract, prohibited from supporting myself in any field of entertainment or other profession as long as my contract was valid. Nor could I select my own films, guide my career. Brian and I were both painted into a corner. The rose-colored glasses were off our eyes. Brian was undoubtedly bored with all my career brouhaha, my tensions and frustrations. I was just plain bored.

It was at breakfast at the Indio ranch that I told him I saw no future in our marriage. I had hoped that he would be jarred enough to review our life together and to try to construct a positive plan. I was twenty-four. I wanted affection, tenderness, even romance . . . to live a life with someone whose main concern was his family and a life together. A solid relationship of mutual understanding and trust, of communication. I wanted someone to care for me . . . and take care of me.

Sitting in the garden outside the adobe ranch house that morning,

Brian hardly looked up from his newspaper. He said only that I should think it over. I said I had, a great deal. His indifference led me to believe he also felt we had reached the point of no return. By noon I had packed a few of my things and driven out of the ranch gates. Looking back at Brian's figure standing by the house, I did not realize that it was the last time I would see him for many, many years.

Back at Rodeo Drive, pacing the garden and my bedroom, I waited for Brian's phone call from Indio. After three days of silence, I telephoned my mother, who was now with G.M. in Saratoga. I didn't want to end our marriage without another try, without a family conference, without even a farewell drink or a good-bye kiss on the cheek.

Mother, suddenly very Victorian, said my marriage problems were none of hers, that she adored Brian and would go on seeing him anyway. No, she couldn't possibly phone him, she wasn't an interfering mother-in-law. As Olivia was in the Pacific with the U.S.O., out went the family powwow. That was that.

Alternately depressed and relieved, I remained at Rodeo Drive in seclusion. I had no new man in my life, not even a girl chum to talk to, as Leslie Allen was busy with her family in Hartford. By the end of the week I called my dear, close friend Harry Crocker. He came over immediately. He dried my tears, told me to pull myself together, get dressed, comb my hair. That evening he took me dancing at Mocambo.

The next morning the phone rang incessantly. Not one call from Brian. But every columnist in town seemed to have gotten wind of our separation. Louella, motherly when it served her purpose, got the story out of me.

Brian's version was that the first he knew of our planned divorce was by reading it in the *Examiner*. What did he think I'd been talking about during breakfast at the ranch? Why had I left? What was I supposed to be doing alone in our house in Beverly Hills?

I filed suit for divorce when there was no attempt at *rapprochement* on his part. I did not ask for alimony—only the house on which I'd spent so much of my salary redecorating.

32

SECOND TIME AROUND

NOW I WAS A BACHELOR GIRL, FINDING A WARM WELCOME WITH WHAT was known as the international set. Among the many party givers were Edie and William Goetz, Sir Charles and Lady Mendl, Sam and Frances Goldwyn, Jack and Ann Warner, Cole Porter. On New Year's Eve, producer Sam Spiegel (once known as S. P. Eagle) always gave a party, as did the Charles Lederers—and I went to both! I wrote a friend:

"I'm reveling in spoiling ME. Awaking in the morning, asking ME what I want to do today. My own house, my own garden, but most of all, my own friends who come to see ME!"

Six months after the divorce I met writer-producer John Houseman, who would be my fiancé for the next many months. John was half French, half English, an intellectual. He was a liberal politically, had charm, wit, a subtle sense of humor. He was kind, understanding, an enjoyable companion, a tender friend.

John and I would have married but for one incident. In the country town of New City, New York, we often hid away from Hollywood, spent precious moments in his cottage on the large hilly property he owned there. His mother, May, and his aunt would join us. New City was an ideal place to build a house of our own and make it our permanent residence away from the turmoil of Hollywood, a place to bring up the children we both wanted.

Painter-architect-neighbor Henry Varnum Poore drew up plans for a hilltop house on Mountain Road. John's mother, of whom I was very fond, as I believe she was of me, was with us in John's cottage the night Henry showed the blueprints: a large kitchen-living room overlooking the valley, a wing for John and me, another for the children we hoped to have.

After John and I went over the plans, May rolled them up, tucked them under my arm, and beckoned, "Come, Henry, I have a few alterations to make of my own." After half an hour they returned from the adjoining room. "There," said May, beaming. "Now my room is closer to the children's."

I said not a word. The next day, in late autumn, I was called back to Hollywood to make a film. John saw me off at Grand Central Station, making faces through my drawing-room window as the Twentieth Century Limited pulled out of the depot. Years later, when I did see the house on Mountain Road, it was the home of another Joan; the children's wing was occupied by her and John's offspring. I never asked where May's room was.

Howard Hughes came into my life again. Hearing I was unattached, he asked me to dinner at a secluded, dimly lit restaurant in Los Angeles. Howard neither drank nor smoked. Nervously, I asked for a daiquiri, lit a Kool. Again Howard proposed. Again, I sensed that marriage to this eccentric recluse, now almost totally deaf, would be plunging into an unknown abyss. I declined. Howard left me on the doorstep of Rodeo Drive only to try again, with greater persistence, in five years' time.

On loan-out to R.K.O., I made a trivial film based on a story by Clifford Odets which was finally titled *From This Day Forward*. Mark Stevens played opposite me. Then came a delightful comedy for Hal Wallis at Paramount, *The Affairs of Susan*. I played four different characters with four leading men, Walter Abel, Dennis O'Keefe, George Brent, Don DeFore. Edith Head, the amiable, highly talented, bespectacled designer, outdid herself. Giving me a smashing, sexy wardrobe, she created a new image that Mme. Karinska's "mouzze" would not have recognized. The giant billboards up and down Sunset Boulevard showed me, full figure, in a brown lace tight-fitting gown, my hair pulled back in a chignon for the first time on screen. Momentarily I was a pinup girl. As this was my first comedy since *The Women,* I hoped the highly successful *Affairs of Susan* would lead to others. It didn't.

About this time my body was doing odd things. My eyes would swell, a dress I'd put on in the evening would become so tight it had to be cut off later that night. My producer arranged for me to see his doctor after rushes one evening. At his Beverly Hills office, the handsome doctor X-rayed me, put me under the fluoroscope, gave me a physical. He followed me home and made many an unnecessary house call every day for the next several weeks. I was flattered, romantic, starry-eyed at his in-and-out-of-bedside manners—until I got the itemized bill for every visit he'd made.

The New Year holidays of 1945–46 found me at St. John's Hospital in Santa Monica undergoing a series of elaborate tests. As I was under commitment to R.K.O. for my next picture, from my hospital bed I telephoned the head of the studio, William Dozier, to say that I would have to cancel the scheduled film.

Bill responded by visiting my hospital room. The next evening he brought his teen-age son, Bob. The third evening he proposed, saying his present marriage was in name only, that a divorce was pending and would soon be final. With tears in his eyes, Bill said that he badly wanted another child, a daughter. He wanted a wife with whom he could discuss his work, who knew the film industry, who liked to entertain, to travel . . . a friend and a companion. He wanted to take care of me, guide my career, build a life together. Wasn't that what I wanted, too? It was. Besides, he was very attractive. I fell.

Out of the hospital, I went into the Convent of the Sacred Heart in Menlo Park, as my doctor thought that part of my health problems might be caused by outside pressures. For three weeks I saw no one but the kindly Mother Superior and the nun who served my solitary meals.

Bill got his divorce. On May 1 Mother and Olivia professed great happiness for me as Bill and I dined with them at La Rue's Restaurant the night before we flew to Mexico City and our wedding. They toasted my future with my newfound protector, someone who would give me an anchor, roots. At the home of friends we were married in a quiet garden ceremony on May 2, 1946.

After the wedding we drove off to Taxco. Bill had asked me once where I had been most unhappy during my previous marriage. I said that it was at an enchanting inn above this picturesque Mexican village where I'd stayed on one of my trips with Leslie Allen. Leslie was an inveterate bridge player, often leaving me to my own devices after dinner. I would wander in the moonlit gardens alone, feeling very sorry for myself, feeling that life and romance were passing me by.

Bill arranged to have us stay there the night of our wedding, confident that he would make up for all those lonely hours. Unfortunately, I mistook the name of the hotel. At Taxco, in our rented car, Bill and I drove up to a totally strange inn, one I'd never seen before.

Too eager for a drink, a bath, dinner, to be alone, we made the best of our unfamiliar quarters. By midnight all sorts of fireworks went off. The Mexicans were celebrating their Fourth of July early. Cinco de Mayo was two days away, but their anticipation was as great as ours. Mrs. William Dozier had a wedding night to remember!

33

SECOND HONEYMOON

WE CONTINUED OUR HONEYMOON IN A PALM-SHELTERED COTTAGE IN Acapulco, then returned to Mexico City. It was midnight when the phone rang in our hotel bedroom. I awoke and accepted the call from the United States. A woman's voice announced that she was a syndicated reporter from Hollywood. Did I know the details of a certain damaging episode in my new husband's past? She had never liked me, she went on, and was going to blazon the story in the next morning's Los Angeles newspaper. How did I like that? Did I have anything to say?

Holding my hand over the receiver, I repeated the conversation to Bill, now awake in the other bed. He took the instrument from me. "Of course Joan knows all about it. I was just out of college . . . a youthful aberration . . . a kangaroo court. . . ." Placing the phone on the hook, he nonchalantly said to me, "Don't worry, I'll have all the editions bought up in the morning." After phoning his lawyer and instructing him, Bill casually peeled a banana from a bowl of fruit given us courtesy of the management. Having eaten it, he promptly fell sound asleep.

My world had splintered. The man I'd chosen to take care of me, to be the father of my children, had been less than frank, to say the least. I lay awake all night, trying to glue my life back together. An annulment? A divorce? What would I do then? An admission to the public that would damage us both? As on the night before my wedding to Brian, I didn't know how to stop the wheels once they'd been set in motion.

At breakfast that morning, I asked Bill why he hadn't told me, why he hadn't given me the choice of facing the truth, of deciding whether it mattered more than our future together. He replied candidly, showing no emotion, "I thought you might never find out. What you don't know can't hurt you." Had I only suspected that this attitude would prevail throughout our future together!

Numb, I returned to Rodeo Drive with my new husband. Once we were under the same roof, it was too late to turn back. Mother and Olivia had known all along, they said, even as they had drunk the toast to my future happiness at La Rue's during the pre-wedding dinner. I might be able to patch up my world, but the seams would always be there.

I gave myself a mental anesthetic. As I would do before going onstage on an opening night, I blocked out everything but the immediate future, reduced all action to a minute-by-minute response. One step at a time.

First step: As Bill felt uncomfortable being in the same house where Brian and I had lived out our marriage, sell Rodeo Drive and find a new house. After looking at several, we found a delightful, sprawling, many-windowed, shingle-roofed house on Fordyce Road, clinging to a hillside in Brentwood. The pond-sized pool with an island in the middle, waterfalls cascading into it from rocks above, a tropical garden, an orchard reminding me of La Paloma, a hothouse —all these things beguiled me. I could cook while looking out over a valley, the U.C.L.A. campus in the distance, glimpse the Pacific from our bedroom windows. The anesthetic began to wear off, the pain to subside.

Second step: Move in, play house, decorate, compile guest lists of mutual friends. Entertain.

Third step: Business as usual.

I started *The Emperor Waltz*, produced by Charles Brackett, directed by Billy Wilder, as my last film under the Selznick contract. Much of it was shot on location in Canada. Bing Crosby, whom I'd met only once before, was the leading man. Though he was pleasant to work with, I felt I scarcely knew him when the picture was finished. The results looked like it.

While the cast and crew frolicked in the evenings after work, I would go to my lakeside cabin and try to sort myself out. Bill flew up at the end of location shooting and together we returned to Hollywood. The pain diminished to a nagging ache that was never to leave me.

Bill was resilient, efficient, amusing, gregarious, confident. He had an acid wit, charm when he wished. He made an excellent, expansive host. He was boss at Fordyce Road. He also became my boss at R.K.O.

After *The Emperor Waltz,* which did not do well at the box office, Bill signed me to a long-term contract. Again . . . a repeat pattern. Just as Jesse Lasky had put me under a personal contract, then sold it to R.K.O., now no sooner was I again at that studio when Bill Dozier left to produce at Universal. But he didn't leave me entirely behind. We formed our own film company, Rampart Productions, and made two fine films under its aegis, *You Gotta Stay Happy* with James Stewart, and Stefan Zweig's story *Letter from an Unknown Woman* with Louis Jourdan, produced by John Houseman. With Max Ophuls, who directed *Letter from an Unknown Woman,* I communicated intuitively. After a take, Max would come over to me and start to speak in German, which I scarcely understood. I would nod before he had said six words and he would then resume his position behind the camera. After the next take was completed, he would rush over and say, "How you know egg-zactly vot I vont? Preent dat!"

I made two other films at Universal during those first years, *Ivy* and *Kiss the Blood Off My Hands* with Burt Lancaster.

Ivy was notable for the exquisite costumes designed by Travis Banton and the song of the same name written by Hoagy Carmichael. It was on this picture that I made one of my most embarrassing gaffes. Herbert Marshall had lost a leg in the First World War, but did very well with an artificial one, about which he was very sensitive. One day we were shooting a scene together on shipboard. "Bart," as he was called, tripped over a coil of rope on the deck. In chagrin and probably some pain, he dropped into a deck chair. I sat beside him, trying to ease the situation, chatting gaily to cover his embarrassment. At that moment, columnist Sheilah Graham appeared on the set. "Don't look now, Bart," I whispered. "If she joins us, she'll talk your leg off!"

The Doziers' personal life was filled with activity. We traveled, entertained, chartered yachts. Bill had a Cadillac, I had a four-door Lincoln Continental convertible. No longer with Selznick, I was now able to command a respectable sum of money. Bill's salary at Universal was sizable.

One trip to Bermuda found us houseguests in Hamilton. A large party was planned in our honor. Before the dinner guests arrived, the host, who had been celebrating our marriage too juicefully, was in no condition to assume his duties. As the party began, our hostess appealed to Bill to be surrogate host: "Bill, dear, please see that all the guests have cocktails, that the canapés are passed, that the fireplaces are lit, that the musicians are playing."

Half an hour later, Bill reappeared and announced, "All the guests have drinks, the canapés have been served, the fires are lit, the musicians are playing. Now what would you like me to do?"

The grateful hostess replied, "Thank you, Bill. Now just talk to the guests."

Without a pause, Bill quipped, "That's where I draw the line!"

Having an excellent Japanese chef and his wife in our Fordyce kitchen, we often gave sit-down dinners for twenty. One evening I gave one with an all-Russian menu, starting with caviar and vodka, served in chilled Orrefors shot glasses. One of the guests got to his feet, proposed a toast, and then suggested that, as in the Russian manner, we break our glasses after drinking from them. Crash! Twenty exquisite glasses were hurled against the wall. Our impervious Norwegian butler brought out the vacuum cleaner, swept up the broken glass, and proceeded to serve the cutlet Kiev as though smashing hundreds of dollars' worth of crystal was a daily Hollywood occurrence.

One Sunday the Doziers were about to give another dinner party. Late that afternoon, I ventured into the kitchen and opened the refrigerator door. There sat the dessert for the evening, one small mousse, barely enough for four and certainly not enough for the twenty we had invited. The chef, occupied with the rest of the dinner, ordered me from the kitchen. What to do!

Bill and I piled into his car, found a "Mom and Pop" grocery store that was open on a Sunday. We bought eggs, sugar, milk, vanilla bean. Rushing home, we found a hot plate in the laundry room and smuggled an eggbeater and bowls from the kitchen. The Universal producer and his film-star wife set to work in the library. By seven we had completed making two heaping bowls of *oeufs à la neige*, just in time to dress and receive our guests. The dessert was a great success.

David Niven, in one of his two excellent, amusing memoirs, recalls that he attended a party by a Brentwood pool when the butler, carrying a tray of hors d'oeuvres, fell into the water. The assembled guests dove in, nibbled the canapés from the depths. Sorry, David. That was not at Joan Caulfield and Frank Ross's, it was at the Doziers'!

In August 1946, Olivia's agent had telephoned me after reading of Olivia's marriage in Westport, Connecticut, to writer Marcus (*Delilah*) Goodrich on the previous day. Did I know anything about the groom? Searching my mind for wisps of information, I volunteered, "All I know about him is that he has had four wives and written one book. Too bad it's not the other way around." The agent couldn't resist spreading the remark around town until it finally reached the indignant novelist.

Both Olivia and Marcus were very sensitive. Soon there were many who found themselves ostracized by the Goodriches, including Mother. Olivia refused to speak to her for fifteen years, so my mother told me.

One day the telephone rang. It was Olivia, calling from somewhere in the East. She and her new husband were coming to California. Could they stay with us? I explained that our guest room as well as part of our bedroom was torn up because we were adding a large upstairs balcony linking the two rooms; however, Bill and I would be delighted to have them to dinner. The day and time were agreed upon.

On the appointed evening as seven o'clock went by, Bill and I consoled ourselves that Olivia was not known for her punctuality. We bet each other: Bill gave her an hour's tardiness, while I wagered him that she would not turn up at all.

Neither of us won: at seven-forty-five the Goodrich car pulled up into the driveway, but the couple did not alight. Bill refused to go out to be doorman to a brother-in-law he had not yet met. I, feeling that a newlyweds' quarrel might be under way, kept my distance and attempted to placate the irate cook.

By eight-thirty Olivia and her groom entered our front door. The evening was ruined. The atmosphere, try as the hosts might, was as cold as the dinner had now become. It was the first and last time that the Goodriches suggested a family get-together.

Shortly after this disastrous occasion I was asked by the Motion Picture Academy to present an award at the annual ceremonies, which was the usual invitation extended to a former Oscar winner. The evening arrived. Mother and Bill sat beside me at the Shrine Auditorium until I was requested to go backstage. After I placed the statuette in the hands of winner Harold Russell, the Academy director asked me to remain for photographs. The next category was announced . . . "The winner of the best-actress award for 1946, in *To Each His Own*, is Olivia de Havilland!"

After Olivia delivered her acceptance speech and entered the wings, I, standing close by, went over to congratulate her as I would have done to any winner. She took one look at me, ignored my outstretched hand, clutched her Oscar to her bosom, and wheeled away just as *Photoplay*'s photographer Hymie Fink captured the moment with his camera.

I fled to the privacy of an empty theatre box, where I remained until the entire ceremony was over. Olivia's reaction was totally inexplicable to me. Mother did not go backstage at all as she, though she knew not why, had been previously placed in Coventry.

34

MOTHERHOOD, HOLLYWOOD VERSION

OUR RAMPART PRODUCTIONS AT UNIVERSAL WAS JUST TAKING SHAPE . . . as I was about to lose mine. The frog test revealed nothing. Puzzled, my doctor admitted that sometimes one had to wait three months before a positive reaction appeared. I was signed to do *Kiss the Blood Off My Hands* at Universal, to be followed immediately with *You Gotta Stay Happy*. I tried to beg off. Lying on the sofa in our library, feeling more than queasy, I pled with Bill to cancel both productions. He replied that the act-of-God clause could not be invoked because there was no medical proof of my pregnancy, and gave me the standard "show must go on" routine.

The studio car arrived at dawn each day outside the house. Lying on the back seat, I would be driven over Sepulveda Pass to the studio in the San Fernando Valley. At the top of the grade, the driver would stop the car, hold my head as I retched, then go on to deliver me to my dressing room, where I would repeat the embarrassment. Halfway through the film, the doctor's frog obligingly came through with the proper verdict. In *You Gotta Stay Happy*, the brilliant dress designer Jean Louis did a masterful job of disguising my bulging midriff. Toward the end of the film, the script luckily specified that I wear a man's leather flight jacket, which afforded a splendid camouflage.

One day on location, director Hank Potter wanted me to jump off a hay wagon in my high-heeled cowboy boots. I protested. He stood firm. I jumped. Half an hour later I was rushed to the emergency ward of St. John's Hospital. Two days later, I was back on the set.

During the months of my pregnancy, I'd earned well over a quarter of a million dollars, but would have definitely preferred a gestation period of tranquillity, and to be the hothouse for my child under less trying circumstances.

With the house in shambles as we were adding on a nursery and enlarging the kitchen, Bill moved me into a suite at the Bel Air Hotel. It was only to be for a short while. The Dozier-ette was due mid-September. Then it was October 1. Then in time for my birthday, October 22. Then November 1.

I was a prisoner in a stranger's body. I now weighed fifty pounds more than usual. My clumsy, swollen body kept me confined to my bedroom. My days were spent alone, knitting, doing needlepoint, reading Dr. Grantly Dick-Read's *Childbirth Without Fear* and Dr. Spock. Mother was in Saratoga, Olivia was away with husband Marcus Goodrich. So many of Bill's evenings appeared to be occupied with business meetings, leaving me alone to cope with room service.

On the night of November 4, ten months after I knew I was pregnant, I felt the first twinges. In his car Bill sped me through the midnight streets from Bel Air to Santa Monica, frightening me so that all the calm I had been working on in accordance with Dr. Dick-Read's instructions was totally destroyed.

At dawn, in my hospital room, Bill sat and tried to read. As the pains grew in intensity, he flung down the magazine. "If it's a natural function, why does it hurt?" Next time I saw him was late that afternoon and he was a father for the second time.

Now began the worst part of the ordeal, something that few women have to go through. Because of my career, curious nurses and interns barged into my hospital room in a never-ending parade. They would insist on examining me with rubber gloves every few minutes. I'd protest to the white-jacketed interns to no avail. Childbirth at St. John's Hospital in 1948 was for me an entirely humiliating, embarrassing, degrading experience.

By two that afternoon the nurse prepared me for a special visitor. An angry, healthy, blanket-wrapped bundle came into my life and my arms. Deborah Leslie Dozier was an independent lady from the moment we met. She would have none of me, thank you. The water from a bottle she'd been given in the nursery was easier than nature's way and she was going to be fed from a bottle or she would scream down the hospital. She got her way.

From my hospital bed I called Mother in Saratoga. She did not seem exactly thrilled at being a grandmother. Nevertheless, she managed to make a gay jest of her newly acquired but not coveted status, suggesting she be called "Gams" because of her beautiful legs. I couldn't call Aunt Olivia, for we, at that time, were having a *frisson*.

Three days after Debbie was born, Bill and I brought our daughter home to Fordyce only to find reporters and cameramen waiting for us at the front door. Bill proudly carried his blanket-wrapped bundle across the threshold to the click of cameras. I hung back in my maternity clothes, trying to look invisible . . . an impossibility as my figure had hardly snapped back to its accustomed shape.

Following months in a hotel room and my sojourn at the hospital, it was thrilling to be home again. After Debbie and her nurse were installed in the new blue-and-yellow nursery, I roamed through the house and garden. Atop a ladder, I managed to hang two paintings in the guest room before withdrawing to my bed for what used to be known as the lying-in period.

Soon it was time for Deborah's christening. The ceremony promised to be a sticky one. Louella had to be invited since she was a Catholic, as Bill's daughter must be. Yet Hedda couldn't be snubbed. Wily William solved the problem. Louella came to the church, holding Debbie throughout the service. Unbeknownst to the columnist, our infant was wearing Hedda's own christening robe, loaned for the occasion.

At home, Debbie had nervous parents. She was not an affectionate, cuddly baby. Like a puppy, she preferred whoever was feeding her. Mindful of my own mother's strict nursery routine, I would wait outside my daughter's door until the nurse gave me permission to enter. I'd rush home from filming at R.K.O. to be told the child could not be disturbed. Both Debbie and the nurse ruled the house. Bill and I felt like intruders. Debbie's hungry howls in the night did not add to our attempted *rapprochement*. Before Debbie was eight months old, her parents were estranged.

35

HOWARD HUGHES

THE FIRST FILM I MADE AFTER THE BIRTH OF MY DAUGHTER WAS *Born To Be Bad*. Joan Harrison, Hitchcock's writer, had shown me the novel *All Kneeling*, by Anne Parish, and suggested it might make an interesting vehicle for me, one that would give me a chance to break away from the English lady heroines that I'd been playing. I bought the rights to the book and sold them to R.K.O. Despite a cast that included Robert Ryan, Zachary Scott, and Mel Ferrer, direction by Nicholas Ray, the only acceptable part of the film was my wardrobe designed by Tina Leser.

During the making of *Born To Be Bad*, Howard Hughes bought the R.K.O. Studios . . . lock, stock, and Fontaine's contract, too. My boss was now the same man who had been proposing to me for over ten years. I was summoned to his office.

There Howard informed me that we were to see the rushes together every evening and that he had heard the Doziers were breaking up. Was it true? Again he proposed.

"Why me, Howard? Why *me*?"

"Because you know the business, because you like to travel, you like to fly . . . why, I haven't even been to South America! We could read scripts together, play golf, see the world." Then he added a remark that was to explain his reclusiveness. "Since my accident in 1946, I can't bear to look at my face in the mirror when I shave. I'm getting ugly and don't want to be seen. And with my deafness, I haven't much more time to be among people."

At Fordyce that evening, I recounted to Bill the entire conversation I'd had with Howard. He looked thoughtful. "I'd like to run R.K.O. again," he confessed, "and our marriage isn't any good anyway. . . ."

I was never in love with Howard. As a matter of fact, I was a little afraid of him. Certainly one could not be relaxed and at ease with a man of so much wealth, power, and influence. He had no humor, no gaiety, no sense of joy, no vivacity that was apparent to me. Everything seemed to be a "deal," a business arrangement, regardless of the picture he had tried to paint of our future together—but money is sexy and he certainly had a blinding overabundance of cash appeal.

The next afternoon I went into Howard's office again to explain that Bill might be willing to give me a divorce under certain terms. But before I could even consider another marriage, I would have to get to know Howard much better, to see if the life he envisioned for us was possible. And there was Debbie. What about her?

Howard pressed the intercom button on his desk, mumbled into it, and said, "Let's go." A shabby, inconspicuous car was waiting below. We got into it, Howard driving along Sunset Boulevard, eventually turning toward the hills. At a white stucco, red-tiled house, he got out and ushered me into an indifferently furnished living room. The front door had been unlocked.

"What's all this, Howard? Whom are we visiting?"

Cocking his head to one side as he so often did to hear better, in his quiet, level monotone, he answered, "It's yours. Until your divorce is final, we can meet here."

I turned quickly and raced out the front door. Back in his car, Howard soon learned that I had my own house, thank you, and was not about to lead a shady double life with anyone. Even though I was not a lawyer, it was obvious to me that if I did so, Debbie's father would have justifiable grounds to gain her custody. Howard obviously couldn't have cared less.

Undeterred, Howard began telephoning me at the house, undoubtedly to bring matters between the Doziers to a head. Sometimes Bill would answer and hand me the phone. "God calling." Bill even seemed amused by the situation. I was not. California laws are very protective about children. If it could be proved that I was having an affair, even after divorce proceedings had begun, I most certainly would have lost custody of my child. Too, the newspapers could have had a field day, and I would end up in a monumental scandal: no child, no career, no anything.

One evening Howard telephoned me to say he wanted to discuss our situation further and would meet me in his car in Brentwood. Bill agreed to have dinner with friends while I was out. At eight o'clock, I parked my car behind Howard's and we set off in his along the coast highway. Howard had a solution. Because of his own legal situation, a year-long California divorce would be less chancy than a quick one obtained in Reno or Mexico. I was to live at a ranch he would rent for me in Nevada or Arizona while I got the divorce. He would fly in on weekends to visit me.

What! Coop me up for a year? No friends, no films? And what about Debbie? I thought of the Cole Porter song "Don't Fence Me In."

"Sorry, Howard, it won't do."

Howard kept looking in the rearview mirror as we approached Malibu. I, too, could see exceptionally bright lights that shone steadily in the mirror. Howard abruptly turned the car southward. We were being followed. I saw a black limousine with white wall tires turn in the half circle we had made and resume its tail behind us.

Back in my own car again, I waved good-bye to Howard as the limousine stopped at the corner. Howard had a fair idea of who had had us followed. So did I. I recognized the driver. I was to see him again.

Ten minutes later, back at Fordyce, I telephoned Bill at the number he had given me and told him of the conversation with Howard and of the black limousine. He was not pleased. His bewildering comment was "You've botched it." Then silence. He hung up the receiver abruptly.

Bill did, eventually, get his old office back at R.K.O., but I was to wait for some time before getting a divorce. I was one of the few girls pursued by Howard Hughes who never had an affair with him.

36

EUROPEAN INTERLUDE

I HAD CHOSEN THE RIGHT PATH. I WAS SOON TO BEGIN ONE OF THE MOST fascinating periods of my life. God and Mrs. Bruiner were about to make amends for the long pregnancy, the ignominious hospital experience, the problem of the persistent Howard Hughes, the broken marriage. Even the disastrous *Born To Be Bad*. Hal Wallis would select me to play in his *September Affair* for Paramount, one of the first American films to be made abroad after the war.

September Affair was a delightful, escapist romance about an established American architect and a celebrated pianist who meet aboard a transcontinental flight. The plane crashes over Italy. Among the survivors are the architect and the pianist, Manina. The list of passengers, all of whom are supposedly killed, is published. Joseph Cotten and I, in the script, realize that Fate has given us the opportunity to flee from family and commitments, to start life over in anonymity, together. We change our names, take a villa in Florence, and, cut off from all former ties, live together in clandestine happiness. At last, Joe's conscience forces him to return to his wife and son, my career lures me back to the concert stage. "September Song," from *Knickerbocker Holiday*, ran through the film and helped set the mood. The film was a big box-office success.

The night before I was to leave for New York and Paris en route to Rome to film *September Affair*, Bill slept in the guest room and did not awaken when the studio car arrived to pick me up early that morning. We had agreed that Bill would live in the house with our daughter and her governess until he had found an apartment. He would move out before my return.

Debbie was asleep in her crib at Fordyce as the studio car headed toward the house of Hedda Hopper, who would accompany me on my first European visit. Both Bill and I thought Hedda would be an excellent traveling companion as she, a businesswoman and former actress, would understand the exigencies of studio locations, publicity assignments, coping in a foreign language.

On the New York-bound flight Hedda chatted incessantly. From my window seat, I looked down at the red and mauve cliffs of the Grand Canyon, at the golden sea of wheat fields over Kansas, and wondered just how I'd arrived at this point in my life. I was aware that it was entirely my own doing. I could blame no one else.

My daughter would have divorced parents. As my parents had been divorced, I knew that numerous problems exist in a divided home, none of which are of the child's making. Even though I hadn't liked it that much the first time around, I would be a bachelor girl again. On my return to R.K.O. I was going to have interesting problems with Howard Hughes still as my boss. I was heading toward unknown territory and not only in Europe. Over my preprandial martini, I shed a tear or two that rolled down my cheek on the side away from Hedda. I needn't have been sorry for myself. Not since my school days in Japan was I going to be so free, so happy, or feel so young!

From my New York hotel suite, I talked on the phone to Howard. "Come back home immediately, or I'll cut out all your close-ups in *Born To Be Bad*," he commanded.

"If you promise to do that, Howard, I'll stay in Europe forever!" Now that I was away from Hollywood, the whole Hughes-versus-Dozier situation seemed almost funny. Howard promised to come to Italy once I'd settled into the role. He never did, I'm delighted to say.

From the moment that our plane landed in Paris all the oppression of my domestic life left me. No longer was I running a large house and staff, overseeing a child and nurse, answering stacks of fan mail, paying endless bills, attending business parties because it was good business, giving parties for much the same reason, talking shop with Bill over breakfast, dinner, and around the pool. Now I was a single woman, thirty-one, of some position and financial security, about to see Europe for the first time . . . and on a lavish expense account, too. No writer of soap opera could devise a better situation.

At the Ritz in Paris, Hedda bobbed her flowered hat around the bar, collecting social friends from San Francisco on holiday. Many expatriates lived on the Continent. I took off with Leslie Allen's son Walter, who knew Paris well. In dirndl and sandals, I climbed the Eiffel Tower, sailed around the Île de la Cité on a Bateau Mouche, lunched at a bistro on the Left Bank, spent the afternoon at the Louvre, walked in the gardens of the Tuileries, sauntered through the Bois.

When I returned at six that evening, Hedda was still holding court in the Ritz bar. She had seen Paris before and was amused by my childish enthusiasm. By nine we were on an Air France plane bound for Italy.

When our plane was about to cross the Alps, the stewardess beckoned me forward. The pilot invited me to share the cockpit as we flew over the snowcapped mountains, still visible in the summer twilight. The lights of Milan twinkled below as we turned south down the boot toward Rome.

We were about to deplane. Hedda handed me an armload of her fur coats to carry down the ramp. I dutifully followed her as she waved gaily to the *paparazzi* waiting below. They had a field day. Flash bulbs popped in all directions: "Hollywood film star arrives in Rome in midsummer covered in furs." A photo on the front page of next morning's Rome paper showed behatted Hedda, with Joan trailing behind, head sticking up over a pile of assorted minks and sables.

One of the cameramen at the airport was George "Slim" Aarons of Time-Life. In customs, he came over and whispered to me to put down the furs and be photographed on my own. He had caught the situation immediately and knew far more about the press than I. Hedda knew a good story, too, and hadn't hesitated to go for it. I realized that Miss Hopper was going to be more unwieldy than an armload of furs!

At the Excelsior Hotel the Paramount reception committee awaited us in a suite assigned to Hedda and me. I knew sharing quarters with Hedda would be a grave mistake with my early work calls and with Hedda on the phone, calling in her column at all hours of the day and night. Handsome, tall Slim again came to my rescue and had the management find another suite just for me. Hedda sulked.

Still too exhilarated to turn in, I slipped away with Slim to the Via Veneto and a midnight espresso. There he warned me that I could expect trouble if Miss Hopper dared put her foot on the set. Both Joe Cotten and director William Dieterle cordially disliked her, while tactful producer Hal Wallis had to pretend to play ball with the powerful lady. Slim and I both realized that Hedda was going to stick to me like adhesive plaster.

Next morning, more interviews, more photographs, more adhesive plaster. Hedda was a businesswoman first, friend second, helpful duenna not at all. She arranged lunch and dinner parties and ordered me to attend. My shooting schedule prohibited me from this sort of extracurricular activity. Besides, I wanted to see Rome, to dash about in the country with Slim in his midget convertible whenever I had a free moment from shooting. It was an angry Hedda who finally announced she was taking the train back to Paris, hats and all. Slim and I saw her off at the station. He predicted that her column would print that I'd treated her badly. He was right. I knew that her slanted publicity wouldn't help my legal situation. I was also right. Dozier had moved out of Fordyce, but now, after the Hughes debacle, was unwilling to give me a divorce.

With Hedda now gone, I was fancy-free to roam about the galleries and museums, to hear *Aida* under the moonlight at the Baths of Caracalla, to eat fettucini from the gold spoons given to Alfredo by Mary Pickford and Douglas Fairbanks when they visited his restaurant on their honeymoon. Free to do all the tourist things that postwar Italy had to offer.

Slim was an excellent guide and tutor. He had been assigned to the film by his magazine, and he protected me from making further mistakes with the press. He understood my sight-seeing ardor and was as keen as I to keep away from social life.

Shooting scenes in Florence, using the exterior of Bernard Berenson's villa and having tea with the owner, was an experience to remember. The mayor of this glorious city invited us to dine and had the tower where Savonarola was incarcerated lit up with bowls of flaming oil. Moonlight carriage rides with Slim along the banks of the Arno, strolling in the piazza while musicians played Verdi and

Puccini, gazing at the pictures in the Uffizi Galleries made me fall as much in love with Florence as I had with Rome.

Shooting the film was pleasant. Dieterle and Cotten were civilized and amiable. Hal Wallis was a producer of charm and concern. Arising at dawn, I would go to the temporary makeup room, where thimble-sized white china cups of espresso started off the day. I didn't even mind the redolent smells of garlic and nocturnal pleasures emanating from the hairdresser and makeup man.

Naples, Milan, Capri . . . all were location sites for *September Affair*. In Venice, Joe Cotten and I donned costumes and became extras in Orson Welles's *Othello* when that quixotic director shot a scene in the Piazza San Marco. Joe played a wealthy Venetian, I his page. Often I go back to all those glorious places in Italy that I first visited in 1949—to Portofino, to Rapallo, to Positano, to Sorrento—and I feel sixteen all over again.

37

CALIFORNIA, HERE I COME

THOUGH THE FILM WAS ENTITLED *September Affair*, THE NINTH MONTH in 1949 was the only time the cameras didn't turn. July and August were spent shooting exteriors in Italy. A layoff in September was scheduled while the cutters in Hollywood reviewed the reels of film flown over. The interior scenes were to be filmed in October at Paramount in California.

After spending part of September in England, visiting my de Havilland family, I flew back to California, to Fordyce and my daughter. Arriving early in the morning after a night flight, I rushed into the nursery only to be told that Debbie was asleep in her playpen by the pool. I ran through the garden. Debbie was under the poolside gazebo, all right, but so was a fan, camera in hand, waiting to catch the reunion of mother and child.

I'd forgotten! I'd forgotten all that fan-magazine business, the autograph seekers, the photographers popping out from unlikely places. Not that there wasn't the same thing in Europe, but somehow, here in my own garden, when I wanted to hold my child in my arms again after three months' absence, I felt the intrusion keenly. And my servants obviously had not only condoned the trespass but had informed the fan of my homecoming.

I realized that my house had now become theirs, that perhaps I was the outsider. With Bill gone, I would now have to be the boss at Fordyce, run the house, do what I thought best for Debbie and me, take a page from G.M.'s book of rules. It would be a question of being away at the studio all day, up in the morning before the staff, home at night after the rushes, just in time for bath and dinner with lines to learn before lights out. It was not going to be easy to be the single parent, the housekeeper, the billpayer in the short time I was home in the evenings. It wasn't.

Being single again was, as I suspected, not much fun. It was all work and no play. Several bachelors helped break the monotony by squiring me to parties or weekends in Santa Barbara or Hillsborough, but it was not until I went to a party at the home of Dru Mallory (now Mrs. H. J. Heinz III) that I met a man who attracted me. Collier Young was a perennial Peter Pan, a wit and a wag whose avocation was writing and producing. Give him a lampshade and he'd wear it. He was just what I needed after losing the mutual humor Bill Dozier and I had once shared.

Conrad Hilton had asked a group of us to fly with him for a week of fishing at the opening of a posh hunting lodge on Prince Albert Inlet in British Columbia. I soon discovered that the lodge's totem poles were going to be more fun than the guests. At the millionaire sportsman's paradise, I found I was the only fisherman. Collie, who had professed to be the Compleat Angler, turned out not to know which end of the pole to bait. It didn't matter, because the fish weren't biting. What did matter was that there was nothing else to do. I began to laugh. The whole situation seemed ludicrous. Ann Miller, dressed in American Indian regalia, entertained by doing war whoops and rain dances for the photographers. We were captives, miles away in the forest from the nearest town, smothering in total luxury and total boredom.

Collie and I found we were on the same laugh wavelength. We stimulated each other until we became as giddy as children on a roller coaster. Everything was funny, even trying to figure out how to extricate ourselves from a whole week of ennui.

Suddenly I remembered that my father and Yoki-san, whom I hadn't seen since Japan in 1934, had moved to Victoria, B.C., after their enforced stay at Colorado Springs during the war. I sent myself a cable saying that dear ole Dad was fast fading: a last glimpse of his cherished child would allow him to die happy.

Conrad Hilton obligingly had us flown to Victoria by private plane. Now where to find my pining, declining pater? At his chess club, of course. Telephone directory. Directions from friendly policeman. Knock on door of Victoria Chess Club. Ask for Walter de Havilland. Out comes Father! Easier than pulling fish out of Prince Albert Inlet.

Father, who had always looked like Methuselah to me, seemed bent and frail in 1950, but he was to live eighteen more years. I found now that he had no power over me, I was only sorry for him. For a moment, Collier and I stopped laughing.

Father was no less eccentric, I discovered. After all those years, he was no less haughtily aristocratic. He still wore his navy pinstripe as though he were strolling from his tailor's on Bond Street. He still damned my mother, still looked down on Americans as though we were a crude, illiterate tribe of vulgarians. Collie and I made a hasty retreat, heading for Southern Vulgaria with all speed and much relief.

When we eventually arrived at Fordyce, Collie repaired to his red barn of a house on Mulholland Drive, packed his bags, and returned within the hour. There was a lighted candle in the window when he entered the front door, to stay for many years.

Now I had someone to share my days and nights, to laugh with, a shoulder to cry on when needed. Debbie would have a sense of family, a surrogate father. We would both have a playmate.

Not-yet-two-year-old Debbie adored "Uncle" Collie and treated him as someone her own age. She was right.

38

SOUTH OF THE BORDER

EARLY IN THE SPRING OF 1951, I WAS ASKED TO GO ON A STATE Department-sponsored film junket to South America. The purpose was to attend the film festivals, promote good public relations between our hemispheres, and, of course, renew interest in American movies now that European films had begun to vie with Hollywood productions.

The film festival in Rio de Janeiro occurred simultaneously with Carnival and was followed by another film festival at Punta del Este in Uruguay. On the chartered flight from Los Angeles to Brazil were many Hollywood celebrities, including Robert and Mary Cummings, Irene Dunne, Fred MacMurray, Patricia Neal, June Haver, Rhonda Fleming, Evelyn Keyes, Wendell Corey. Harry Crocker went along as my escort and as a member of the press. Errol Flynn joined us briefly at the Brazilian festival. The plane trip was uneventful except that Bob Cummings' wristwatch alarm would regularly resound through the plane. He was a vitamin addict and took his pills every four hours, night and day, awakening the sleeping passengers.

The Carnival in Rio was a unique experience, especially the uncontrollable enthusiasm of the crowds. Policemen tried to hold back the milling celebrants. When too many happy Brazilians surrounded us, we Hollywood visitors were carried like logs of wood high over the heads of the populace to the safety of police cars.

At the hotel one morning during the three-day celebration, I came out of my suite just as Irene Dunne stepped out of her neighboring one. "How did you sleep last night, Joan?" inquired beautiful Irene.

"How could I sleep with all those thousands on the beach chanting under my window 'Joanna Fontana, Joanna Fontana!'" I wearily replied.

"Not at all." Irene smiled. "I heard them, too. They were calling out 'Irenee Doonee, Irenee Doonee!'"

At Punta del Este, the film festival was taken very seriously. Many kind Uruguayans entertained us. Edward Miller, Undersecretary of State for South America, joined our party. He, Harry, and I, at the end of the festival, stayed at the U. S. Embassy in Montevideo while the Countess di Frasso and Patricia Neal, among others, stayed with *bon vivant* Alberto Dodero in his villa.

One evening, at a large buffet at his house, host Alberto, an old friend of mine, came up and whispered that he felt unwell, was going upstairs to lie down, and would I see to his guests? That was the last time any of us saw him. He died during the night.

Dorothy di Frasso telephoned me at the Embassy at seven the next morning to tell me the news. "What should Pat and I do? Ask the ambassador." As my host was not up yet, I suggested that they eat a hearty breakfast, tip the servants, pack and leave . . . a thank-you note would not be expected!

In Argentina, Harry and I had hardly arrived at our hotel when the phone rang in his room. It was the Buenos Aires Chief of Police, demanding I appear at headquarters immediately. Harry, bearing our passports as requested, went in my stead. Evita Perón, the President's wife, had heard that I had balked at attending an audience with her that had been arranged for our group. Harry explained to the *jefe de policía* that we were no longer traveling officially, but would be happy to meet her individually. Since our passports were withheld we were now prisoners of the country.

At nine the following morning, very official cars called for us at our hotel. Very official gentlemen escorted us to all of Evita Perón's "good works." The first stop was at her school for actresses, for she had been one, too . . . in a manner of speaking.

On her trip to Spain after the war, one story goes, she was riding with General Franco in a welcoming parade through the streets of

Madrid. The populace shook their fists at her, calling after her open car, "*Puta, puta!*" Evita supposedly turned to her escort and tearfully asked him why they called her a whore. "Never mind, dear Señora Perón." He patted her hand respectfully. "I've been retired for years but they still call me General."

Next we visited Evita's hospital and were shown the latest medical equipment, including an oxygen tank, rare in those days. Vases of wilted flowers were everywhere, left over from Eddie Miller's inspection tour two days before. We saw no patients, no doctors, no nurses. "They are on other floors," we were told.

Next on the agenda came the nursery school for small children of the *descamisados*, the "shirtless" people of the country. I noted that the manufacturers' stamps were still on the socks, the sheets on the tiny cots. Obviously they were still unwashed. "The children are out on a sight-seeing tour," we were told.

At noon we were driven to a very official building where, amid marble columns, we were left to cool our heels and to consider the honor about to be bestowed upon us. Exactly one-half hour later, we were ushered into a huge hall. A red-carpeted aisle led to the end of the room, to a huge vermeil desk, behind which Evita was busy on a French telephone.

The First Lady of Argentina looked up and scrutinized me closely as I traversed the mile of carpet, stopped in front of her desk, and waited until she hung up. "You're not afraid of me, are you?" she asked with some incredulity.

"How do you know I'm not?" I replied as politely as possible.

"By the way you walked down the aisle," said Evita, smiling. (Oh, dear G.M., thank you for all those toeing-out exercises. Mother . . . for all those book-on-the-head posture lessons.)

"Come sit beside me." Señora Perón patted the brocaded chair behind her desk. "People say we look alike. I think so, too." Our hats bobbed close together. Her blonded hair and brown eyes, my fair skin and hazel eyes were compared by Harry as he stood patiently overhearing the conversation but totally unnoticed by Brown Eyes. In a garble of English, French, and Spanish, we might have been two matrons talking over old school days.

Evita asked my advice. Realizing she was as direct as I, I gave it: She'd made several international public-relations mistakes on her European postwar tour. All the jewels, the elaborate ball gowns, the parade of wealth, when orphaned children in Italy and Spain still had little to eat. Argentina had kept out of the war and thrived economically. I said she would have been far more welcome if she'd brought wheat and beef, two of the principal Argentine exports, instead of empty splendor.

Evita listened intently. Instead of showing rancor, she immediately understood. She was an excellent propagandist in her own country, as President Perón well knew. She instantly grasped what I said. "Be my adviser. I shall speak to your ambassador. You must be cultural attaché to my country. I want the world to understand me." More than that, I knew she wanted to be a movie star, to be loved the world over.

That night Harry and I attended a banquet with the Peróns, the next day the Pan American games, sitting in their box. A mosquito lit on the forehead of her husband. I pointed it out to her. "Slap it away," she suggested, and giggled. "He's only the President." Juan Perón smiled at her indulgently.

Harry and I, passports restored, were relieved to depart the country, but not before saying good-bye to all our Argentinian friends, who realized we had had no alternative but to socialize with the dictator and his señora.

(When I returned home to California, a large autographed photo of Evita was waiting for me. Later her biography arrived, bound in gilt and leather, a flowery inscription above her signature. Pleading family and career matters, I politely turned down invitations to come to Argentina, and never again entered the country during the Perón regime.)

After a brief stop in Chile, Harry and I stayed with the Harold Tittmans at the American Embassy in Lima. At dinner on our first night there, the ambassador insisted that we visit Cuzco and Machu Picchu before going home. On the telephone after dinner, he persuaded the brother of the Peruvian ambassador to Washington, Gustavo Berckemeyer, to act as our guide the following morning.

The flight to Cuzco in the unpressurized plane was unexpectedly pleasant, due partially to the charm and aristocratic mien of our handsome Peruvian guide. Gustavo, a most eligible bachelor, was thoroughly knowledgeable in the lore of his country, its conquest by Pizarro, the capture and death of the Incan king Atahualpa.

After stopping in Cuzco long enough to view the architecture, the canals dug by the ancient Indians, we made our way through a mountain gorge on a narrow-gauge railway train. When we could go no farther by rail, we mounted mules and wound our way up perilous paths to the mountaintop, to Machu Picchu, the last stronghold of the Incas.

I couldn't wait to explore the ruins, consisting of giant stones fitted together without mortar, and to try to visualize what it might have looked like before the Spanish arrived. As I strode ahead of our group a small ragged child darted out from behind a rock. She pointed, "*Mira, mira! Mi casa, mi casa.*" I looked over in the distance and saw a one-room, dirt-floored, thatched shack, perilously perched on a crag over the river far below. It was the only house amid the ruins, except for the inn at which we were staying.

The tiny girl shadowed me, chattering away in Spanish as though we were old friends. Her wispy pigtails were tied with white string, her sandals so worn that they hardly held together. Her sleeveless patched cotton dress was insufficient to keep her warm at this altitude, nor did it cover the sores and insect bites on her arms and legs. Taking my hand, she led me through the ruins like a seeing-eye dog. I was even more captivated by Martita Pareja than by the view of the Andes surrounding us.

That night I could not sleep. Something troubled me. In the vivid moonlight outside my room, a tall yucca stood like a sentry by my window, casting a shadow over my cot. Eventually I did sleep, but awakened with a start. That child! Martita! I couldn't leave her there! She, somehow, belonged to me, too, and I to her. I lay awake, exhilarated now, planning her future. It opened before me without effort: she was a Catholic, Debbie was, too. She had a beautiful and distinguished name, Martita Valentina Pareja Calderon, as she had pronounced it that afternoon. I wouldn't change it. I wanted to take her back to Fordyce as a sister for Deborah, as a small friend for me. To educate her, heal her poor sore arms and legs, her swollen belly, to give her a bed of her own, to clothe and feed her. And, perhaps, one day, when she returned to her own country and family, she would, because of her education, help others of her race. Neither of her parents could read or write.

At breakfast next morning Gustavo and Harry had already had their coffee when I entered the rustic dining room. I told them of my vision. They scoffed. "You've got enough to think about. You don't need an Inca in Hollywood. Don't play Lady Largesse. The publicity won't do you any good. In race-conscious America it can only harm you. You're being emotional and impulsive." They both thought I'd gone crackers.

I *was* being emotional and impulsive. I realized that I was undertaking an enormous responsibility, but Martita had captured me and I was helpless. Reluctantly, Gustavo sent for the parents. Eugenio Pareja, hat in hand, came as far as the door. Deferentially, Martita's father would not enter the inn, but stood in the pouring rain as Gustavo explained to him in Spanish the crazy lady's request.

To everyone's amazement except my own, Martita's father answered without hesitation, "Yes, we know. My wife has gone to the village to sell a chicken, but before she left she told me to say that Martita may go with the señora."

To me, it was another proof that Mrs. Bruiner had been busy in the night. How else could the parents have known that I wanted to take Martita to the United States, to raise her as a member of my family?

I could only think that the poverty-ridden family had too many mouths to feed, envisioned too many more births in their Catholic aerie. At least now one of their children would have enough to eat, would have some sort of life other than begging from tourists, never going to school, never having medical or dental attention, never having a bed to sleep in. It is difficult to imagine such poverty, for the head of the family was, I was told, earning eight cents an hour, working on the tiny railway. Señora Pareja was old beyond her years, her face lined from the climate, her body distended from childbirth and malnutrition.

That morning I promised Eugenio Pareja that, if possible, I would bring Martita back for a visit every year and that I would help out with their financial situation. That was volunteered by me, for never did the proud Parejas ask for money at any time. As difficult as it was for them to give up their child for a few years, they, too, hoped that she would return and be a source of pride and happiness to them and their people.

Flying back immediately to Lima and the American Embassy, all the necessary papers being obtained in record time, I became Martita's legal guardian under Peruvian law. She soon had a Peruvian passport of her own, an entry permit for the United States. Gustavo wasn't an ambassador's brother for nothing. All of his friends in Peru who were sympathetic to Martita's cause were extremely helpful.

Gustavo worked miracles, as did our ambassador, Harold Tittman. All around, it had been a week of miracles.

Over the telephone to California, I told Collie of my dream, asked him to explain to Bill Dozier that I was bringing home a sister for his daughter, to tell Debbie she would soon have a playmate to share her nursery.

Collie knew that I had been asked to stay with the Joseph Kennedys in Palm Beach on my return to the United States via Florida. Perhaps our host could find a Spanish-speaking nursemaid for Martita, that is . . . if we were both welcome? There was a polite reply by cable from the Kennedy residence that the house was unexpectedly full. There was no room at the inn.

(Two years later, as I was lunching one day with Joseph Kennedy at his favorite restaurant in New York, he congratulated me for adopting Martita, saying that I had done so much for relations between the two hemispheres, so much, by example, for Catholic children of impoverished minorities. Over our *poulet à l'estragon*, I did not remind him of the March 1951 weekend, when his Florida house had suddenly burst at the seams.)

On the flight to America, five-year-old Martita, who had never seen a flush toilet, a seat belt, a dinner served on a tray before her, seemed totally at ease. She used her knife and fork, her napkin, more elegantly than most of the passengers. Then, and as long as she remained with me, her manners were always impeccable, learned through natural inclination and observation. She was modest, considerate, soft-spoken, gentle. When she laughed, she threw her head back, closed her eyes, and smiled inwardly.

After our dinner trays were removed, I watched her carefully. Not a flicker of homesickness seemed to cross her face. It shone with pride in her new station, in anticipation of the adventure before her. She chatted away in a mixture of Quechua and Spanish. Somehow I understood her and replied in pidgin Spanish and English. Somehow, she understood me. Soon she curled up in the seat beside me and slept soundly until the stewardess awakened us for breakfast and our arrival in her new land.

39

FORDYCE FOURSOME

IN PALM BEACH, COLLIE MET US AT THE PLANE, TAKING US IMMEDI-ately to the Colony Hotel before anyone knew we had landed. Here I bathed Martita and bought her dresses for our journey homeward. Next I took her to the hotel beauty salon, where, fortunately, there were Spanish-speaking operators. Her hair was trimmed, per-manented, and arranged in a soft bob about her face. The duckling turned into a swan! With her gold skin, straight teeth, hazel eyes, red-black hair, Martita was a fetching, adorable, laughing, affec-tionate daughter. Not once did I regret my impulsiveness. Though my Palm Beach friends longed to see the new addition to my family, I quickly smuggled her aboard the first plane to Los Angeles and the seclusion of Fordyce before the press and the curious might upset her.

At home at Fordyce, Debbie, in her blue Dr. Dentons, met us at the front door that evening. She put her arms around Martita and gave her a wet kiss. And, just as Martita had beguiled me with *"Mira, mi casa"* in Machu Picchu, Debbie took her new sister by the hand and showed her the nursery, the toys, and the bed Martita would occupy. Debbie showed me a side of herself that I hadn't seen before. Collie, who unfortunately couldn't have children, now had a daughter, too.

There were four very happy people at Fordyce that evening.

Martita learned English quickly. She learned everything quickly. She had an intuitive sense about most things. About me. Whenever I came home from the studio tired or upset over the day's shooting, she had only to lay her hand gently on my shoulder and I could feel her empathy. For a time I thought we read each other's mind, for often I wouldn't have to tell her what to do. She looked at me and did it.

I never had to scold Martita, for she never disobeyed. One day in the children's dressing room, I found she had squirreled away in a drawer various eye-catching objects . . . a silver spoon, red tissue paper, a colored ribbon. Taking her by the hand, I led her through the house, through the garden to the pool, the hothouse, the gardener's cottage. I explained that it all was hers . . . more than she could ever hide in a drawer. Nothing was ever missing again.

The results of her former diet, principally of corn, gave us a problem. After the doctors had healed her sores, removed the parasites from her stomach, straightened her legs with braces, it was a year before milk, eggs, fresh meat, fruit, and vegetables changed her body chemistry. Fortunately, she liked the American diet, though she was never greedy, never ate to excess.

Bed was a problem. Martita had never known a mattress in Machu Picchu, where she had slept sitting cross-legged on the floor, leaning against the bare wall, as did her parents, her brothers and sisters. I would go into the nursery at night to find her sitting asleep on her bed: the covers pulled up over her shoulders like a serape, her legs crossed, her head against the white plaster wall. Gently, I'd put her down in a horizontal position and rearrange the bedclothes. She seldom woke.

One by one, curious friends came to see my adopted daughter. They, too, were enchanted and soon accepted the little foreigner with grace. And three-and-a-half-year-old Debbie flourished. No longer did I overhear her threaten to fire the servants if they disobeyed her. No longer would she test me to see how much she could get away with before the gentle but inevitable spank on her rubber bottom. No longer were the contents of the refrigerator or the cookie jar her sole interest. The girls seldom quarreled. Obviously they enjoyed each other's company.

Until birthdays and Christmases, that is. As Martita's birthday was November 3, Debbie's November 5, we celebrated on the fourth, giving equal presents to both. But try as I might, I could never even up the gifts Debbie would receive from her father and stepmother, Ann Rutherford, and from Bill's friends. To balance the count at the end of the celebrations, I would keep extra presents, already wrapped, hidden away for Martita. Intuitively, Martita knew this, was always hurt and perplexed that Debbie's father did not follow the same code of equality practiced at Fordyce. She never felt comfortable at the Doziers' house on Greenway Drive or with Debbie's half-brother, Bob.

But I loved Martita and so did Collie. I loved both my children at Fordyce in those days when Collie's black standard poodle and German shepherd, plus Calico, the gray Persian cat, would romp in the nursery, the playroom, the garden. Often we'd all splash in the pool together . . . except Calico, of course.

Yet someone had to pay the butcher, the grocer, the music teacher (suitably named Miss Schwinger), the gardener, Louis, the housekeeper, Frances.

Since *September Affair*, all I had done were some dreary retakes of *Born To Be Bad*. I was still under contract to R.K.O., and out of pique Howard Hughes was simply going to let me sit and wait for a new assignment. No good scripts were arriving at Fordyce from independent producers. Even though paychecks were coming in regularly from R.K.O., they would not go on forever. Bill Dozier was not contributing to his daughter's keep at Fordyce. Divorce proceedings had already begun, but I had not considered asking for alimony. I doubt if it would have been granted, considering my past earnings, and there would have been a bitter legal battle.

One sunny day in May 1951, I sat in the garden, watching the children taking their swimming lesson. Looking at the gold-skinned, dark-haired girl splashing water at the younger blond child, I realized they might well be Olivia and her sister and I might be my own mother observing her children at play.

Unconsciously I had re-created the very situation my mother had found herself in at approximately my present age. Here was I, a single woman with two girl children, two years apart in age, uncertain of my future, hoping to give them the advantages of education, travel, the security of a home and companions, roots, stability, church. I wanted them, too, to have what I hadn't known: demonstrative love and laughter in the home, friends who came to the garden and pool to play, animals to love. I wanted them to have the companionship of their mother as well as her supervision and affection.

Like my mother, I was in legal limbo. My parents' divorce took years. Here was I, still legally tied to William Dozier, unable to marry Collie, the man I had chosen to be stepfather to my children. I was the sole breadwinner at Fordyce and I knew that Collier Young would never be able to help me with the financial burden. It was, and always would be, on my shoulders alone.

"One, two, kick, kick." The swimming instructor's voice echoed over the water. I looked around at the serenity of the garden, the dancing light on the pool edge as the bamboo reeds swayed in the breeze. Music was coming from the hidden amplifiers in the trees. Hazber the poodle and Fang the German shepherd rushed up and down the flagstone terrace as the children swam the length of the pool in the Australian crawl.

As my mother had, I, too, had the same fear and suspicion of my daughter's father, the same dread that he might try to separate us, that he might try to denigrate me in my daughter's eyes, just as Father had done. An exact replica of the pattern.

Though the noonday sun beat down on the hibiscus hedge behind my canvas chair, I felt a chill run through me. The road ahead would be paved with rough stones.

It was clear that the insecurities I had felt all my life arose from the schism between my parents. In California I had felt an alien and longed for my father. But when I was united with him I found him a stranger. I had no family ties in America, was allowed no friends in the Saratoga house. Mother always reminded us that G.M. had no financial responsibility toward either sister and that we should be obedient and grateful to him for his benevolence.

I resolved that Debbie and Martita would have as carefree a life as I could give them, that I would try to keep the innocents in paradise as long as I possibly could. I vowed, too, that I would never deprecate Debbie's father to her, regardless of his comments about me.

"In, out, in, out," came the instructor's voice. I gazed down the flower-lined walk toward the hothouse, then across to the lawn and the Oriental garden surrounding it to the rambling shake-roof house, looking out at us through picture-window eyes. How long could an actress in her midthirties continue a movie career, give her children an idyllic childhood? What was the alternative?

I could give up my career, sell this place, move into a small apartment, live on the salary I was getting from my long-term R.K.O. contract, and single-handedly raise the children, driving them to school, doing their homework with them each evening, being their housekeeper, chauffeur, cook, maid, drudge. And when they had grown up and left the nest, what then? Or I could continue my career as best I could, marry Collier in order to give the children a father, live in Fordyce whenever my pursuit of the dollar allowed me, and, at the same time, squirrel away for all those rainy days that must inevitably lie ahead. There was no choice.

Fortunately, I would be free to marry within a year. Though Collier Young was charming, amusing, a gay companion to both the children and me, I realized I would have to be disciplinarian for both of us. It was I who would have to fix the furnace, hire and fire, remind the children to brush their teeth and to say "thank you" and "please." Collie would be a delightful guest who made us all laugh and who would take nothing seriously. Well, not a bad bargain . . . for a while. But the depth, solidity, and permanence of our relationship would be up to him.

The girls dried themselves with giant towels. The swimming instructor agreed they'd both turned into fish and were now as completely at home in water as they were on Fordyce Road.

I resolved then and there that I would try to keep my family together, no matter where my work led me. But at the same time I could not allow myself to be inextricably painted into a corner, to be buried in domesticity as my talented mother had been. And since there seemed to be no films for me in Hollywood, I'd search elsewhere. As I could not take Debbie out of California during divorce proceedings or again uproot Martita, I would have to leave the children behind. I picked up the phone in the garden gazebo and dialed my travel agent.

40

EUROPE REVISITED

JUNE 1951 FOUND ME EN ROUTE TO PARIS, THIS TIME TO BE THE HOUSE-
guest of Norman and Rosita Winston on the rue St. Dominique.
Paris in June is the racing season, the time of fashion shows. English,
American, and South American horsy types crowd the courses at
Chantilly, then flock to Deauville, and later to England for the
Derby.

The night I arrived in Paris, the Winstons took me to a party
given by interior decorator Jacques Franck. There I met a dark and
dapper charmer by the name of Prince Aly Khan. Next day my room
at the Winstons' was filled with red roses. Over lunch at Maxim's,
Aly handed me a small package from Cartier's: a gold-and-crystal
desk clock in a red morocco-leather case. Aly became my escort at all
the parties and racing gatherings.

In his Ferrari, we dashed to his horse farms to name his foals. We
raced to Deauville, where we galloped along the beach on hacks
hired from local stables. We attended galas at the casino with his father, the Aga Khan, and swam in the Mediterranean at his villa at
Juan-les-Pins. Usually there was a group of friends with us, for Aly
was gregarious and generous, liked the "jet set," and thirsted for admiration from the opposite sex.

One day, as we were lunching at Coq Hardi in Bougival, I took out my cigarette case and lit a cigarette.

"Are you enamored of that case?" inquired the Moslem prince.

"No, not particularly," I replied.

"I thought not." Thereupon Aly took a small object from his pocket, placed it before me: a gold-and-diamond case.

Elsa Maxwell reigned as international hostess in Paris when she could afford it. At her Spanish Ball that year all the international set turned out dressed to the teeth, the ladies in their freshly laundered diamonds. That evening I was with Aly and Mr. and Mrs. Byron Foy. Thelma Foy, of the Chrysler family, always on the best-dressed list, cared considerably about her appearance and spent endless hours fitting her wardrobe several times each year at the Paris couturiers. This night she had on a stunning black tulle ballet-length Dior and looked supremely radiant. As we entered Pré Catelan in the Bois, which Elsa had taken over for the occasion, Thelma to her horror spied seven ladies in the identical dress. She promptly sat down on the nearest banquette in the foyer as her faithful friends quickly surrounded her. After greeting several of the guests from a sitting position, she led us through a side door and into the park. We spent the rest of the evening dancing at the fashionable nightclub Jimmy's. There hers was the only black tulle Dior evident.

Ivanhoe was about to go into production at London's M.G.M. studio. Jules Stein, my agent, who had a house in Paris, asked me at a party if I would like to play Lady Rowena. With Elizabeth Taylor, George Sanders, Robert Taylor, and Finlay Currie in the cast, I jumped at the chance. After all, wasn't that the reason I had come to Europe?

Cutting short my whirlwind fling with Aly, I flew to London and reported to producer Pandro Berman and director Richard Thorpe, as well as to the wardrobe and hairdressing departments. Between fittings, I would fly back to France and Aly. After one weekend riding horses at Deauville with Aly, I returned to London so stiff from the unaccustomed exercise that I could hardly move. But Noël Coward was escorting me to the first night of *Sleeping Beauty* with Margot Fonteyn dancing the leading role. In a glorious Griffe creation of tight-fitting chartreuse satin dripping with velvet grapes, I painfully sat through the first act at Covent Garden. Suddenly everyone in our box stood up and bowed deeply. The Queen Mother entered. I tried as best I could to execute a curtsey, yet the dress and my aching muscles held me in a vise. From his bent position, Noël snickered. The Queen Mother's eyes twinkled at me, for she could clearly see my dilemma.

Taking a flat at 15 Grosvenor Square, I settled in for five months' shooting of *Ivanhoe* at Elstree, where I found that director Thorpe cared more about the performance of the horses than the actors. Elizabeth Taylor was being wooed by Michael Wilding. Bob Taylor was nursing his vanity over his divorce from Barbara Stanwyck. George Sanders was his laconic, moody self.

One evening the phone at Grosvenor Square rang. An English hostess was sending around an escort. She'd only just learned that I was in London and insisted that I come to her party. Hastily donning an evening gown, I soon opened my door to a handsome youth wearing a betasseled Spanish hat cocked over one eye. It was Prince Nicholas of Yugoslavia, who would become a great friend and dear, platonic companion, even to sharing my apartment with me while he attended Oxford. His brother Prince Alexander often did the same.

Despite long hours huddled in studio caravans on location, waiting for the clouds to lift so that Richard Thorpe could photograph the battle sequences and the jousting tournaments, I spent happy weekends with Nicky, flying in his rented plane above the English clouds. Aly would send a D. H. Dove for us to join him in Deauville or the South of France.

One weekend at L'Horizon in Juan-les-Pins, Harry Crocker and I were about to try out Aly's hundred-foot slide into the Mediterranean. No one warned us of any danger. Harry went first. I slid down, head first, close behind him. As Harry struck the water, he was stopped short by the impact. I hit his well-padded shoulder with my head, collapsing a disk in my spine, accordioning the vertebrae in my neck.

Harry dragged me, temporarily paralyzed, to shore, where I realized from the excruciating pain that I was in for trouble. Concealing my agony, I sat through luncheon listening to the latest gossip as told by Elsa Maxwell and her lifelong companion Dickie Gordon, to the chatter of Jules Stein's daughters, to the laughter of Aly's sons, Karim (now the Aga) and Amin. I wondered whether I had permanently damaged my spine.

Back in London after a painful midnight flight, I called Noël Coward, who sent me to his doctor, Guy Beauchamp. Fortunately,

Dr. Beauchamp knew what to do. He "hung" me daily during the weeks I was on the film, stretching my neck and spine until the split disk fused by itself.

As we were still shooting *Ivanhoe* in late November, I could not get home for Thanksgiving with the children. Therefore I arranged with the service kitchen at Grosvenor Square to prepare a real American Thanksgiving for a few of my friends. Mary Martin and her husband, Dick Halliday, were staying at the Savoy Hotel during her highly successful run of *South Pacific*, so I invited them, as well as the cast of *Ivanhoe*.

Although I had stressed that the gathering was to be very informal, and I was in slacks, Mary Martin arrived in a black cut-velvet Mainbocher. Mary took over. Standing in what is called in the theatre "fireplace center," she directed us all, the conversation, even to where we should sit at table. As the Hallidays left that evening, Dick said his thanks with "We had a nice time. Not *very* nice, but nice."

One weekend Harry Crocker and I were guests at Warwick Castle with Vincent and Minnie Astor. The Earl of Warwick showed me to my room, containing the bed slept in by the first Queen Elizabeth, and pointed out that his room was next to mine. After he left, I realized that there was no key in the door between our rooms.

After I'd gone to bed that night, sure enough through the unlocked door appeared his lordship clad in nothing but a multicolored bath towel. Fortunately, I was reading Churchill's *History of the English-Speaking Peoples*. With cold cream on my face, my horn-rimmed spectacles firmly in place, I asked him if he had trouble with sleepwalking. Fulke sat on the end of the bed as I read aloud various passages from the book. Every time he moved closer, I seemed to find a paragraph of even more interest as I straight-armed him back to his original position, never taking my eyes from the text. Eventually, as the temperature of the room got steadily cooler, the Earl took himself off to a warmer bed.

One evening Harry Crocker and I motored to Stratford-on-Avon, where we were electrified by a young Welsh actor by the name of Richard Burton in *Henry IV*. At the London restaurant Les Ambassadeurs, during dinner the following week, we told Darryl Zanuck of our discovery, and he promptly signed the actor to a contract at Twentieth Century–Fox. His first film at that studio was *My Cousin Rachel* with Olivia de Havilland.

By the first week in December, *Ivanhoe* was completed. I was in New York, anxious to get to California for Christmas. An early present to Joan from Joan was a Jaguar Mark VII. With the help of Elizabeth Taylor's secretary, I drove it across the country. At Needles, near the California border, I called Fordyce and heard Debbie's chirps and Martita's lilting laughter, then I called Collie at his house on Mulholland Drive. My five months abroad had been a lucrative and fascinating experience, one which I hoped would help my career and which undoubtedly had broadened my horizons. But this Christmas was going to be very special, for I had two daughters to share it with.

41

TRIALS AND TRIBULATIONS

EARLY IN THE SPRING OF 1952, I HAD GIVEN THE CHILDREN A NEW puppy. John Falter, the talented illustrator, had business to conduct in Beverly Hills and was staying for a few days in the guest room downstairs. During the night the puppy, on the veranda outside the girls' room and adjoining mine, began to whimper. I got out of bed, went through the curtained french doors, and picked him up from a playpen where we kept him at night until he was house-trained. Taking the puppy into my bed, I crooned to him until he quieted down. Suddenly the french doors were flung open. A huge figure of a man was silhouetted against the midnight sky. The intruder took a step toward the bed. I screamed.

Rushing to the head of the stairs, I yelled, "Frances! John! Come quickly!" Then I bolted for the children's room, standing sentinel at the door until both bathrobe-clad adults appeared from belowstairs. The man evidently vanished the way he had come, for at dawn we found scuff marks on the bark of the tree leading to the second-story veranda.

After I stopped shaking and returned to bed, John sat in an armchair in my room, across his knees a shotgun I had purchased after a dog of mine had been bitten by a rattlesnake in the garden. Frances, the housekeeper, served us coffee. She appeared as shaken as I.

John and I tried to piece together the events of the night. Had I recognized the intruder? Of course! He was the man who had driven the black limousine, tailing Howard Hughes and me up Highway One after Bill Dozier and I had agreed to separate. He obviously had been hired to spy on me again, hoping to catch John and me in a compromising situation. Apparently, when I spoke to the puppy, the trespasser had assumed John was with me.

John and I were old platonic friends. Only Frances and Collie, who was absent on business that night, knew he was my houseguest. Collie was in no way possessive about me, nor I about him. Frances was, I thought, loyal. Then who was the informant?

Mike Frankovitch, then an independent producer, had just offered me a film to be made in Spain, *Decameron Nights*, written by my dear friend George Oppenheimer. It was to go into production as soon as I could get myself and the children ready for the journey. Though my divorce had become final in February, the custodial agreement stated that I could not take Debbie out of the county or state without her father's consent. He refused permission. I decided to take the matter to court.

Upon the advice of those I trusted, I contacted a non-Hollywood lawyer to represent me. On the way to the Los Angeles airport to catch a plane for San Francisco to meet Jake Ehrlich, I observed behind my taxi the black limousine with whitewall tires that had tailed me before. Clearly I was being watched. Perhaps someone was tapping my phone, perhaps even bugging my bedroom.

As the trial was about to begin, Frances the housekeeper, avowing that I was her "only gen-u-wine friend," begged not to be my witness: she was too nervous. Jake Ehrlich agreed that she was to go on a holiday out of the state until the ordeal was over. She left in tears, giving me her blessing in anticipation of the forthcoming trial.

The next time I saw Frances was when she appeared in court on the witness stand on behalf of Debbie's father! Jake Ehrlich realized we had no case. Frances would testify that Collie had been living in my house for the last two years. Though a father might have as many affairs as he wished, under California law a mother under the same roof as the child must live a totally monastic life, even though she is supporting the child.

My witnesses were aghast to see Frances on the stand. They had often heard her profess her devotion to me. Maureen O'Sullivan Farrow, who had come to court as Debbie's godmother, threw pennies to the floor that Frances might recognize the biblical significance. The judge ruled against me. Debbie was to live with her father in my absence. Regardless of what was best for my daughter, I had to give her up for the time being.

After renting out the Fordyce house, I was forced to leave Debbie with her father and with Frances, whom Bill had now hired as his housekeeper. Martita and I flew to Madrid. My dream of keeping the family together was temporarily shattered.

With my small adopted daughter beside me, I made the best of a sorry situation. The film was shot in Avila, Barcelona, the Costa Brava, and the gardens of the Alhambra in Granada. Martita played a tiny role in it, shooting a half day in all, but it was an illuminating experience for her: I hoped she might understand what kept me busy from dawn to dusk. Martita, wherever we went, behaved with poise and exquisite manners, though she was naturally bewildered by the strange surroundings, by the uprooting from our Eden in California.

I wondered each night as I lay in bed just what Debbie would be doing at that moment. Until I was sure that she would be returned to me without another court battle, I decided to stay in Europe. It would be legally unwise to go home to Fordyce and have the children together until I married Collie, and I was not yet sure that he was the one pillar upon which to rest my life.

Collie came over and settled us into an apartment in Paris at 11 *bis* Boulevard Delessert. I had intended to see if I could establish myself in films in England and Europe until I could untangle my life from the web that Dozier and Frances had spun around me.

But now, in Paris, Martita was enrolled as a day student at Notre Dame, learning French overnight, as she had English. She missed Debbie, missed the fun, the informal country life at Fordyce, as chilly autumn settled in over Paris. I missed Fordyce, too. Most of all, I missed my own daughter and wondered about her life under her father's roof. She, too, no matter how much attention she might receive where she was, must have felt the wrench as Martita and I did.

I resolved to marry Collie, no matter what our relationship might eventually turn into, in order to unite the children. I returned to California, opened the house, and had Martita flown from Paris to Los Angeles as soon as I had Fordyce in readiness.

As fate would have it, out of the blue I was offered *From Here to Eternity*, the role that was eventually played by Deborah Kerr. As the film was to be shot in Hawaii, it would mean more separations, more uprooting for Martita, more time before I held Debbie in my arms again. I turned the offer down, much to my regret and to the damage of my future career. Now I had to collect my family, settle them in their nest. This was the first order of the day.

In November 1952, I married Collie in a quiet ceremony at Montalvo, in northern California. Martita was my flower girl. Debbie, still with her father, was unable to attend the ceremony, as was Olivia, who had been out of touch for many months.

The irresponsible streak in Collie instantly showed: he had forgotten the marriage license! His male secretary, telephoned in Los Angeles, hopped the next plane with the document. The wedding was postponed until his arrival late that afternoon.

Mother again planned the wedding reception. Though we might miss our plane to Chicago, where we were to attend the wedding of Collie's brother three days later, Mother insisted we down the wedding cake and champagne she had at La Paloma. We missed that plane. And because of fog, no other planes were taking off.

Martita had returned to Fordyce on an earlier plane with the secretary. Collie and I sped by limousine across the San Mateo Bridge to Oakland in hope of catching a train. It pulled out of the station as we raced toward the last car.

Honeymoons and I are incompatible. My new husband and I had no recourse but to spend our time in San Francisco until the fog lifted. The driver of our hired limousine turned out to be an ex-champion skater. Collie was enchanted. He asked the driver up to our suite in the Mark Hopkins Hotel, plied us both with champagne, and proceeded to take a skating lesson on the living-room rug, doing figure 8's and twirls until I started to sneeze.

I have a strange allergy: chocolate makes me sneeze, peppermint makes me sneeze, and most of all, I sneeze when I'm bored. Watching the two skaters, the bride couldn't stop sneezing that fogbound night in San Francisco. As on my first honeymoon night in that city in 1939, I slept on the window ledge, this time with my head out of the window, gasping for air. Collie, in his twin bed, slept like a bear in winter.

Eventually the fog over the Golden Gate cleared sufficiently for us to catch a plane in time for the Chicago wedding. After the ceremony I took to my bed for twenty-four hours of remedial sleep. I'd traveled a long distance and over many hurdles since the beginning of 1952.

Christmas 1952 found us all together again. The lights on the Yule tree at Fordyce burned brightly. Debbie seemed to bounce from parent to parent like a tennis ball, no visible signs of trauma yet apparent. Martita forgot her French as easily as she had learned it. Passable students at St. Martin's parochial school in Brentwood, she and Debbie soon got back into their scholastic routine as though they had never left it.

Because I had to support the family, I had signed a contract without script approval for a number of films at Paramount. I was soon forced to make several mediocre pictures. When I was given the script of James Barrie's *Alice Sit-by-the-Fire*, I took it to my advisers of the moment, Ethel Barrymore and Charles Brackett. They both thought the treatment was a good one and that it should make a distinguished film. Little did we all guess that the title would be changed to *Darling, How Could You?* and that the studio would hide the fact that it was a classic. It was written off as whimsy-arty by the publicists and front office. It was a typical Hollywood example of what may happen from original concept to finished product.

In *Something To Live For* I was directed by George Stevens. During the shooting of this dull film about an alcoholic who falls in love with her rescuer from A.A., Ray Milland and I often did takes that lasted nine or ten minutes at a time. I had to play half of one such scene in my nightgown, go off-camera, completely dress, and reappear while the camera was still running.

As both Ray and I always made it a practice of seeing our rushes after work each night, we filed into the projection room at Paramount when this scene was processed. After two-and-a-half hours we stumbled out into the dark, bleary-eyed, never again to return to the rushes during that film. One hour had been spent looking at takes of the scene through a lace curtain . . . George had placed a camera so as to catch Joan changing in and out of nightgown and dress over and over again. No more than fifteen seconds of that shot could ever have been coordinated into the finished film. I always had a sneaking feeling that George Stevens had considerable shares in the raw-film companies!

Ray and I not only had photographic memories but could retain lines read aloud to us. One morning at eight-thirty we were enmeshed in a life-and-death game of gin rummy in my stage dressing room when dialogue director Ivan Moffatt appeared, waving a sheaf of pink pages, rewrites of the day's scene. "Go ahead, read them off," said Ray as he plucked another card. Disgruntled and perplexed, Ivan proceeded to read our new lines. "Gin!" chortled Ray as the ten-page reading ended.

Ivan retorted, "You two haven't heard a word I've said."

"Try us!" we chimed together and proceeded to recite, word for word, exactly what we had just heard. Ivan quietly vanished from the dressing room.

Ray Milland, during the shooting, showed me a sensitive, unselfish side of him which I will always appreciate. One morning on the set just before the first take, I confessed to him that I was wrung dry from the previous day's shooting, that the final close-up we were about to make would be almost impossible since I hadn't a tear left.

"What makes you cry in a scene, Joan?" inquired the handsome Welshman.

"When I've exhausted the impact of the actual situation, then perhaps thinking of my mother dying, or myself dying . . . and when that no longer works, I recite the Lord's Prayer."

As the take was about to begin, from behind the camera I heard Ray's whisper, "Our Father, who art . . ." My tears gushed forth in gratitude. It was a one-take print.

Flight to Tangier with Jack Palance got no better than it deserved. *Casanova's Big Night* with Bob Hope should not have been made at all.

The Bigamist I did solely for my husband. Independent producer Young came home one night in distress: Jane Greer was to play in his forthcoming production, to be directed by his ex-wife, Ida Lupino. That afternoon Miss Greer had telephoned his office to say that she was unable to do the picture. Collier's independent company could afford neither a lengthy delay in the shooting schedule nor my salary, but I felt it was my wifely duty to leap in and save the day.

Production began. After shooting all my scenes, director Ida saw the rushes, didn't like the photography, and changed cameramen before actress Ida began her own scenes!

The children thrived. My days were occupied in emptying ashtrays, foraging in supermarkets, tidying the house, weeding the garden, inspecting the laundry, feeding the dogs and children, and entertaining occasional guests. Any creativity in me went into making spaghetti sauce, into devising parties and Easter-egg hunts for the children, planting the seasonal flower beds.

The frequent visits of Debbie to her father's house or her trips with him to Palm Springs made life difficult for Martita, for me, and, indirectly, for Debbie. She had two sets of parents, two sets of rules. She took advantage of her situation. She was indulged in both homes and her attitude soon showed it.

Collie and I stopped laughing as the web of domesticity tightened about us, as the daily minutiae of life at Fordyce rasped, forcing me to be parent first, fun-loving wife and mistress second. Bernard Shaw is reputed to have said that marriage is the deathbed of love. Might he not have included parenthood, too?

The year yawned by. Debbie broke her leg as a neighbor's Ping-Pong table collapsed on her. I wore a brace from neck to waist as the pain from my old injury at L'Horizon returned with savage intensity. Collie and I played double solitaire by Debbie's bedside as the champagne bubbles of our union evaporated into the aridity of householding and child care. My wings were clipped. I was grounded.

42

TEA AND SYMPATHY

IN THE SPRING OF 1954 I WAS OFFERED THE PLAY *Tea and Sympathy*, then running on Broadway with Deborah Kerr. I replaced her as she took the successful vehicle on a national tour. The original cast, with the exception of Deborah and young actor John Kerr, remained in New York to continue the run. Anthony Perkins and I rehearsed in California on the Warner Brothers lot under Karl Malden's direction. When we reached New York, the original director, Elia Kazan, put us through our paces with the rest of the company.

During rehearsals, I was feeling my way from just "being-and-feeling" in front of the camera to the projection of voice and personality across the footlights, beyond the proscenium arch. Elia Kazan, in reply to my question as to how much more the stage actor gave, replied, "With my direction, you do no more," while the author, Robert Anderson, said, "With my dialogue, you do no more." Movies may be a personality medium, but I have yet to watch a stage actor totally immerse his own personality into the character he is playing. I doubt if it can be done.

Betty Furness was kind enough to lend me her apartment during rehearsals. My debut at the Ethel Barrymore Theatre was a most terrifying experience. Brooks Atkinson of *The New York Times* reviewed me very favorably though I hadn't been on the stage since 1941. Tony Perkins also got excellent reviews, starting him on a long and successful career.

After the success of opening night, I rented a charming Park Avenue apartment. This time, Dozier allowed Debbie to join Martita and me and we soon settled into our New York life, a threesome again. Collie had to work in Hollywood and would visit us only occasionally.

My daughters, enrolled at Marymount, were a comfort to me at home, but at the theatre every performance was a torture. I'd awaken in the morning, relieved that last night's show had gone without incident, but by noon stage fright would begin to tighten my stomach. By the time my five o'clock tray of lamb chop and salad arrived, I would have lost my appetite. At the theatre, by "half hour," already in makeup I would lie in my dark dressing room and pray.

Sometimes during the entr'acte, my phone would ring. It would be the housekeeper to tell me that Debbie had a raging fever, Martita had a sore throat, the dishwasher had broken down. After the final curtain I would jump into a cab even before the audience had left the theatre and rush to the apartment to play Miss Florence Nightingale and Miss Fix-it.

One glorious Saturday night, S.R.O. at the box office, the audience stood and cheered at the end of the play. Word was sent to us backstage that Olivia was out front and would be coming to my dressing room at any moment. Leif Erickson, who played the headmaster in *Tea and Sympathy*, had acted with Olivia before, many years ago, in the stage production of *A Midsummer Night's Dream*. He was curious, as we all were, about her reaction to the play and the cast. Assembled in my dressing room, the actors tried to be casual as we awaited our distinguished visitor. What would she say?

Miss de Havilland was ushered in as we all stood as though for military inspection. "Well! Isn't it something!" volunteered the Hollywood superstar as she shook hands with the group. Then she quickly turned and left the cast gaping.

Isn't it something? Something is what? We all put our heads together, pondering Olivia's enigmatic statement, giving it every inflection, every intonation, accenting first one word, then another. Finally we decided it was like gazing at someone's newborn child in its crib and, wanting to be polite, cooing, "What a beautiful bassinet!"

Regardless of the haunting stage fright and the one-parent responsibilities, I was grateful to be in New York. I was no longer living the station-wagon-and-dogs life that I had left in Brentwood, waiting for the phone to ring. New York I found an exciting place, gay, varied, with innumerable fascinating things to do by day or night. The tempo of the city was my tempo. Before going to the theatre, I learned to delay my stage fright by knocking off a cocktail party or two en route, drinking only coffee and chatting with friends. In Hollywood I would have had to spend the whole evening in an automobile, just going from one gathering to another. In New York, most of my friends were within walking distance. After the evening's performance all of Manhattan was mine. Greenwich Village dives, dancing to "Mister Sandman" at El Morocco, having supper in its Champagne Room. Dropping in at "21" or the St. Regis Maisonette, the Plaza for a midnight floor show. At Sardi's, the whole of Broadway would congregate to discuss the latest openings, the rewrites on the road, the newest theatrical imports from London or Paris, the foibles of David Merrick.

Many hostesses asked the theatre people in "after dinner," which for me meant eleven-thirty in a Balmain or Balenciaga, squired by an attractive bachelor picked by me or the hostess. At the Byron Foys' just before Thanksgiving, I saw Aly across the marble dance floor. An exciting and unexpected reunion for both of us.

Next afternoon Aly and I went shopping. He wanted to bring American presents back to his friends in Paris. At closing time for Saks the management obligingly shut the doors on the public, allowing Aly complete freedom throughout the store. Thousands of dollars' worth of gifts were bought that evening as Aly prowled about, pointing out "This and this and three of those" to the starry-eyed saleswomen who jotted down the purchases. In the negligee department, Prince Charming seemed to be buying for every woman he'd ever made love to . . . little was left on the racks and shelves when we departed. I was presented with a white ballet-length tulle nightgown and matching negligee, wide apple-green ribbons dripping from every possible seam. I wore it once: it scratched and imprinted its pattern of tiny lilies of the valley on my skin, which baffled my wardrobe lady as she dressed me for the stage the following evening.

After the Saturday-night performance, I always felt free as a balloon, ready to soar wherever the wind blew. Southampton to stay with friends. To Seabrook, New Jersey, to ride in horse-drawn coaches. To Newport, to the Pennsylvania Dutch country, to Fishers

Island, to Bedford Village. Often the children came, too. All of New England, all of Manhattan captured and held me. This was my native home. This is where I belonged. Always, in Hollywood, I had felt a transient: "This, too, shall pass. . . ." The East was my habitat and I longed to stay forever.

Thanksgiving 1954 was jam-packed with adventure . . . or misadventure. John "Shipwreck" Kelly, the football player from Kentucky, divorced from Brenda Frazier, was at the same Foy party where Aly and I had chanced to meet again. After Shipwreck had asked me out several times, I finally agreed to attend a party with him on Thanksgiving Eve. He picked me up at the stage door after the performance and drove me to my apartment, where he waited in the library, still in his overcoat and scarf, for me to check the children, to bathe and change for the party. Impatient, impulsive Shipwreck, hearing me splash in the tub, flung open the bathroom door. Shoes, tweed overcoat, scarf, wristwatch, and all, he made a flying tackle, landing neatly beside me in the foamy bubble bath.

I spent most of the night drying out his clothes in the kitchen oven. Since traditionally he had always spent Thanksgiving with the William Paleys, after breakfast I got out the iron and tried to even up the length of his water-soaked trousers, the sleeves of his shrunken jacket. Shipwreck went straight from my apartment to the Paleys' house in Manhasset. That Thanksgiving the Paleys had two turkeys at their dinner table . . . one roasted, the other drip-dry.

At Christmas, Collie arrived. The cast of *Tea and Sympathy* were given a well-earned week's holiday which Collie, the girls, and I spent at the Black Bass Inn in Lambertville, New Jersey. I welcomed my freedom from the eight-a-week schedule, yet each evening about eight I would plunge into a deep depression. Longtime friend, author Budd Schulberg, who lived in nearby New Hope, was a frequent guest and noticed the change in my demeanor. Of course! we decided. Pavlov's dog! It was curtain time.

One morning Budd and Collier disappeared, only to show up at noon. Both were dressed as George Washington, complete with wigs and swords. As they lifted their goblets in the taproom to toast the Revolutionary heroes, they murmured something about crossing the Delaware as soon as the ice melted. If they meant the ice in their constantly replenished glasses rather than on the river outside, they are still standing by the bar at the Black Bass Inn.

* * *

Even in New York I was not free from disloyal servants, from surveillance inside my apartment as well as outside. One day my secretary informed me that she had picked up the phone to hear, over the extension, the children's nursemaid giving, in minute detail, my plans for the day. That I intended to return a package to Saks, to lunch at such-and-such a place with so-and-so. The nurse had obviously inspected my date book, eavesdropped on my telephone calls. I fired the girl on the spot. Like Frances at Fordyce Drive, she was rehired by Mr. Dozier.

With the passing of New Year's and Collie's return to Hollywood, I knew he had found other playmates in my absence as I had in New York. Separations, under the best of circumstances, can be lethal to marriage. It was inevitable that we would both go our own ways, seek companionship where we could find it. But a European marriage formula had its compensations. After all, we were both adults, neither of us believed any longer in "until death us do part."

By New Year's the lease on the Park Avenue apartment had expired, and the girls and I moved into the Basil Rathbone apartment on Central Park West. As a housewarming present, Shipwreck bought the girls an entire electric train set, whose tracks took up most of the library floor. He also brought along his daughter by Brenda Frazier, brown-eyed, serious-miened Victoria, with whom I became enchanted.

Sliding down a snowy hill at the Paleys' one morning with the children and Shipwreck, I went over a rough bump on my aluminum flyer, Debbie riding on my shoulders. Late that afternoon, our first at the Longacre Theatre (the play had had to move from the Ethel Barrymore), "Gadge" Kazan rehearsed the cast in our new surroundings. Feeling intense pain, I somehow got through the night's performance. By morning both my shoulders felt as though splinters of glass had been imbedded in them. Acute bursitis held my arms stationary. The theatre physician injected novocaine and cortisone into the bursae and called a rehearsal before the show that evening. As he watched me try to climb the scenery stairs, one arm in a sling, maneuvering my way through the maze of stage furniture, he stopped the rehearsal. My understudy, Mary Fickett, was alerted. She went on that evening and all the rest of the evenings of *Tea and Sympathy* on Broadway to considerable and much deserved acclaim. I returned to the Central Park West apartment and spent many painful days in bed until I was able to pack up my family and return to California. I had paid the rent in advance for six months, but I had stayed only three. Before leaving I had the windows washed, the floors waxed, the entire apartment thoroughly cleaned. Then I phoned the delighted Rathbones to say they were welcome to move back in. When I reached California and Fordyce, I found waiting for me on my desk a bill from the Rathbones for two missing dish towels and a chipped glass tabletop which had been damaged before I moved in. I paid the bill.

Now, in 1955, it was back to the station-wagon-and-dogs life. Emptying ashtrays and waiting for the phone from my agent to ring. As director Edmund Goulding said of Hollywood, "It's always up Gower and down Fountain."

43

MOTHER AND DAUGHTERS

BEFORE GOING TO NEW YORK AND *Tea and Sympathy,* I HAD TAKEN Martita back to visit her parents in Peru as I had promised. When our plane landed at Lima, cheering crowds had gathered at the airport. Martita in her white dress and coat, her sailor hat with its streamers, her white cotton gloves was a national heroine. Lindbergh's triumphal return to America after crossing the Atlantic must have been like this. Hundreds of peons pressed against the glass windows of our limousine to stare at their enviable countrywoman, their Cinderella. Martita's face darkened. I saw a gathering storm. Martita was in no-man's-land. She belonged neither here nor in California.

When we reached the end of the narrow-gauge railway, Martita was reunited with her parents, her brothers and sisters, her numerous relations. I journeyed up the mountain to the inn at Machu Picchu, leaving Martita below to spend the night with her family in their new cottage.

Within the hour Martita's father brought the now stoic child back to me, saying she had been protesting *"Mi madre, mi madre"* the moment I had left her sight. Poor Señora Pareja, how she must have felt when her own daughter now called someone else "Mother" in front of her.

Martita slept on a cot in my room that night. It was the very same room in which two years before I had had the vision that caused me to adopt her. Now suddenly she was remote, taciturn, uncommunicative. I felt that I had lost her. So had her parents.

Next day the Parejas, in gratitude to me and to honor their daughter, were married in the cathedral in Cuzco. Martita was the flower girl, I the matron of honor. The white wool lace shawl that Martita had brought her mother covered the bride's head, partially concealing the bulge at her waistline that presaged another little Pareja, another mouth to feed.

The Parejas, realizing the traumatic effect the reunion had had upon Martita, suggested that she remain with me in California, to visit them again only when she was sixteen. I felt the decision was a wise one, the best for Martita. I promised that Martita would visit them when she was better able to understand their unselfish love and devotion, when her values had broadened and she could see what noble, kind people her parents were.

Observing Martita closely on the trip back to Fordyce, I noticed a marked change in her, a stubborn silence, a sullen withdrawal, a steel-like set to her jaw. Though she had matured early, she was still a child. . . .

The girls soon got back into their schedule, but they were growing apart. Debbie was at the beck and call of her father. Any discipline I might try to enforce was vitiated by undisciplined weekends and holidays at the Doziers'.

Martita was left out of the invitations or she chose not to tag along. The situation was unhealthy for them both. Debbie was getting brash and arrogant. She talked through her nose and became critical of everything and everyone. Martita sulked in silence.

Feeling that Collie and I could not cope with the family situation, I sought neutral ground, sending both girls to a woman psychiatrist; I hoped she would balance both households in the children's minds and bring objective order and purpose into their lives. Instead I found that the children had a willing ear to complain to, that in place of one household criticizing the other the children now could have a field day while they criticized both factions to their paid listener.

My only hope was to get them both away from the atmosphere between the Capulets and the Montagues, from the Hollywood environment.

Meanwhile in 1955 and 1956 my career continued with no particular distinction. I made *Serenade* with Mario Lanza and Vincent Price for Warner Brothers, *Beyond a Reasonable Doubt* at R.K.O. with Dana Andrews, with Fritz Lang directing; *Until They Sail* at M.G.M. with Paul Newman, Jean Simmons. Director Robert Wise, who had been a cutter, literally used a stopwatch on one of our scenes. I knew then that the picture would be a pompous, plodding failure.

Collie was writing and producing for T.V. and would do most of his script work around the pool on weekends. Bob Altman (who later produced and directed *M*A*S*H* and *Nashville*) would often confer with him on scripts, then swim and have a lunch of hot dogs and hamburgers from the poolside barbecue with me and the children.

Spring of 1957 found me in Barbados and Grenada, filming *Island in the Sun* with Harry Belafonte, Dorothy Dandridge, John Justin, Joan Collins, and the enigmatic James Mason. This might have been a good picture, but Darryl Zanuck, despite the protestations of author Alec Waugh, who was with us on location, felt that it was too soon to tackle the race question with honesty. As it was, Harry Belafonte and I had an embrace, a kiss toward the end of the film.

Later hundreds of reviling letters poured into Fordyce. The hate letters, many containing dimes and quarters, read, "If you're so hard up that you have to work with a nigger . . ." They were postmarked from various parts of the country but they were obviously dictated by one organization, as many of the phrases were identical.

On my return home a close friend telephoned me. "Aha," she chortled. "So you're back from all those romantic location spots, all those moonlit nights strolling on silver sands with Harry Belafonte. . . . How was he?"

I found myself saying, "Well, you see, he was black and I was yellow!"

I had dreaded returning to the complexities at Fordyce. The girls were not particularly interested in anything, they did not excel at anything. They had developed lazy minds, a parochial apathy, the Hollywood syndrome. Their values had become those of their classmates . . . sheeplike, T.V.-indoctrinated. They never opened a book except when necessary for schoolwork.

Joan with her two girls

Collier completes the Fordyce Foursome.

The crooner and the countess,
The Emperor Waltz

With Joseph Cotten in
September Affair

Elizabeth and Robert Taylor, J.F.,
and Emlyn Williams in *Ivanhoe*

Black and white in color—*Island in the Sun*

g run of
nd
thy

Arrowhead retreat—detectives
behind the trees

Christmas in Maine, 1960

A Certain Smile, with
Rossano Brazzi

20TH CENTURY–FOX

Pierre Balmain designed the
clothes for *Tender Is the Night*

20TH CENTURY–FOX,
COLLECTION OF
R. BOWERS

Frightened member of winning team at the
International Balloon Race, Rotterdam

With Charles Addams in his Bugatti

Brentwood paradise—before. Bill and I could see the Pacific from our bedroom window.

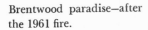

Brentwood paradise—after the 1961 fire.

John O'Hara, Mrs.
Charles Byrd, Bride-
groom, Bride, Sharman
Douglas, Sister O'Hara,
Charles Byrd, Drew
Dudley

With Alec McCowen
and director Cyril
Frankel on the set of
The Devil's Own

Politician and actress—tickling Adlai's funny bone

Ben Goodrich, Aunt Joan,
Gisele Galante, Mother, Olivia,
and cousin Ann

With President and Mrs. Marcos,
1968

At home with
Carnoustie

Last family portrait

Something had to be done. In May of 1957 I made a compromise arrangement with Debbie's father. Let me take Debbie out of the country, to Europe. Expose her to a different life from the one she knew at St. Martin's parochial school, from Fordyce Road and Greenway Drive. To another language, another milieu. The penalty? At the end of summer Debbie would return to live with him and Ann for six months.

I hoped that by the time Debbie had come under new influences, she would be prepared to judge for herself, select the best of all she had experienced and observed, that she would be able to create her own standards and values. My exposure to a new life when I returned to Japan as a schoolgirl had been invaluable to me. I hoped the same would be true for her.

44

AT HOME ABROAD

In June, Martita, Debbie, and I, accompanied by a nursemaid, flew to New York and sailed to Cherbourg on the *Queen Mary*. Martita and Debbie were thrilled at the prospect of a sea voyage. All difficulties seemed to vanish as they became the eager, adorable girls they had once been.

Paris was a delight for them. I showed them the Eiffel Tower, took them through the Louvre, the Bois, walked along the stalls on the Left Bank. We motored through the French countryside, where Debbie showed much aptitude as we translated kilometers into miles and back again. She could figure the 6-into-10 ratio with rapidity as I gave her problem after problem to work out in her head. Martita did not find our game absorbing.

By evening we arrived at Le Joko, an enchanting *moulin* at Le Cannet, above Cannes, which I had rented for the summer from Parisian couturier Jacques Fath. With lawns and a millpond where frogs burst into a cacophonous uproar as *l'heure bleu* settled over the Mediterranean, it was an ideal place for the girls, a French Garden of Eden. So far, so good. At least I had them to myself, away from the tug-of-war which had been going on since Debbie's birth.

A French tutor was waiting for us. He would also drive the rented car and be with the children constantly when the nursemaid had other duties. The staff, which came with the house, lined up to greet us at the front door. We explored the millhouse with glee, the garden, the pond, the guesthouse under the trees. By nightfall I felt that I had my girls back again.

The girls enrolled for water-skiing lessons at the Carlton Hotel and became proficient immediately. I showed no aptitude at all, falling off my skis constantly—to the delight of the camera-addicted tourists who lined the shore. From then on, the girls went skiing daily, while I stayed home, played solitaire, and waited for the promised arrival of Collier.

I had many friends in the South of France, but I did not like to go to lunches or dinners unescorted. One evening the phone rang. It was a hostess who was sending an escort to bring me to her house for dinner. As I sat in the garden playing idiot's delight, down the stone garden steps sauntered the tall, athletically built Peter Viertel. Poised, cool, multilingual Peter was unimpressed by movie actresses; he had lived in Hollywood many years as his parents, Berthold and Salka Viertel, were both screenwriters like their son.

Peter became my guide, showing me St. Tropez, Portofino, Biarritz, Carcassonne, Madrid. On weekends, when the traffic between Cannes and Monte Carlo would be bumper-to-bumper, Peter and I would drive off in his gray convertible Porsche, taking in the bullfights at Pamplona or Grenoble. When the matador honored me by presenting an ear or a tail at the end of the corrida, I would airmail it back to Collie at Mulholland Drive with a plea for his presence at Le Cannet.

One weekend found Peter and me at Miguel Dominguin's Spanish finca, overlooking a lake. We all decided to go for a swim, and I unfortunately struck out for a motorboat anchored offshore. How was I to know that the boat had a slow leak and was waterlogged? I climbed up on the stern to rest. *Woosh!* Up went the prow, down went the stern. The leaking boat rapidly disappeared from sight, while life preservers popped to the surface all around me. I swam back to my hosts astonished, embarrassed, and nonplussed as to how to make amends. But Miguel and Lucia were charming. They assured me their workmen would refloat it—and even thanked me for bringing the faulty hull to their attention!

I realized that I needed a set of wheels, too, unless I was going to be a prisoner at Le Joko or deprive the children of their tutor and

car. I purchased a nifty Facel Vega. Black, with tan leather seats, the
car had a high-powered Chrysler motor. Now, surely, Collie would
join us. He did.

The children and I met him at the airport in Nice. Collie, still in
his black linen shorts from a lost Long Island weekend with Budd
Schulberg, looked like something the cat had dragged in. We
whooped with laughter, took him back to Le Joko, and dumped him
into the tub. Debbie brought him a martini as Martita clipped his
nails. I trimmed his sideburns and the nape of his neck. Collie
wallowed in the water, being his bright and amusing self. This was
going to be fun. We there sat on the edge of the marble tub, gig-
gling at his quips.

With Collie behind the wheel of the Facel Vega, we visited
friends, took the children on picnics and excursions. Our family was
together again . . . but not for long.

As *Island in the Sun* was selected for a command performance, I
flew to London and was presented to the Queen, Prince Philip, and
Princess Margaret. Back at Le Cannet I broke my little toe while
kicking a football with the children in my bare feet. Back to London
and Guy Beauchamp for repairs.

Autumn was fast approaching. Debbie was due to return to her father at Greenway Drive. At a family conference we decided that
Martita would go to school in Switzerland. Though scholarship did
not interest her, she would learn to ski and perhaps major in lan-
guages, for which she showed a marked aptitude.

In the Facel Vega, all four of us took off for Milan, the Brenner
Pass, Innsbruck, Montreux. The girls were thrilled by the Alps, and
Martita actually showed excitement at the prospect of her new ad-
venture. At Villars we looked at several schools, selecting one that
pleased Martita, too. She beamed in anticipation as we drove back to
Le Cannet through Geneva, Chambéry, Digne, and Grasse.

Collie and I talked over our future. I would remain in Europe to
have Christmas with Martita, to visit her at her school and observe
her progress. I would stay with widowed Charles Mendl in his Paris
apartment on Avenue d'Iena. Collie would live at his house on Mulholland Drive (the "Mouse House," to the girls). Debbie and the
nursemaid would fly back to Greenway Drive, where my daughter
would spend the next six months, as previously agreed upon, with
her father. Fordyce would be rented.

*   *   *

I flew as far as Denmark with the children, where we spent a glorious last day at the Tivoli Gardens. As I watched Debbie scampering about the playground, I beckoned to the nursemaid. I said that Martita and I would slip away before we had an emotional farewell that could only scar us all. Out of sight of my nine-year-old daughter, I sat down on a park bench and burst into tears. Martita stroked my head as the yellowing leaves drifted down from the trees overhead.

From Paris I drove Martita to Villars. Martita was warm, our old closeness had returned, and I felt, though Debbie was returning to her same life in California, that at least Martita's horizons would be broadened, that she would benefit from the breakup of the Fordyce family.

Returning from Switzerland, I drove through the maze of streets leading into Paris and wondered what was ahead at Avenue d'Iena. Living with a charming but very old gentleman in a wheelchair would not be easy. Charles Mendl had grown forgetful, crotchety, often called me "Yvonne," the name of his last wife.

After I parked the Facel Vega in front of the apartment building, Charles Gordon, secretary of the Traveller's Club and close friend of Sir Charles's and mine, welcomed me and showed me to Yvonne's bedroom and her paneled dressing room with its sunken bathtub. Later, over cocktails, we planned small dinners for Sir Charles, who felt that his friends had deserted him.

I planned the menus, Charles Gordon selected the wines. We drew up a guest list, and during the winter months of 1957 many of Sir Charles's old friends sat around his lunch or dinner table. The Duke and Duchess of Windsor, Prince Paul of Yugoslavia and Princess Olga, their son Alexander and his wife, Maria Pia, the daughter of King Umberto of Italy, Mme. Schiaparelli, Ludwig Bemelmans, and many others returned to Avenue d'Iena. Sir Charles would nod over cocktails, fall asleep during the first course, snore through the entrée. By dessert we would all raise our voices until he awakened and continued the conversation at the point where he had fallen asleep. None of his friends minded. We all loved the affable knight and wished to make his last days as pleasant as possible.

When Sir Charles died, I was in the United States and unable to attend the memorial service. Alexander of Yugoslavia was there with the faithful Charles Gordon. No one else attended. Somehow the British Embassy had given out the wrong date of the ceremony,

Alexander told me. After the service, Charles and Alexander proceeded to the mortuary, where, to satisfy French law, they witnessed the body being placed in the furnace. After an hour an attendant, dressed in a blue smock, wheeled a cart in front of them. Pointing to several black-cloth-covered urns, he gruffly inquired, "Which one is yours?" He might have been a waiter in a restaurant asking what one wished from an hors d'oeuvre cart, recounted Alexander.

The two friends carried Sir Charles's ashes to Père-Lachaise cemetery. Here they requested the urn be placed in the niche next to that of Sir Charles's first wife, Elsie. "Lady Mendl, Lady Mendl," muttered the caretaker as he pored over the yellowing pages of the register. "Ah, yes, here she is," he exclaimed. "But no one has paid the rent for several years." Charles and Alexander asked where they might locate her niche. "Zut! When the rent is not paid, they cannot stay here. We threw her away." The Frenchman shrugged and wrote down the name of Sir Charles at the end of the long list before him.

I loved Paris but I loved Ireland, too. Peter Viertel had taken a house at Kilcock, for the hunting season. In Dublin, at Dudgeon's Riding Academy, I took jumping lessons, falling off my horse every few minutes, much to the amusement of the five- and six-year-olds in my beginners' class. By the fourth lesson gallant Colonel Dudgeon felt that I was ready for my first day in the field, with the Kildare hunt, on condition he rode beside me. It was he who took the spill that day. I was too frozen with fear to have any air between my cream-colored riding breeches and the leather of my saddle.

Double banks, stone walls, wooden gates. All were jumped during the twice-weekly hunt. Peter and I also hunted with the Meath and the Ward. The challenge of this new sport was exciting, it was dangerous, it was fast; like New York, it was my tempo.

I flew to England and had a lesson in dressage from Brian Young at the Silver Hound Riding Club at Stoke D'Abernon. Just as had my flying instructor at Mines Field, Mr. Young could not understand why I always did exactly as he told me. Heels down, knees in, hands on the reins eight inches apart. Sit forward on the jump. It was easily explained: after years of hitting one's mark before the camera, of never moving one's head an inch out of the baby-spot light, a film actor should be in total control of his body movements.

I adored hacking around the Irish countryside on the days between hunts. After a day in the saddle, the cheerful maid at Kilcock would fill my tub, pouring in a cup of sodium bicarbonate to ease my aching muscles. My navy-blue hunting jacket from Hawkins on Cavendish Row, the heather tweed hacking jacket from Johnson and Marie in Paris, my black riding boots given me by Lady Brownlow were always taken belowstairs, to be returned next morning in spotless condition. After breakfast, all the guests would find their riding hats, their crops and gloves neatly laid out on the tripod table in the hall. On evenings after a day of hacking, Peter and I would go into the woods and shoot dove from the sunset sky. The cook would then serve them for dinner. In Ireland I found a life-style that was fast-vanishing.

I must have comported myself without disgrace on the field, for at the end of the last hunt after the kill, the master rode over to me and placed a spot of blood on my forehead from the tail of the fox. I had been blooded, which meant that I now qualified as a genuine rider to hounds. I mailed the tail back to Collie in Beverly Hills.

On some weekends I would drive to Villars to check on my Inca Princess, take her for lunch at the Palace Hotel in Lausanne, read to her Byron's poem "The Prisoner of Chillon" before going to visit the castle about which it was written. Other weekends would find me at Fleur Cowles Meyer's country house in Surrey, where her husband, Tom, dispensed genial hospitality. To the Cotswolds, to London to be escorted to the theatre by various bachelors about town, to stay in manor houses in Lincolnshire.

One afternoon, in Gloucestershire, I was following the Beaufort hunt on foot with friends as none of us had our riding gear with us. I was wearing a fox-lined raincoat. As I plunged over the countryside in my borrowed rubber boots, I heard indignant cries from the huntsmen. The baying of the hounds. The Duke of Beaufort rode up to us. From his saddle, "Master" politely suggested I get the hell out of there: the hounds were after my coat instead of their quarry! As the hounds closed in on me and my coat, we made a flying retreat to the safety of our car.

In Switzerland at Christmas, I rented a chalet in Klosters, where Martita and a charming classmate from Villars came to spend a snowy vacation. When they returned to school, I attempted skiing lessons. My legs felt like iron weights as I dragged myself up the snowbanks. Surely skiing wasn't as arduous as this. Everyone around me on the slopes seemed to be enjoying himself. As the lesson continued, I felt my body was encased in a suit of armor. Something was obviously wrong.

That evening a cable from my agent arrived. A *Certain Smile* was going into production at the Fox Studios in Beverly Hills. I was to take the next plane to Los Angeles.

45

CLIPPED WINGS

STAYING WITH COLLIE AT MULHOLLAND DRIVE, I FOUND I COULDN'T eat, was rapidly losing weight. I had difficulty walking, a slight temperature, a constant depression. Somehow, I got through the picture with Rossano Brazzi and Christine Carere. Johnny Mathis sang the theme song.

My humor returned briefly when I was told how Mrs. Brazzi had reacted when informed that her husband and Miss Carere had become romantic on location in the South of France. "What took him so long?" replied the actor's wife, thoroughly used to the peccadilloes of her handsome Italian husband.

By now I knew I was headed for a serious illness. I could no longer sleep, there was a constant ringing in my ears. An inner vibration, as if I had a motor inside my body, constantly plagued me. As soon as my part in the film was completed, I flew back to Europe to fetch my daughter, stopping briefly in Vienna to see Peter Viertel, where he was working on a film directed by Anatole Litvak. Deborah Kerr was the leading lady. Peter had discovered her, she had discovered him. They later married.

At Geneva, Martita and I stayed overnight at a hotel before taking a plane to California. In our bedroom I suddenly fell to the floor, unable to move. I heard Martita go to the phone, telephone the concierge. In French she pleaded for a doctor. One appeared almost immediately and injected Adrenalin into my arm. My heart had stopped and Martita's quick action had saved my life.

Next morning as Martita and I waited for our plane, I lay in the lounge at the airport. The ground seemed to sway under me.

Back at Mulholland Drive, the doctors pronounced undulant fever, then mononucleosis. Debbie and Martita, now reunited under Collie's roof, both ran a mild temperature as mine climbed. I stayed in bed most of the time, reading Dostoevski, his gloomy writings being compatible with my mental state. Soon I could only see in black and white and gray. I could only grasp the subject, verb, and object of a sentence as subsidiary clauses were too difficult to follow. My writing became a scrawl.

To get away from the summer heat of Hollywood, Collie and I, with the girls, drove to Lake Arrowhead in the mountains above San Bernardino. The cool, smog-free air and the altitude seemed temporarily to relieve my fever. I felt I could go no further.

As Fordyce was rented and the Mouse House was too small for the family to live in during the coming school year, here was the perfect place for me and the children. We'd be away from Hollywood, in a rural atmosphere, yet close enough for Debbie's father to visit her, or for Debbie to go to Greenway Drive on weekends when invited. Collie could easily drive up to see us.

Mrs. Bruiner seemed to be at work. A rental agent showed us a charming rustic house on the lake, and handed over the key to me on the spot. The girls rushed off to explore the paths in the woods, to paddle the canoe.

I put in a call to my business manager, who was also Bill Dozier's manager. I explained the situation and asked him to discuss it with Debbie's father, to assure him that I was in no way depriving him of his daughter, that he could visit us when he wished, have Debbie visit him at his convenience. I also asked Collie to deliver the same message, as I was too ill to cope with the contentious Mr. Dozier. Neither of them told him, I later learned.

Now, as continuous flu-like symptoms settled in, I was confined to bed almost continually. The local doctor diagnosed hepatitis as he injected me with gamma globulin.

I would get the children's breakfast, see them off on the bus to school, fall into bed until I hobbled to the bus stop to meet them on their return. In the evening I would cook their meals, help with homework, and turn their lights out. The long, sleepless nights kept me sitting upright in bed, gasping for air, my nightclothes wet with perspiration.

Occasionally the fever would abate for an hour or two. Then I would cook enough food to last us until the next siege. Somehow I managed to become a den mother when the children became Girl Scouts, and we attended field trips and sewing classes. Collie would drive up from Beverly Hills on weekends, once bringing puppies for each of us.

The children thrived in their alpine surroundings; they had never seemed happier, closer to each other. They learned to drive the motorboat. My mother joined us from Saratoga and read to the children in front of the fire as I knitted away on a colorful afghan. My Bedlington caught fish in the lake and deposited his gift on our front doorstep each morning before breakfast.

One day as Collie and the children were boating on the lake, they observed a speedboat following them closely, a man with a long-range camera lens snapping pictures of them, the dock, the house. As I limped down to the shore to meet them, the girls shouted, "Go back, go back," frantically waving me toward the house. What? More spies? Not again!

Next afternoon as I hobbled to the bus stop, I heard a camera click from behind a pine tree. The children stepped off the bus, spotted the observer, and hooted, "Olly, olly, oxen-free. We see you . . . you can come out now!"

Fox now offered me a film. I hoped I had enough strength to do it. As I swung my Facel Vega down the mountain and into Collie's Mulholland driveway, a car loomed behind me. Through the driver's window, an arm tossed a subpoena onto the lawn as the car turned and sped away. Another custody battle with Debbie's father, because I had removed her from the county.

Collie and I hired Jerry Giesler, the prominent Los Angeles lawyer, to defend me. Too shaken to accept the Fox assignment, I returned to Arrowhead and the girls next afternoon. At dinner, I broke the news to my daughters. We stared out of the window at the moonlit lake. No one spoke.

The eve of the court trial in Santa Monica, I drove back to Mulholland Drive to confer with my lawyer. There his assistant informed me that Jerry had heart trouble and would be unable to appear in court. The substitute confessed that he had not yet read the complaint because the typing was so smudged that he could not decipher it. Next morning, accompanied by my doctor, my business manager, and Collie, I made my appearance in court. The judge had not yet entered. Through a crack in the door leading from his chambers I heard a voice commanding, "Get out there."

Then the black-robed judge, his shoulder just appearing, replied to his unseen companion, "This case shouldn't even be in court."

Nevertheless, the verdict was that I must return Debbie to Los Angeles County within two weeks or face an immediate prison sentence. As I left the courtroom that morning, photographers snapped away and one reporter shouted after me, "You wuz robbed!"

As Collie drove Debbie and her puppy away from the Arrowhead house, she didn't look back. Martita and I stood tearfully on the doorstep. I knew that Debbie now was as resigned as I . . . our family had come to an end. I could no longer go on with the fight. For her sake, for Martita's, for my own sanity, I resolved to give up the battle. Dozier had won.

My fever abated, returned, went through quiescent periods, reappeared with brutal intensity, bringing with it the same symptoms of flu and fatigue, the same vertigo. But I could not remain in Arrowhead forever. The coffers were running low. The court case had cost five thousand dollars in legal fees.

Collie and I selected a light comedy with Broadway potential. I tried *Hilary* out at Coral Gables, then Miami, took it across the country on a nationwide tour. Martita continued her schooling in Arrowhead and joined me during the summer months. Debbie was allowed to be with us briefly.

As the play closed outside of Chicago one night, to reopen in Rhode Island the following Monday, I took the children to O'Hare Field. As our plane was delayed, we went to the desk of a motor inn at the airport. I requested a room for the children to rest in until our plane took off. The lady behind the desk eyed Martita, her black hair, her gold skin. "Sorry, but we're all booked up," she sniffed, as she handed a key to the man who had been standing behind us. In 1959, race-conscious Chicago had no room for my Inca daughter! The gentleman saw my dilemma, handed me his key, and the three of us went quietly upstairs to rest.

The children returned to California, Martita to live with Collie at Fordyce, which was now tenantless; I continued on with *Hilary* through the strawhat circuit, then to the major cities, finally closing in San Francisco forever just before Christmas.

Grateful to be back at Fordyce at last, I cooked Christmas dinner for all of us. Mother came down from Saratoga to join us, but I knew the reunion was only temporary. As I had to work in the theatre—since my last Hollywood film offer had been the role of Elvis Presley's mother!—I would be out of the state most of the time. Debbie, therefore, would have to stay at Greenway Drive. I would have to rent Fordyce again. Martita was now attending boarding school in La Jolla, at Bishop's. I somehow sensed that this would be our last Christmas together at Fordyce. As things turned out, it was the last we ever spent anywhere together.

This Christmas, thanks to my earnings from the tour, I was able to give Collier a Thunderbird. After dinner the girls and I arranged a paper chase for him, winding all about the upstairs room, finally leading down to the garage. In place of the old Cadillac he'd driven for years, he found a shiny black convertible with a red ribbon festooning the radiator.

Excitedly, Collie backed his present out of the garage. "Come on, kids, jump in!" Off the three of them went down the hill as I stood in the driveway, still in my apron, pondering the nature of man and beast. My Christmas gift from Collie had been a copper frying pan. . . . I would have preferred a single white rose.

46

LOST AND FOUND

By spring Martita was having serious psychological difficulties at Bishop's. The headmistress telephoned me and I drove down to consult with her in her study. She and the school psychiatrist felt that Martita should have constant therapy, should finish the term, but that Bishop's was not the place for her to continue her studies.

Collie and I consulted two other psychiatrists. One advised me to place Martita in a simple atmosphere, as near as possible to the one she had known as a small child in Machu Picchu. She had physically matured too fast, at the same time suffering from deep-seated inhibitions and preoccupations which kept her from reaching the mental stability of her classmates. The other psychiatrist painted a gloomier picture.

During Martita's last weeks at Bishop's I filed for divorce from Collie as, without the girls, our life together held no purpose. I also became a member of the winning team at the International Balloon Race over Rotterdam. Aviator friends had dared me to join them for the flight, knowing that I suffered from acrophobia. Naturally I had to accept the challenge.

I was frankly terrified. Four of us climbed into a basket not unlike a large laundry hamper as the ground crew let go the ropes. There was no turning back now. I crouched down on the sandbags at the bottom of the gondola and dared not look out for several minutes. The soles of my feet burned from apprehension.

After half an hour in the air, we found ourselves becalmed over the city. Having been a pilot, I felt that we had absolutely no control. With a plane one can always put the nose down and attempt a landing when the motor is dead. In a balloon, one has only two controls . . . up and down. The wind dictates both speed and direction.

I was in charge of ballast, which meant that on the captain's orders I was to throw a cupful of sand over the side from one of the bags. One cup of ballast overboard meant about a hundred-foot gain in altitude. One of the others was in charge of the shortwave radio, receiving reports of wind currents and their altitudes. Another crew member in tennis shoes walked along the rim of the basket, frightening me even more than the sight of oil tanks and high-tension wires a thousand feet below us. Our captain controlled the air trap which provided us with the means of descent.

As May 6 is Liberation Day in Holland, the country lanes were filled with celebrating Dutch, either on foot, astride bicycles, or behind the wheel of automobiles. Tulips festooned hats, buttonholes, handlebars, car radiators. When I had successfully dispensed two cups of sand over the side, so that we had gained altitude and were no longer becalmed, my courage returned. I was able to peek over the brim of the basket. As a small child, my favorite book had been *The Blue Bonnet Babies in Holland.* Now it all came back as I gazed down upon the thatched roofs, the storks nesting in the chimneys, the dikes, the fields of spring flowers.

The pungent, tangy scent of freshly turned earth, salt marshes, ice-cold streams wafted up to our balloon as we glided over the tiny, manicured country. As we traveled with the wind, there was no resistance against one's face. It was as though one were dreaming, as though one were a visitor from outer space . . . an angel winging low over the earth. The sensation when aloft in a balloon is very like one's dream of being able to fly.

As we looked at our map, calculated the perimeter for our point-to-point race, touchdown time approached. Our captain pulled the cord, opening the air trap and letting gas escape. Slowly, our balloon deflated. We heard shots. Children with B.B. guns were having their sport. Our inflammable balloon was their target! Fortunately, the captain sighted an open field directly ahead of us and again pulled the trap. A few minutes later we landed with a jolt and jumped out as the deflated balloon completely enveloped the basket we had just been in. Out of the eighteen contenders in the race, we had touched down nearest the point on the perimeter previously established. We had won.

I took Martita on my *Susan and God* tour that summer, never leaving her alone between performances, sleeping in the same room with her at night, giving her the title of dresser and a salary to make her feel important. My secretary accompanied us and took charge when I was with friends or having interviews.

In the autumn Martita was placed on the secretary's farm in Kennebunkport, Maine. The farm was an ideal place for Martita to live, if I was to believe her psychiatrist. The village provided a quiet, simple environment for her to go to school.

With Debbie at Greenway Drive, Collie at Mulholland, with Martita at Kennebunkport, with Fordyce rented, where should I go? At the end of the tour I would stay in New York, in an apartment I'd located overlooking Central Park.

On the last day of *Susan and God*, I said good-bye to the cast and crew at the Westport Playhouse. The next morning, as the first autumn frost nipped the fast-coloring leaves, I climbed into the station wagon I used on tour and headed toward Manhattan, toward my new home, toward a new life.

As I circled Central Park in my station wagon in search of a garage that autumn afternoon, a crosscurrent of emotions swept over me; for the first time in my life I was totally alone, totally without roots, without business commitments, without a plan for the future. Half jubilant, half frightened, I parked the car in a garage, loaded my luggage into a taxi, and pulled up in front of 36 Central Park South, my home for the next three years.

Unlocking the fifth-floor door, I surveyed the dusty flat. From the huge living-room windows, I gazed across the lake at the park, stretching like a green carpet, surrounded by skyscrapers to the horizon. Next I opened the grimy single window of the tiny bedroom, looked out into the dingy pigeon-infested courtyard, the soot-stained walls that surrounded it. The bed was only a mattress on four legs. I lay down on the faded blue-and-white ticking and burst into uncontrollable laughter.

After all the luxury of Fordyce—the pool, the projection room, the mirror-lined dressing room with its closeted bidet and hair dryer, the hidden bathtub—now this! Alone in a vast city without a single person who was close to me. The beginning of another volume of my life. I hugged myself with glee. I felt free. I felt ME!

Before the week was over, I found a yellow-and-white Fortuny canopied bed at Bloomingdale's. Several interesting painted antique Italian pieces of furniture. I re-covered the chairs in the living room with lake-green velvet; sent for paintings, silver, and china that I had stored in Beverly Hills; brought in logs for the white marble fireplace; dusted the crystal chandelier which hung over the small, velvet-skirted dining table; familiarized myself with food and wine shops in the neighborhood.

By the following week I was having open house. New and old friends arrived to toast my new home, which had now become an attractive *pied-à-terre*.

Hollywood called me back to do a T.V. series. I returned for one night. By next morning I knew I had finished that chapter of my life. I telephoned the producer to say that my home was now New York. I could not contemplate a long series which would necessitate arising at five each morning, day after day, week after week, only to return home exhausted each night, too tired to read anything but next day's lines. Besides, I would have to live too close to Debbie and Greenway Drive. I'd already been through all that too many times. I couldn't wait to get back to New York, to new friends, new surprises, new interests.

To pad my income, I spent summers in stock, made a horrendous film for Irwin Allen with Walter Pidgeon, *Voyage to the Bottom of the Sea*. I invested in oil drilling, bought citrus groves in Florida, an apartment building in Beverly Hills. Now that I was comparatively free of financial obligations other than to Martita and my now-widowed mother, I could begin to think of my own future.

Charles Addams, whom I'd met years before, soon appeared to share my evenings and weekends. We amused each other, were both hobbyists. At his house in Westhampton I would paint in oils while he tinkered with his ancient Bugatti. Evenings, we would take his speedboat on a "cocktail cruise," stopping off to see friends along the canal. On holidays we would motor up to Kennebunkport to visit Martita. I would bring the provisions and cook the meals.

One evening at 36 Central Park South while I was giving a cocktail party in honor of painter Orville Bulman, Mrs. Jules Stein arrived. Doris announced that one of the scourges of southern California, a brush fire, was sweeping the hills of Hollywood. The fire was out of control, racing toward Beverly Hills. Since Beverly Hills is a long way from Fordyce Road I felt little anxiety as I greeted late arrivals.

The phone rang in my bedroom. It was my business manager. His first words were "It's gone. It's completely gone!" Anxious to see to my guests, I asked him to call in the morning. I couldn't concentrate on business at the moment.

"You don't understand," he insisted. "Your house is gone. Fordyce is in ashes . . . there's nothing left!" Hanging up, I wandered like a sleepwalker into the living room, and, parrotlike, repeated his message. Doug Fairbanks was later to say that he had never seen such poise, such total sangfroid. It wasn't noble behavior at all, just paralyzing shock that made me incapable of fully absorbing what had happened.

Later, at dinner with Charlie Addams and Orville Bulman, I suddenly realized the extent of the holocaust. With the clarity that comes only after two strong martinis, I surveyed my loss. Other than in memory I would never see that pool with the island again, the children's room, the white beamed ceiling in my bedroom, the fruitwood living room with its tile-bordered fireplace.

Then there were material things that I would never touch again. The English antiques, the Georgian silver, the oil paintings: a Corot pastoral, a Marie Laurençin portrait, a Henry Varnum Poore still life. My portrait by James Montgomery Flagg, a series of Hogarth prints. Two oils by the mime Angna Enters, the Pascin watercolors. A sixteenth-century map of England given me by Geoffrey de Havilland.

My mind's eyes swept every room in the house, opened every cupboard. The three rooms filled with bookshelves. First editions, signed copies by author friends, reference books now out of print. On my imaginary tour I went to the storeroom belowstairs. No longer would Debbie receive the needlepoint frame I'd made for her before she was born . . . all those minute stitches in blue silk, the French roses on the border. The long white organdy-and-linen embroidered tablecloths and napkins I'd used at parties. The dress and sandals that Martita wore when I first met her in Machu Picchu were stored there, too.

My ghost walked into the kitchen. I would never see that cookie jar, shaped like a pig dressed in a bolero, the "Pink Tower" Spode the children had eaten their porridge from, the copper frying pan Collie had given me the Christmas I gave him the Thunderbird. The leather banquette I had sat in, making out grocery lists and menus before going to work, as dawn awakened the birds in the tall sycamore outside the windows.

Doug Fairbanks should have seen me now!

When the shock wore off, I realized that I'd started life anew many times in my forty-three years on earth. I was becoming accustomed to it. Friends gave me a "fire sale" party at the Stork Club, bringing both funny and serious presents. One wag entered the restaurant carrying a fire extinguisher.

Even today in my present apartment I search for something in a closet or cupboard only to remember that it lies amid the rubble at Fordyce Road, somewhere on the land which I sold after the fire but which has never been cleared or rebuilt upon. Now whenever I visit Beverly Hills, my taxi from the airport turns from Sepulveda east on Sunset Boulevard. Over the treetops on the hill I see two chimneys standing like tombstones, marking the site that was once our home. He giveth and He taketh away.

I find another miracle: friends, fans, total strangers, one by one seem to send me many of the things I lost. An identical tray, a photograph of a friend or one of the characters I played, a scrapbook with snapshots and clippings. A picture of my mother I had never seen before. I value these gifts more than I would if I'd acquired them again myself.

47

POWER AND GLORY

TWENTIETH CENTURY–FOX WAS AGAIN HEARD FROM. NOW IT WAS TO make *Tender Is the Night* in France and Switzerland, to be finished at the studios in Beverly Hills. Jennifer Jones was cast as the feminine lead. I played her sister Baby. Her husband, David Selznick, had masterminded the production, though Henry Weinstein was the titular producer, Henry King the director.

On location Betty Bacall accompanied the still-married Jason Robards, who played Dick Diver. One day while waiting around on a Zürich See yacht for a scene to be shot, Betty became very sisterly toward me, giving me kindly advice. She said that I'd botched up my life, that a girl should never marry without thinking of herself and her future. Love was a thing apart from the marital state. First, the man must never be an actor; second, he must not have had a previous marriage. He must be financially independent. The woman must give up her career. . . .

At the end of the film, Betty married Jason, juggled her children with his by a former marriage and eventually one of their own, made a Broadway success in *Cactus Flower* and *Applause*, and has been working ever since. But their marriage foundered.

In Zürich, Jennifer would be on the phone every day to Hollywood, discussing the shooting with David, who saw the rushes at the Fox studio as soon as they were flown over. Paula Strasberg was with her constantly, coaching her in every scene. Talented, charming Jennifer was the most insecure actress I ever worked with. Despite her Academy Award for *Song of Bernadette*, I felt that acting was a torture to her.

I, who had always played the feminine lead, found it difficult to wait around until David, Paula, and Jennifer had come to agreement as to how the scene should be played, what clothes Jennifer should wear, even how the sets should be dressed. Jennifer's double-sized dressing room with its private phone was always on the stage, always filled with flowers. My little portable was outside the stage door, lined up with those of the other actors. When Jennifer was ready for a take, the assistant director would yell, "Bring in the girl," and I would be called to take my marks. This was in no way Jennifer's doing, yet I found it extremely galling.

F. Scott Fitzgerald's novel *Tender Is the Night* is most certainly an American classic, known to millions of readers. When a member of the cast pointed out that Scott intended his two main characters to be lovers before their rocky marriage, that they most certainly had been sleeping together, Henry King replied, "Maybe that happened in the book, but not in *my* movie!"

Gratefully returning to my aerie overlooking Central Park, I found and accepted an invitation from U. S. Ambassador and Mrs. Edwin O. Reischauer to go to Japan for the inauguration of the new American School in Tokyo. I believe they both had attended the old school, as I had.

It was good to be back in Japan again, to attend the ball at the Embassy, to see old chums from my school days, even the amah who had tended me as a baby.

Before departing, I had given Charles Addams a set of keys to my apartment. In my absence he would drop by occasionally to inspect the mail and check on important telephone calls. Upon returning to New York, the building superintendent waylaid me in the lobby. "Miss Fontaine, please don't give your keys to anyone without advising us," the meek man said hesitantly. "You see, some stranger could let himself into your apartment and I wouldn't know him from Addam . . . er . . . I mean . . . excuse me."

* * *

In October 1962 I was invited to dine at the White House with President and Mrs. Kennedy. At the ball that evening were many friends. Marion Javits, Clayton Fritchey, political columnist for *The Washington Post,* and the guests of honor, Mr. and Mrs. Eugene Black. In a corner Lee Radziwill whispered with her sister, the First Lady, as the guests entered, eyeing us all, what we were wearing, with whom we had arrived.

At dinner that night I was at the President's left. I confided to him that his father had often taken me to lunch when I was in New York, usually accompanied by "Wild Bill" Donovan of the O.S.S.

On one occasion when I had been living at Fordyce Road, Joe had called me from New York, saying he would be spending a few days at the Beverly Hills Hotel, and, since I was between marriages, could he have a date with me. I replied that I was giving one of my obligatory dinner parties and I would be delighted if he could attend. Joe readily accepted.

Sitting at my right at the table at Fordyce, Joe got up before the dessert was served and beckoned me into the living room. "I like it. I like your guests, your children, your house." He went on, "Tell you what I'll do. I'll live here whenever I come to California. I'll invest your money for you . . . just as I did for Gloria Swanson." With one eye on my guests, chatting over the dessert, I listened as he continued. "You can do what you like when I'm not here, but there's only one thing . . . I can't marry you!" I was stunned. Joe had never even held my hand. I simply laughed it off, chucked him under the chin, and returned to the table.

President Kennedy listened to my story with great interest and then smiled. "Let's see . . . how old would he have been then? Sixty-five? Hope I'm the same way when I'm his age!"

During the dancing that evening, both Lyndon Johnson and Hubert Humphrey asked for my New York telephone number. I beat a hasty retreat. Washington was too sophisticated for a simple girl from Hollywood!

The next day was October 20. Charles Addams and I, as guests of the Assistant Secretary of the Navy, Paul "Red" Fay, and his attractive wife, Anita, were invited for cocktails and dinner aboard the presidential yacht *Sequoia,* as were French Ambassador and Mrs. Hervé Alphand, the Robert Kennedys, and Clayton Fritchey.

As we steamed leisurely down the Potomac, Red and his old Stanford schoolmate, architect John Warnecke, toasted their football days together, telling jokes on one another and generally having a fine collegiate time. Charles Addams was then called upon to speak. As I knew it would be an ordeal for him, I jumped up to cover his embarrassment with a few words off the top of my head. I said that our wise President had ordered the captain to take this facetious group all the way to Cuba and to leave us there. The country would be better off without us. Robert Kennedy looked grave. The French Ambassador got to his feet, and to my astonishment said that he totally agreed with Miss Fontaine, this was no time for trivia. With that, the boat docked, a messenger boarded and whispered into the Attorney General's ear. Mr. and Mrs. Kennedy hurried off the *Sequoia*. By midnight all the world knew of the discovery of a missile site in Cuba, that war with Castro was imminent.

When I next saw Clayton Fritchery, he asked me how the devil I knew in advance such dire news. Of course, my remark had been nothing but intuition.

In the Sixties friends from Hollywood began to make their residence in New York, as I had done. Van Johnson, Joan Crawford, Robert Ryan, Joan Bennett, Barry Nelson, Claudette Colbert. Without miles of macadam between us as in southern California, it was far easier for us to keep in touch.

With friends on Broadway, at the U.N., in Washington, New England, New Jersey, my new life was gayer than it ever had been during my twenty-five years in Hollywood. Though living alone, I never have a sense of loneliness in New York. I can close the door of my apartment, turn off the phone, light the logs in the fireplace, turn on the hi-fi, and feel miles away from humanity under the shadows of the tall buildings.

Adlai Stevenson once had a house destroyed by fire as I had. After my fateful cocktail party he rang me to offer his condolences and ask me to dinner. Soon the Ambassador to the U.N. and I began a warm and sympathetic friendship which grew into one of more serious aspects. After we had had several dates, the press took up our friendship, expanding it into one of marital possibilities. Adlai asked me to lunch with him alone in his U. S. Embassy in the Waldorf Towers.

After lunch and over coffee in his many-windowed drawing room, Adlai said he regretted the necessity of telling me that he could not marry an actress: he still had political ambitions and the "little old ladies from Oshkosh" would not approve of such a liaison.

I froze. Such unthinking prejudice is ridiculous and outdated. Taking a sip of coffee, I replied, "It's just as well. My family would hardly approve of my marrying a politician."

My theory is that all good lawyers, clergymen, and politicians must be good actors to start with. Adlai and I both sobbed a little, professed lifelong adoration and friendship . . . it was a heartbreaking scene which both of us enjoyed immensely.

In his black chauffeured limousine, Adlai and I headed toward the River Club, where he had a date to play tennis. Rapping on the glass partition that separated us from the driver, he told the chauffeur that he had forgotten a present he meant to give his passenger and instructed him to return to the Waldorf Towers before taking Miss Fontaine to her apartment. He would telephone his housekeeper from the club and ask her to leave the package with the doorman.

Depositing Adlai, the driver returned to the hotel, where the doorman handed me a small white box marked "PORTER BLANCHARD, BEVERLY HILLS." Resting on a bed of cotton were two pewter cuff links resembling a pair of shoes, the soles with the hole in them that had been his trademark during his unsuccessful presidential campaign.

48

WRIGHT AND WRONG

IT WAS TIME FOR SIXTEEN-YEAR-OLD MARTITA TO RETURN TO PERU FOR the long-promised visit to her parents. I bought her a round-trip ticket, and advised our Peruvian friend Gustavo Berckemeyer and her parents of the date of arrival. Thinking it better that she meet her father and mother without me after the last disturbing reunion, I contacted a State Department official whom Martita and I had met in Lima. He volunteered to escort her safely from New York to her parents, waiting at the end of the flight.

The day before she was to come to New York, Martita telephoned from Maine to say she refused to go, that she was no longer of an age where she had to do my bidding, that she had gotten herself adopted by a Kennebunkport couple. After telephoning Gustavo in Lima to tell him the distressing news, I drove to Kennebunkport, only to find that Martita was in hiding and would not see me. My ex-secretary was enigmatic: it was Martita's life to live as she wished. As I was not her adoptive parent by U. S. law, there was nothing I could legally do. Unfortunately, Gustavo had not been able to reach the parents in the Andes in time to stop their trip down the mountains to the Lima airport. I dread to think of the emotions that were experienced by Martita's family that day.

Child-guidance centers which I consulted told me they'd had many cases such as this, that I'd best leave well enough alone. I have never heard from or seen Martita since, but a year later the couple who had supposedly adopted her appealed to Collie and me for help. The same lack of communication and affection that we had previously observed was now apparent to them.

Next Martita found a home with the family of the local minister. He wrote me, saying that though he refused to let me see Martita, it was my duty to provide for her financially. I wrote back, explaining my promise to the Parejas, quoting the biblical "Honor thy father and mother." He replied with another line from the Bible about fulfilling one's obligations. I did not answer his letter, and that is the last communication I have ever had concerning the Inca child I befriended.

I understand that Martita is married, has children, and is living very simply in a coastal town in Maine. I hope she is happy. I hope the Parejas have become reconciled to their daughter's attitude. I hope they have forgiven me for breaking my promise, through no fault of my own, that Martita would return to Peru.

My mysterious illness returned. As I sat under the hot T.V. studio lights doing such panel shows as "To Tell the Truth" and "Match Game" my clothes would be soaked, the fever would flush my face under the pancake makeup. The vertigo, the flu-like symptoms returned with a vengeance. On the advice of friends, I consulted an expert on tropical diseases whom I shall call Dr. Noh—as my friends came to do.

About this time I bought an apartment on East Seventy-second Street. On Labor Day weekend, 1963, with the help of Charles Addams and Mother, who had driven my Facel Vega from California, I moved in. I finished the decorating and gave a dinner for fifty people in mid-October. The rest of the month I spent in bed with a raging fever. By November 22 I was well enough to have lunch with a publisher friend of mine. We returned home and were sitting in my library when Mother entered. She had been out shopping, had left her gloves in a taxi. Describing the gloves to me so that I might telephone the taxi company in the faint hope they might be retrieved, she then said, "Too bad about the President. He's been shot, you know." Stuart Daniels and I instantly turned on the television, where we discovered that indeed Mother was correct. We watched as the ambulance drew up to the Dallas hospital, as doctors gave the American public minute details as the President lay, unconscious, on the operating table. Stuart and I sobbed in each other's arms as all hope was given up. Republican Mother sat in a high-backed leather chair, dismayed at our emotion, fretting about her black kid gloves.

On the day of the funeral, Charles Addams took me for a long drive as we listened to the funeral oration being delivered over the radio by Cardinal Cushing. We both said little. There wasn't anything to say.

Charlie left me at my apartment that afternoon in Mother's care. I knew a sick lady was not his idea of an enjoyable companion, that our romance was finished. I'd always joked with him that he would spawn with anything that twitched. He frankly agreed.

Being an expert psychologist as well as a physician, Dr. Noh inquired into my life and career. He called Charles Addams into his office and, like a prospective father-in-law, asked the cartoonist his intentions. Charlie didn't have any.

After my tests Dr. Noh instructed me to go to bed and stay there until I heard from him. After three weeks in bed and many requests to his office for medical reports, I was told that Dr. Noh was in Nassau. His assistant came around. Was my illness due to the fact that I didn't have a good Hollywood script? Was I going through the menopause? I shook my head. The flu-like chills and fever had been going on for six years. It was not imagination, malaise, hypochondria. My bill for the tests, the original office visit, the doctor's interview with Charles, the house call came to two thousand dollars.

One gloomy winter evening the telephone in my library rang. It was Dr. Noh, back from Nassau. He was jubilant. "Hurray! You've got toxoplasmosis! It's a parasite of the blood. The lab report just came in." "No," he replied to Mother's query, "there's nothing to be done about it at this late stage. She'll have to learn to live with it."

I lay back on the couch. Mother put an afghan over me, stoked the fire. We both wondered, "What now?"

The answer to that question turned out to be Alfred Wright. After our contretemps in Pasadena over his *Life* article entitled "Sister Act," I had scarcely seen him, but we had met again recently. He called for a dinner date and when I said I was too ill to go out, he offered to come and cook. Soon he appeared, a package of hamburger in one hand, a bunch of dark-red carnations in the other. After cocktails, Mother showed him into my blue-and-white kitchen

and re-joined me in the library. Half an hour went by, then another
ten minutes. Mother left the room. I knew that she had gone to
Alfred's rescue. When my tray arrived, she winked, whispering, "He
can't cook at all!"

I was enchanted. I was touched. The helpless golf editor of *Sports
Illustrated* had tried a new approach. With his failure, he had suc-
ceeded. As he carried me to my bedroom at ten that evening, on
Mother's orders, he put me down on the bed, saying, "We're going
to be very happy in this room one day." It looked like we were engaged. My illness had brought out the male protectiveness in him.
He felt needed. And I needed him. My only major mistake was that
eventually I got well.

After Christmas, Mother returned to her new apartment in Saratoga. Late that January, Alfred and I were married quietly in Elkton,
Maryland, as it was close to Princeton and the John O'Haras. After
the ceremony, we all gathered at the O'Haras' for the reception.

On our drive home that evening to East Seventy-second Street,
Alfred seemed gay and sentimental. He thought his father, long
since gone from this earth, would be wearing a white carnation in his
buttonhole in heaven this night. Once home, we telephoned his
mother in Pasadena. I had always been extremely fond of the viva-
cious, attractive Marie and was pleased she was now my mother-in-
law. She, too, felt that it had been a white carnation day.

After cornflakes and milk by the library fire, we rolled into my
canopied bed and I set the alarm for 6:30 A.M. Tomorrow was a
workday for both of us, Alfred reporting to his desk at *Sports Illustrated* and I to the N.B.C. makeup room and "To Tell the Truth."
Only after the show did the cast read in the morning's edition that I
was a bride.

Hearing the news, my friend Clayton Fritchey asked me, since it
was leap year, whether I had popped the question. Replying, "Of
course," I added, "Alfred's answer to me was, 'I'll have to sleep on
it.'"

My toxoplasmosis, or whatever I had, continued to make life
difficult for me, inexplicable to Alfred. He, too, showed signs of an
odd malady, blacking out from time to time, unable to remember
where we'd been that evening. Once I found him unconscious, lying

on the bathroom floor. As he never drank to excess, I became very worried.

That spring, I discovered I was pregnant. We were both quietly overjoyed. As Alfred had never had a child by either of his previous wives, he had secretly longed for fatherhood. For me, it would mean a new family, starting all over again under happier circumstances.

Alfred was at his sister's in Hillsborough when I knew a miscarriage was imminent. I telephoned him and he took the night plane to New York, arriving just as my gynecologist had finished the unpleasant task of removing all evidence of our misfortune. The doctor took Alfred out to breakfast. The disappointed father-not-to-be broke down and sobbed into his coffee. It was clear that he could not have children, as his history had shown the same pattern of miscarriage with his last wife. The doctor suggested we not try again. But I did. After the second miscarriage three months later, I took his advice.

One spring day the telephone rang. Olivia, now married to *Paris-Match* editor Pierre Galante, had come from their home in Paris to New York for business and pleasure. As I now felt a settled New Yorker, I suggested I give my sister a cocktail party, inviting mutual acquaintances as well as some of my new friends. She seemed delighted and set the day and hour accordingly. Fifteen minutes before the guests were to arrive, my doorman, with the help of the elevator boy, brought a huge florist box into my living room, setting it on the floor as it was too large to place anywhere else. Untying the ribbon and opening the coffinlike box, I found a card among the branches of Japanese quince. "Regret I cannot be with you this evening," it read, and then, "Olivia."

I put the tree-tall sprays in a hastily water-filled umbrella stand, placing the arrangement in one corner. The quince blossoms touched the ceiling. Next I got out the vacuum and, in my new Dior, swept up the fallen leaves and buds from the carpet and recovered from the emergency just as the first group of guests arrived. Taking my friends directly to the mammoth floral display, I introduced them to "my guest of honor." They all agreed Olivia had never looked lovelier.

That summer we took a house in Southampton, where Debbie joined us. She now chose to live with Alfred and me. Her father did not protest. I commuted to New York, taping panel shows.

That fall David Merrick started rehearsals for A *Severed Head*, by Iris Murdoch, which, though a successful play in London, would perplex American audiences. We opened in New Haven, then took it to Philadelphia. The play didn't work.

Lee Grant, Elliott Reid, and I were fired. The leading lady who played my part in London was brought over with other replacements to open on Broadway. I was glad to be out of the play, pleased that A *Severed Head* limped onto Broadway, played three weeks to empty houses, and closed forever.

Nineteen sixty-four. Another Christmas. Many friends sat around the Wright table on Christmas Eve. We all exchanged gifts. Much to my delight and everyone's astonishment, Alfred's present to me was a Black & Decker electric drill. I gave him pearl-and-gold cuff links, needlepoint slippers I had made myself, a fur robe for the Bentley that I'd bought to replace the ailing Facel Vega. Debbie spent the holidays with her father.

I could not work and at the same time control a now headstrong adolescent who would diet when she took her meals with us yet raid the refrigerator in the middle of the night. She would type letters until dawn and then be truculent when aroused to go to school each morning. Alfred felt, since he was not her father, that he could not and should not enforce house rules. I called my close friend "Sister," Mrs. John O'Hara, for advice.

Sister had known me, as well as Alfred, for years and understood the situation. As she had raised three children of her own, she was qualified to advise me that Debbie should remain in California with her father, that my life was complicated enough with earning the living, with a new marriage, with recurring illness. Alfred and I after much discussion agreed that if only for our own life together, we should do as Sister had suggested.

Over the telephone to Greenway Drive, Alfred and I explained to Debbie that I was going on tour with *The Marriage-Go-Round*, that Alfred would be away on assignment for *Sports Illustrated* most of the time, that a New York apartment was not the place for a sixteen-year-old girl to live alone. She put her father on the extension. In our daughter's hearing, he called me an unpleasant name and hung up.

I packed all of Debbie's clothes and effects, including two shoe boxes of letters from her father. I only read one. That was enough. He called me "General Fontaine," "Dr. Fontaine," and "Mrs.

Wrong," thoroughly deriding and reviling me to our daughter. Now I knew what the nocturnal typing of Debbie's had been about. She had been reporting our life at the apartment in minute detail. This time he didn't have to pay his spies.

The year went round. Alfred was always away, coming home, as I teased him, only to get his laundry done. After accompanying him to the Augusta National and on a golf tour in Spain and England with Arnold Palmer and Tony Lema, I realized that a golf editor's wife was extra baggage during a tournament. Also, I could not afford the luxury of paying my own way when I should have been working at home.

In Madrid, Alfred and I stayed at the Ritz. I'd forgotten that because of an episode when a North Carolina-born screen queen had reputedly mistaken the elevator for the ladies' room, actors were banned from this elegant hostelry. Even Helen Hayes was unable to register despite intercession from Angier Duke, the American ambassador.

After our arrival, perplexed that none of my Spanish friends had called, I went to the desk in the lobby. Informing the manager that apparently my messages were not being delivered, I said my name was Mrs. Alfred Wright but that I had a stage name. Perhaps the callers had asked for Joan Fontaine? "We are well aware of who you are," stuffily replied the hotelier, "but we choose to forget it!"

Now while Alfred went on assignments covering various tournaments, I stayed at home, needlepointing everything in sight but the walls and ceiling of the apartment. I did T.V. panel shows in the daytime, lunching with friends and occasionally finding a chum who would escort me to the theatre or a movie. It was a dull life.

Once in the middle of the night I was awakened by an irate husband, phoning from Burlingame, California. He demanded to know where he could find Alfred Wright. I whispered that all I knew was that my husband was also in Burlingame. "Speak up, speak up," yelled the angry man.

"I can't," I gasped. "I have pneumonia."

"I don't give a damn what you've got," the voice screamed over the telephone. "Where the hell is my wife?"

I knew another volume in my life was closing.

49

YES AND NOH

With Alfred still in California, January 1965 found me rehearsing for *Dial "M" for Murder*. The night before I left to go on tour, the Richard Clurmans asked me to their apartment for dinner. After dinner, I went on to an anniversary party for the John Drexels at the Carlyle Hotel.

The first dance was requested by Dr. Noh. "How's the baby? How's the marriage?" Dr. Noh tongued his Dentyne to the other side of his mouth.

"No baby, no marriage. How about you?" I queried as the doctor glided me about the dance floor.

"No marriage either. I'm divorced." Stopping in the middle of a fox-trot, he inquired, "How do I locate you?"

I replied that his office had my telephone number, that I hadn't changed my name.

"Neither have I!" He laughed.

We both laughed. I thought I'd forgotten how.

Mid-February in Atlanta, while on tour with *Dial "M,"* instead of flowers on opening night, I received a "Dear Joan" letter from Alfred, postmarked Palm Springs, California. In it he said that our marriage had been a mistake, that he wanted out. That night after the post-theatre party I wrote him, quoting his letter and saying that I agreed. My letter crossed another of his, saying that he had reconsidered, that now he thought he could be a good husband. It was too late.

It was a cold afternoon in late spring. I was playing bridge in the New York apartment when the phone rang. It was Dr. Noh. He was coming right over.

With brief "hellos" to my guests, Dr. Noh led me into the dining room and without a word put his arms around me and kissed me. The psychologist in him knew exactly how to handle me, gave me no time to demur, to think twice. I was putty when faced with a strong man and I knew it. After so many months of neglect from Alfred, I was grateful to have someone who wanted to share my life.

That night he returned . . . to stay in my life for eight years.

Like me, Dr. Noh was romantic, nomadic, suffered from wanderlust. He, too, had tried marriage and failed. He sensed that I expected a god, a father, a lover, a mentor, a companion, a friend in one man. He became all those things to me. He swore to total constancy, expected the same from me. He got it. . . .

At the end of the run of *Dial "M"* in Millburn, New Jersey, Dr. Noh met me at the stage door. A bucket of chilled champagne was in the back seat of his convertible. We drove through the thick fog to Bedford Village, where dear friends often lent me their rambling guest cottage. The doctor unloaded our luggage, brought out two roast grouse he'd had his hotel prepare, a bottle of Château Haut-Brion. He lit the fire, served the midnight supper, poured the wine, lowered the lights. If this was a honeymoon, it was the best I'd ever had. At least I felt attractive, desirable. I felt like a movie star!

That week, as I was preparing to fly to England to film *The Devil's Own*, Dr. Noh went to all my fittings, supervised my purchases. Over luncheon at the Côte Basque, he delighted me with his quick wit, his quixotic humor, his adamant political views. After lunch he guided me across Fifth Avenue to a jeweler's, where to my astonishment he took off the baroque-pearl necklace I was wearing. Handing it to the proprietor, he announced, "I don't like this clasp. See that a proper one is put on immediately and send me the bill."

As we walked out of the shop, a salesman stopped us. Pulling a stethoscope from the doctor's rear trouser pocket, where it had been dangling since he left his office that morning, the salesman, with a

ceremonial bow, handed it to its nonchalant owner. We skipped
down Fifth Avenue, hand in hand like happy children.

Dr. Noh took complete charge of everything. On the morning of
my departure for England, the doctor and his affable Irish driver
stowed my sixteen pieces of luggage into a waiting station wagon, us
in a limousine, and drove to J.F.K. Airport. There, as my flight was
called, the doctor kissed me good-bye, saying, "See you in a minute."
I knew he meant it.

I arrived at Vivien Leigh's flat in Eaton Square, having lent her
my New York apartment while she was playing in *Ivanov* with John
Gielgud on Broadway. A huge bowl of mixed English roses was waiting for me from the doctor. The telephone rang. It was Dr. Noh,
calling from New York to welcome me to London. Soon friends of
his, alerted to my arrival, telephoned to ask if there was anything
they could do. What a contrast this marriage was to my legal ones.
The doctor was right . . . marriage, the formal kind, was not for the
likes of us.

Vivien was a cat fancier. I have an acute olfactory sense. She
evidently did not. The flat reeked of feline proximity. So did the
housekeeper. The hall coat closet contained a box of Kitty Litter
that had not been changed in weeks. When the housekeeper, with
whom the cat slept, brought my 5:30 A.M. breakfast tray each morning, I could scarcely force down the food. Her white uniform sent
waves of odor toward my bed. I gagged my way to the Elstree studio
in a hired Daimler.

Arranging a protracted holiday for the housekeeper and the cat, I
sent for Mother and my personal maid, both of whom stayed in
Vivien's flat as I spent long days on location outside London. The
director was a dream, understanding that fever kept me lying in my
dressing room, coming out only when I was needed, then returning
to a prone position whenever possible.

I was ill again, homesick, and loathed the union's grip on the studios: the deliberate delays, the mandatory coffee breaks which would
interrupt every scene just as it was going well. Already I missed Dr.
Noh and his noncritical support, his concise mind, his immediate
grasp of every situation, his ability to cope with any problem.

"See you in a minute" was true. He came over for a week during
the filming, bought a gray convertible Alfa Romeo for my use, took
me to the London theatres. I found him extraordinarily knowledgeable about the theatre, ballet, every art form.

Since I had left Vivien with my excellent Jamaican housekeeper in New York, had left out all my linens and silver for her use, I saw no reason why I should leave the Alfa Romeo on the street in Eaton Square when her garage was unoccupied. I rang the New York apartment and explained my problem to Vivien, asking for housing of the convertible. "You are *not* to use my gar-rahge," she regally commanded, and hung up the phone. My phone! This was not the last encounter I was to have with Lady Olivier.

While making *The Devil's Own*, I was informed that I had been given the Eleanor Roosevelt Humanitarian Award for my work with children at the New York School for the Hard of Hearing. The scroll was presented to me by Ambassador David Bruce at the American Embassy in Grosvenor Square. I value that award as highly as I do my Oscar.

At the end of the film, Dr. Noh returned to London. Closing Vivien's flat, we took the airlift to Ostend, the Alfa Romeo traveling with us on the same plane. We spent that night in Brussels, rambling in the Grand' Place, dining deliciously at La Maison du Cygne, listening to music in the ancient square as midnight approached.

Next day we motored to Strasbourg. "Walking Through the Black Forest" was, appropriately, coming from the car's radio. At two in the afternoon we stopped at a tower restaurant. "The kitchens are closed, sir." The maître d'hôtel bowed deferentially to the hungry travelers. Undaunted and flashing a ten-dollar bill, Dr. Noh ordered pâté de foie gras, cheese, French bread, and Alsatian wine. Where had he been all my life!

By the time we reached the Drei Könige Hotel in Basel on the Rhine, my fever was acute, my body was numb. I lay in bed as the good doctor fed me grapes and lulled me to sleep.

The next day our destination was the Domaine de la Sylviane in the South of France. Here we stayed several days while I regained my strength before driving on to Portofino and the Hotel Splendido.

At this north Italian port of enchantment, we basked in the sun, took our meals at my favorite restaurant in the world, De Pitosforo. Under its grape arbor we would drink Campari and soda, feast on fish from the Mediterranean. We laughed, sang, listened in the evening to the band in the square as moonlight dappled the boats in the harbor. During the day, the doctor water-skied, explored the golf course at Santa Margherita. I had never been so happy.

Back at the Domaine de la Sylviane, I suddenly became so ill that it was apparent a gynecological operation was urgent. Dr. Noh, first flying to Teheran to pick up specimens for his research on tropical diseases, went immediately to New York to arrange for my hospitalization.

I had long since vacated Vivien's London flat. Her New York show had now closed, but she had stayed on in my apartment. "What am I to do, throw my luggage into the street?" the disgruntled Lady Olivier coldly queried the doctor. As she was leaving next day for Jamaica anyway, he arranged for her luggage to be stored in the apartment until she could pick it up en route to England. Weeks later a mutual friend put Vivien on the phone, cautioning me that she was not well, had regretted her unfriendliness, and wanted to apologize. Over the phone, she dripped icicles just the same.

The last contact I had with her ladyship was through the F.B.I. It seems she had an étagère filled with valuable watches that Laurence Olivier had given her. When I arrived at Eaton Square, I had had the housekeeper put away anything of value. I never saw the watches, but now they were missing. Mother, stopping at my New York apartment on her way to California, was interrogated. My maid, too. No one had seen the watches. The F.B.I. gentlemen smiled and shook their heads. They may have been through this before with the actress. Despite the fact that I never received a report from the F.B.I., or from Vivien, as to whether they were found or not, a New York columnist printed that I had stolen the valuable timepieces.

After my operation I was glad to be home, glad to tootle about with the doctor in the Alfa, which had been shipped over from Nice. Soon the subtle doctor had me walking on the course while he played golf. One day he put an eight iron in my hand. "Why don't you pitch a few to the green as I play?" I was hooked. I joined his golf club on Long Island and soon became an avid golfer, even playing on snowy days with colored golf balls.

Soon I took Dial "M" to the Ivanhoe Theatre in Chicago. Next a tour in Private Lives. Wherever I went, Dr. Noh was sure to follow, always driving me from one theatre to another, returning the following weekend to pack my wardrobe and see me safely ensconced in the next rented cottage, the next dressing room. No husband had ever cosseted me so well . . . if at all.

During those eight years we traveled everywhere. Hawaii, Japan, Mexico. We played golf in California, Florida, Colorado, Jamaica, Puerto Rico, Bermuda, Ireland, Scotland. We even named the doctor's West Highland terrier "Carnoustie" after the famous Scottish course. We played "The Palace." President Ferdinand Marcos of the Philippines has a course outside the presidential palace in Manila where one tees off, shooting across the river to the first fairway, then takes a government launch to the opposite bank. I was the President's partner, and of course we were allowed to win.

Once when Dr. Noh and I were packing our bags for a trip to Europe, an S.O.S. cable arrived from Olivia. She was in both financial and marital difficulties and finding her current bills impossible to pay. Arriving in Paris, I immediately telephoned her, and lunch at her house the next day was arranged. We were greeted at her door by my niece and nephew and ushered upstairs, where I found my sister ill in bed. She listened attentively while I explained to her that the scarcity of film roles now available to us did not mean the end of our earning capacity . . . there was Broadway, T.V., stock, dinner theatre, and the lecture circuit. I gave her the names of my theatrical agent and my lecture bureau. I then left a sizable check, which she was soon able to repay. She signed with my lecture bureau and eventually had so many bookings that I had to find a new bureau to handle mine.

50

THE MILK AND KEY INTRIGUE

At the end of 1969, in order to keep Dr. Noh amused and our life together vital and exciting, I accepted an offer to play in a film to be made in Italy. The script was an adaptation of a successful Italian novel. My role was interesting, the location sites promised to be a traveler's dream, the billing and salary were acceptable. Negotiations were handled by a free-lance agent in Hollywood and his partner in Rome.

Dr. Noh and I spent the New Year's holidays in Great Harbour Cay. As I stepped into the apartment upon our return to New York, the phone was ringing. The free-lance agent had been phoning every hour.

"Hurry," the anxious voice commanded. "You must catch tomorrow's plane to Rome, the starting schedule has been moved up. Your contract will be waiting for you upon arrival."

Hastily packing, I left for the airport next morning, lifted an "*arrivederla*" glass of champagne to the doctor in the lounge as my flight was announced.

The Italian partner of the Hollywood agent met my plane, taking me speedily to the Grand Hotel. Here I was introduced to the producer's sister, a lawyer who was handling the business details while her brother (also a lawyer) was overseeing the filming on location.

Innocent as I was in the ways of Italian film-making, I had had enough sense to insist that I be paid in cash before the start of each week's shooting. However, not only was the contract written in Italian, of which I understand very little, but I am hardly equipped to pass on a contract even in English unless my own lawyer or agent has gone over it first. With eyes of Toledo steel and the charm of a cash register the lady would not hand over the salary for the first week's shooting until I signed the contract. I said I could not sign unless it was approved by my lawyer in the United States, but that I would proceed with the costumes and publicity interviews in the meantime. Reluctantly, but realizing that I was not to be budged, she had the agent sign the contract in my stead. That rather amused me. Little did she know that I had no signed agreement with these agents and thus they had no legal right to represent me at all. Signora Steel Eyes handed over the cash for that week's work and I went on my merry way, glad to be in Italy again, glad to be in the bustle of film-making, delighted by the frequent transatlantic telephone calls from the doctor.

North of Venice, the first week's shooting was pleasant and easy. As we were preparing to leave for Cortina and our next location, I stood at the concierge's desk, collecting my jewel case from the vault where I had it placed upon arrival. As though out of the mist from the Adriatic, the producer appeared at my elbow just when the concierge handed over the zippered case. His eyes had a curious glint as they brushed over the bag.

"I owe you next week's salary. Please remind me this afternoon after we reach Cortina."

I nodded assent. No bulb lit up in my head. It did not occur to me to refuse to budge before I was paid. The cast and crew were swarming through the lobby, paying bills, moving luggage. I dutifully climbed into the car assigned to me and the beret-topped, trench-coat-clad producer.

The drive to Cortina d'Ampezzo was enchantment. Snow crept up the Italian Alps as our car climbed from the orchard-carpeted foothills to the ancient square in the center of the village.

After unpacking in the delightful corner room at the hotel, pleased that the windows looked out on the cathedral on one side and the valley we had just left on the other, I made my way to the concierge's desk in the lobby, turned over my jewel case to be locked in an individual strongbox, and received the key. Just as I was placing the key in my purse, the producer magically reappeared at my side. Since it was a Sunday, the gentleman suggested I dine with him at a local *ristorante*. Here he spread charm over me like a fishnet. During the saltimbocca and Valpolicella, the very first glimmer from a twenty-five-watt bulb lit in my head. . . .

After two more days of shooting and no payment in sight, I informed the producer that I would not work until the money was forthcoming. (I had heard that Orson Welles refused to leave his makeup chair each morning unless his Italian producer placed his day's salary in his chubby fist.) The producer took me into the hotel bar, ordered two Camparis, and explained to his leading lady that by Italian law, once anyone had started a job, no matter in what capacity, he was compelled to finish it, pay or no pay.

I shook my head. I'd been idiotic enough already. Ignoring my Campari, I suggested I fly to the United States immediately, have my lawyer draw up a contract legally binding under American law and have it put on the next plane to Rome. Once the producer had signed it, I would return immediately and resume shooting.

The producer's eyes turned to colder steel than his sister's. He slammed his half-finished drink onto the marble-topped table. Snatching up his beret, he rose to his full five feet and hissed, "We see aboutta dat!"

I was in my room, reading, when the phone rang. The concierge's formal voice crackled against my eardrum. "A gentleman from the *polizia* to see you, Signora."

Aghast, my heart constricting, my knees turning to rubber, I heard my voice nonchalantly replying, "Oh, by all means send him up."

Outside, the cathedral loomed ominously . . . I had never noticed the iron grilles on the hotel windows before. Savonarola, here I come!

The phone rang again. Again the concierge. "Signora Fontana, *prego*. Give quickly your safe-deposit key to the bellboy. They will soon try to impound your jewelry!" I was beginning to understand this scenario. At that instant an out-of-breath bellboy knocked on the door. His white-gloved hand closed upon my key just as a tall serious-miened replica of T.V.'s Efrem Zimbalist appeared around the corner. The bellboy bowed and backed away as the immaculately tailored police representative introduced himself.

Did I know that I was breaking the laws of Italy? Did I know that he had the power to arrest me, impound my clothes, jewelry, passport? As he continued to state his government's case, the suave, cool prototype of a detective opened my armoire, inspected my hats, furs, suits, riffled through my handbags.

Again the phone. Through the receiver my conspiratorial concierge whispered, "Signora. Rest assured . . . we have your jewels in our keeping. They are safe. Now the police will ask for your key. You must give it of course. We now return it to you."

"How?" I muttered, hoping Efrem would think I was addressing an American Indian.

"You will see, Signora." My mysterious new friend rang off.

As my visitor took my mink coat to the light of the window and held it up for inspection, there was a knock on the door. "Your order, Signora." Smiling, the bellboy pointed to a glass of milk on a silver tray. The light bulb in my brain flashed again. Thanking him and closing the door, I excused myself to the mink inspector. Taking the glass into the bathroom, I quickly poured its contents into the basin. Sure enough, there at the bottom of the tumbler was the key to my safe-deposit box. I shoved it under my sweater and reentered the bedroom, wiping an imaginary wisp of milk from my lips. Efrem was now inspecting my other fur coat.

How to get the key back into my bag on my dressing table? Oh, the old handkerchief trick. I was beginning to enjoy myself. Turning my back to the fur expert, I opened my purse, palmed the key from under my sweater as I searched for the lace-trimmed hanky. With an angelic expression, I dabbed off the last traces of milk.

This was getting to be a better scenario than the one I was supposed to be shooting. Replacing the coats in my closet, my gentleman caller now, as if on cue, asked for the key to my safe-deposit box. Without hesitation, I turned once again to my purse, extracted the key after suitable rummaging, and magnanimously handed it over. Efrem bowed courteously, scarcely wrinkling his beige herringbone jacket. No smile crossed his handsome face. (I couldn't remember if American T.V. police and detectives ever smiled. Anyway, they presumably didn't in the films my Italian friend had studied.)

Now I needed a witness. With the gracious permission of my police chaperone, I telephoned the director of our film, who already knew of my contractual difficulties. As his room was on the same floor, he speedily appeared to assure the candidate for the best-dressed list that I was anxious to finish the film, nay, eager to finish it, and he had found me cooperative in every way.

After a long stage wait and a look meant to curdle my blood, Italy's answer to the F.B.I. departed, saying cryptically that he would return. "Perhaps with a warrant next time, *sì?*"

Confiding to the director that I had never walked out on an assignment in my life and didn't intend to now as long as I was paid and had adequate legal protection, I put in a telephone call to New York and Dr. Noh. From doctor to lawyer to agent to actress, the phone was tied up for the next two hours. We agreed to confer again at eight that evening.

The room was now dark. I lay on the bed and stared at the ceiling. Noises of arrival emanated from the room next door. Luggage being unpacked, clothes hung in closets. Two male voices chattered away excitedly in Italian. Now whispers. The handle of the communicating door slowly turned, clicked back into position. The phone rang. As I stretched out my hand to pick up the receiver the room next door fell silent. Tiptoe sounds stopped at our mutual door. I could almost *hear* the brush of an ear against the keyhole.

It was Dr. Noh on the telephone. My lawyer in New York would draw up a suitable contract, have it ready upon my arrival. I could read it, have it notarized and put on a plane for Rome within two hours after my return. Once the producer signed it, I could be on the next plane to Italy and ready to shoot on Monday. Nothing would be lost but the money for my round-trip ticket. If I stayed in Italy under the present circumstances, I had no guarantee of ever being paid and a fairly good likelihood of winding up in jail.

That evening I dined with the author at her house. Later, back at the hotel, when I asked for the key to my room at the desk, two impeccably dressed gentlemen appeared on either side of me, breathing against my neck. So these were my neighbors, *sì?* My bloodhounds followed me all the way to my quarters as inconspicuously as two boys let out of school on a warm spring day. While the inspector had played his part with cool understatement, these two *prosciutti* were overacting monstrously.

In my room, I made a couple of innocuous telephone calls, turned on my portable radio full blast, and sneaked down to my new *amico*, the concierge. "*Per piacere*, Signora Fontana." He would have my reservations from Venice to Rome, from Rome to New York stamped on my ticket. *Sì*, he would arrange everything, even a car to take me to the airport. But it must be done before dawn. No other way would be safe. I could see my friend had not had so much pleasure in years. His cheeks glowed with excitement as he handed over my jewelry. We both winked like conspiratorial children as I shook his hand.

Quietly I let myself into my room, stowed my belongings into suitcases, dressed in slacks for my transatlantic trip, and lay down on top of my bed until the first streaks of day lit the leaden clouds.

A single muffled tap on my door. Two stealthy porters silently removed my luggage and escorted me down the service elevator to the waiting car. Tipping them lavishly, I kissed them on their smiling cheeks as the concierge looked on. He seemed to thrive on intrigue and lack of sleep.

Waving to my three accomplices through the rear window of my hired car, I began the drive down the Alps as the first rays of sun turned the snows to raspberry ice. I had been in Cortina just three days.

The wait at the Venice airport seemed interminable. How long would my absence remain undetected? Were my Abbott and Costello detectives still kneeling at the keyhole? Would my phone ring and, going unanswered, tip them off that their little blond bird had flown the coop?

Venice had been safe. Rome definitely was not. As my plane came to a halt on the tarmac, two uniformed policemen awaited me. I descended the stairs as they converged upon me, each taking an arm, leading me briskly to the airport police station.

Here I was requested to turn over all my baggage checks, one of my two fur coats. I was informed that I could take away nothing but the clothes I was wearing, one coat, and my makeup case, which they searched on the spot. Luckily, my jewelry was in a carrying bag in my left hand, hidden by the fur coats over my arm. I haughtily informed them that I was dining at the American Embassy that evening and the ambassador would have a full report of this embarrassing incident. This rather pleased my two *opera buffa* captors as well as the police captain. This was no everyday, run-of-the-mill airport drama.

Next I lowered my hidden jewelry case and the two fur coats onto a nearby chair. Taking the coat on top, which fortunately was a knock-about lynx that had seen better days, I handed it over to the policeman in charge, scooped up the rest of my belongings, and sailed majestically out of the police station.

Barely ten feet closer to freedom, I was called back by a beckoning policeman. Stashing my jewelry case behind a potted palm, I reappeared at the door. They had forgotten to search me. This time, as a sheepish policeman lightly patted my slack suit, reversed the pockets of my mink coat, rummaged through my purse, all looked at the floor. Had we caught an eye, we might all have burst into laughter.

Being allowed to depart a second time, I retrieved my cached jewelry case miraculously undisturbed behind the sheltering palm. As I scooped it up under my mink, I casually strode out into the chilly Rome night to the taxi stand.

At the Grand Hotel, the kindly manager heard my story and agreed to register me under my married name, to place my jewelry in his own vault. After consulting the American consul by phone, I spent the rest of the evening in the offices of Italian lawyers who only confirmed the verdict of Cortina police: in Italy, one is guilty until proven innocent . . . the producer could accuse me of anything he wished. I would have to defend myself in court. The lawyers looked very grave. More playacting. That night I again slept in my slack suit.

New York! Full speed ahead! My only recourse was an American lawyer, an American contract, American law. In case I was searched again, I left my jewelry with the U. S. consul, who arranged to have it delivered to me in New York the following day. I left Ciampino Airport next morning with no further harassment. The Italian police had impounded everything of value they thought I had with me. They could not legally hold me in the country as I was an American citizen. At least the Italian lawyers had been helpful with that bit of costly information.

Dr. Noh met my plane at J.F.K., had his car drive me directly to the offices of lawyer Arnold Weissberger. The last details of the contract were filled in, exactly as outlined in the original agreement. The document was signed and witnessed within the hour. By evening it was handed over to the special representative of Pan American World Airways and was on the night plane for Rome.

Although the contract arrived as scheduled on Saturday morning, the producer refused to cosign it! Still another twist in the plot! Perhaps he was not yet aware that my impounded luggage did not contain the jewelry he'd eyed so covetously, that the fur coat I left behind was valueless. Perhaps, after a court hearing, I would have had to forfeit all my luggage to him. With my jewelry, he could have financed another film. His hatchet-faced sister might have looked less severe in my mink coat.

In my own apartment at last, I added up the gains and losses. I had worked two and a half weeks, received one week's salary. I had incurred Italian lawyers' bills, American legal fees. I had been threatened, searched, frisked, and had seen the inside of an airport police station. The Italian government was holding my luggage containing used slacks and sweaters and little else.

Still, I'd seen a lot of Italy and received a fair insight into the Italian mentality. Now, at last, I would comprehend more fully the intricate plots of *Don Giovanni* or *Rigoletto*. My new Italian acquaintances had shown me their love of drama, of intrigue, of intimidation. Only . . . they were so delightfully amateurish about it.

I sent gold pen-and-pencil sets to the manager of the Grand Hotel in Rome, to the concierge at the hotel in Cortina.

After years of litigation, the producer declared bankruptcy. No one won, everyone lost . . . except the lawyers.

51

FLAT CHAMPAGNE

DR. NOH SPOILED ME, OFTEN SLIPPING A GOLD PIN OR A BRACELET FROM his pocket with the excuse it was for St. Swithin's Day or Guy Fawkes Day or "just because it's Monday." I took him to tailors in London and New York, supervised his wardrobe, and insisted there be no rear trouser pocket for his stethoscope. Soon he bragged that I bought him everything he was wearing, down to his socks, shorts, and shoes. But he paid all his bills, a different situation from my previous experiences.

During this time I continued in summer stock, continued my panel-show appearances. Debbie, older now, came to live in New York on her own, taking a pad in Greenwich Village, studying drama with Sandy Meisner. She visited Martita in Maine, but was reluctant to discuss her adopted sister.

Then came an offer to tour for three months in South Africa with *Dial "M."* I was excited at the prospect of working in a new country, one I'd never visited. Dr. Noh assured me that "See you in a minute" still applied. He, too, wanted to see South Africa. It was essential, he said, that he come over within six weeks. Too long a separation would be damaging to our relationship.

Taking the excellent actor Richard Clarke, who had played the role of the diabolical husband with me on my previous engagements, we joined actor John Gregson in Johannesburg. Dr. Noh telephoned me in Paris on our stopover there and frequently during rehearsals.

After playing in Johannesburg, we were to open in Cape Town. My old friend from Japan, Copper Hewitt, contacted the producer to say he wished to entertain for me the night of my arrival. Delighted as I was at the prospect, I warned the producer that we had a rehearsal, an opening night ahead next day, and I had learned to garner my strength. He replied that the publicity would be useful and would help the box office . . . that I should attend the party.

After arriving by air at Cape Town, I found the whole afternoon filled with interviews, press photographs. Scarcely able to find time to unpack my clothes at the Royal Britannia, I went to the Hewitts' that evening, had an early dinner, and begged to be taken home straightaway. Copper and his attractive wife, Jean, understood.

Next morning I had laryngitis. By noon, after more interviews with the press, I could hardly speak. By evening, now in my dressing room at the theatre, I asked for a doctor. He examined my throat and diagnosed acute laryngitis, but he knew of no palliative measures, such as we have in the theatre and opera in America, where a temporary treatment enables the artist to go on with a performance. He advised total silence and warned that I might damage my vocal cords irreparably if I went on that night.

I called Richard Clarke into my dressing room and begged his help. Cautiously, Richard tried to approach the producer in the backstage corridor in the hope of persuading him to cancel the performance. The doctor was in a huddle with the producer. Richard was waved away as the stage manager knocked on my door. "Five minutes, Miss Fontaine." My leading man returned to my dressing room, saying that there was nothing he could do and that we all had better get ready.

"Miss Fontaine, you're on."

As I took my place onstage, I knew that my emergency telephone to God and Mrs. Bruiner was out of order. I would have to fend for myself. The curtain rose in the beautiful new auditorium. I attempted to speak my first line. Only a hoarse croak came out. I could not be heard beyond the third row. By the end of the first scene the audience was restive, thumbing through programs, whispering among themselves.

As the curtain came down on the first act, the producer was waiting for me in the wings, red with fury. "You're ruining the show!" he shouted. "I'm canceling the performance!" I was a pariah backstage. All the actors and stage personnel depended on the producer for their future jobs. No one spoke to me as I left the backstage door with the Hewitts.

In my suite at the hotel, Jean and Copper fed me honey and lemon juice and ordered supper for me, forbidding me to do anything but point to the room service menu. All next day and the next I stayed alone in my rooms, not even using the telephone, in order to rest my voice for the following performances. Then I learned that my pay for the aborted opening night had been docked.

In the American theatre, if an actor reports by half hour, the legal time limit to arrive backstage, he is paid regardless of whether the curtain goes up. Not only had I appeared, was I forced to go on, but, regardless of what risk it might have been to my vocal cords, I had performed as well as I could under the circumstances.

On principle, I fought for restitution of the opening night's salary. Lawyers were hired on both sides. There was no efficient actors' union to do battle for me. Thank God Dr. Noh arrived in the midst of the fray to calm the troubled waters, to persuade the hostile producer that a night's salary meant little to me in terms of money, that I spent twice as much giving parties for friends in each city I played. But it was the principle that mattered. I was begrudgingly paid so that the show would continue. Psychologist Noh had shown his mettle again. But the battle royal between the producer and me continued. He even threatened to sue me over that one night's pay in the United States, a course he finally gave up when he was apprised of American court costs.

After closing night I was smuggled out of Johannesburg on an Alitalia flight which I changed to at the last minute lest the producer serve me with papers at the airport.

Before I left Johannesburg, friends had taken me into Soweto, the native compound of huts surrounded by barbed wire where the inhabitants were confined from six in the evening until six in the morning. I was told that Soweto, built to house 750,000 people, had twice that number. The official explanation was that the natives were much better off here than in the jungle where they came from.

The school system insisted on uniforms being worn by the students. Many black families were too poor to afford them. . . .

Coming from democratic America, I was shocked and enraged. Furious that Eartha Kitt was not allowed to sing in Pietermaritzburg. The mayor said that they would have been delighted to hear Miss Kitt sing, but, unfortunately, the laws prohibited her from using the backstage toilet facilities. Her light-skinned daughter could enter the public playground, while Eartha could not. To my surprise, Miss Kitt, who had delivered a sharp diatribe to Mrs. Johnson while she had been a guest at the White House, never issued a controversial statement.

In Cape Town, at the Nico Malan Center, where Dial "M" was playing, Margot Fonteyn was dancing at the adjoining opera house. Dame Margot, at her own expense, rented a hall on her day off to dance without charge for the blacks. Few dared to turn up.

In June, Dr. Selma Brodie, city councillor for Johannesburg and niece of Helen Sussman, the only woman member of Parliament, and I landed in Nairobi. Here we were welcomed by the politically minded daughter of President Kenyatta and taken through the Parliament of this all-black-ruled country. I, coming from white-ruled South Africa, found the situation mind-boggling.

Next Selma and I stayed overnight at Treetops, where we watched the animals all through the night, as they came out of the jungle to drink and defecate at the artificial lake. I felt like a fly on the ceiling of a vast public toilet. It was difficult to choke down breakfast before leaving the next morning.

After a two-day reunion with Olivia in Paris, where she visited us at our hotel but did not invite me to her home on rue Benouville to see my niece, Gisele Galante, or nephew, Benjamin Goodrich, I flew back to New York. Dr. Noh met the plane and drove me to the apartment, which I had not seen for almost four months. The inevitable bottle of iced champagne rode in the back seat of his convertible.

Glorious New York! Free people, mingling together in the streets. Next day Dr. Noh escorted me to a matinee of the Czechoslovakian ballet at Lincoln Center. I was thrilled to see Chinese, Japanese, Puerto Ricans, blacks all sitting together around the outdoor fountain, eating hot dogs, drinking soda pop. All laughing together, all relaxed and happy . . . all equal under the spring sunlight.

I'd almost forgotten, after those months in South Africa, what democracy was like. Just as when I had left the Iron Curtain countries of Hungary, Yugoslavia, and Czechoslovakia, I could have knelt down and kissed the ground outside the New York State Theatre. America . . . how truly beautiful you are.

Our *Dial* "M" tour continued in the United States for two more months. Dr. Noh sent me off with "See you in a minute." But . . . this time . . . he didn't. I'd been gone too long. I sensed that I had been supplanted. I was right. The seven-year itch had broken out one year late. Dr. Noh was drinking champagne with someone else. Despite our earlier vows, he had broken his word. I had kept mine.

At the end of the tour we met again. This time the champagne was lukewarm. Within days it was flat. So was I.

The fever returned. This time it was partially emotional. I couldn't eat, couldn't sleep, couldn't think, didn't care. Olivia, in the United States on a lecture tour, and Sister O'Hara nursed me at Sister's house in Quogue. Because of her marital difficulties with her second husband, Pierre Galante, my sister seemed able to understand what I was going through. Olivia undressed me, put me to bed, held me in her arms as she sang a Japanese lullaby from our childhood . . . "*Nen, nen, korori, okororiyo.*" Still the tears would not stop.

52

THE LAST GOOD-BYE

ON A SNOWY JANUARY DAY IN 1975, I WAS REHEARSING *Cactus Flower* at the Chateau de Ville Dinner Theatre in Rhode Island when the stage manager whispered into the ear of the director. Next he came over to me and said there would be a ten-minute break while I took a call from Santa Barbara on the wall phone backstage.

Over the telephone I heard Mother's doctor saying that his patient was desperately ill with terminal cancer and he did not know how long she could survive. I explained that I was contractually bound to the Chateau for some weeks, but that I would immediately cable my sister.

I was not taken by surprise at this sudden call for I had discussed Mother's rapidly declining physical condition with the producer months before, when I had signed for the twenty-six-week tour. Though sympathetic, the producer had then pointed out that he could not provide an understudy for his only star, and that if I left for my mother's bedside, not only would it throw the other actors out of work but he would be forced to cancel the run. I would be liable not only for the actors' salaries, but the box-office losses as well. Since I was sending monthly checks to Santa Barbara, I felt it was advisable to sign and hope for the best. The producer agreed to give us Easter week off (which was never a lucrative time anyway), during which I planned to fly to California to spend the holiday with my ailing parent.

After cabling Olivia in Paris, I resumed the rehearsal very much like a sleepwalker, marveling that some instinct could send out the memorized lines through my lips and tell my body where to stand and sit while kaleidoscopic visions of my mother down the years were flashed on the screen of my mind.

During the rehearsal period I sent Mother flowers and amusing cards but her nurse would not put her on the phone, explaining that her patient's hearing had deteriorated. I sensed I would never hear that golden voice again.

One morning two weeks later the telephone rang as I was cooking breakfast in my rented cottage near Warwick. It was the first I knew that Olivia had arrived in Santa Barbara. "How is she? How is she?" I blurted, my heart beating fast.

"Well," too calmly replied my sister, "she's sitting up in bed. I've put a ribbon in her hair and given her a manicure." She continued without hesitation, "I don't think she has cancer at all."

Trusting the doctor's diagnosis, I was astounded. Olivia then went on, "I think other doctors should be consulted and she should have an exploratory operation."

I was horrified. Mother, the last time I had seen her, quietly and with no dramatic overtones, had said that as she could no longer hear, see, or enjoy her food, she was no longer interested in life. "Consult as many doctors as you like, but the decision is entirely Mother's," I replied, and hung up.

How many times in the last two months had I held long telephone conversations with Mother as we prepared each other for the inevitable . . . and now Olivia was suggesting that Mother go through pain and indignity, possibly to die on the operating table. Olivia, who had not been in touch with Mother for many, many months and knew nothing of the stages of her worsening condition, was now taking charge of the life and death of our eighty-eight-year-old mother.

During the second week of the run the phone rang. (I had pneumonia but had managed to crawl to the theatre, missing only one matinee performance.) Again it was Mother's doctor in Santa Barbara. All thought of an operation had been abandoned, as her heart could not stand the ordeal. But she was sinking fast. If I wanted to see her again I must come at once. With pneumonia, with such severe legal and financial penalties if I should leave the show, I could only beg the doctor to give my mother my love and explain my absence.

One week later my daughter called me from Beverly Hills to say that her grandmother had died in her own bed and in her sleep. "Thank God! You've brought me blessed news," I replied. Olivia had telephoned her niece, but her telegram sent to Warwick had not reached me. I could only feel, "Atta girl, Mother. You were always a good stage manager and you handled this last performance with your usual style and did it your own way."

I continued on tour, now playing in Boston, flying home on Mondays (our day off) to collect mail and check telephone calls. A letter from California was on the hall table when I arrived one morning. It came from a close friend of Mother's, one whom she had appointed as executor of her will. The letter stated that Mother had been cremated and the memorial service for her would be held at Montalvo in two weeks with Olivia, Brian Aherne, and Collie delivering eulogies. There was no suggestion that Deborah and her father be present . . . and certainly not me.

It was obvious that Olivia and the executor had taken full charge, making all arrangements, disposing of Mother's effects as well as her body without bothering to consult me. I telephoned the executor, saying that as much as I had always shunned any publicity concerning my relations with my sister, unless the memorial was delayed until my Easter vacation—only a week away—I would call the press and give them the whole story. After several demurs, one being the availability of parking space, the executor finally agreed to postpone the service two days so that I might attend.

Bill Dozier and our daughter met me at the San Francisco airport, driving me through Saratoga to Montalvo. As the guests arrived (I had not been told who was invited or what the formalities would be), Debbie and Bill escorted me to the front row of the tiny country theatre in the woods where Mother had directed so many productions and where the ceremony would be held.

As the formalities began, Olivia and the executor took places in the same row. The minister opened the service, then Olivia got up on the dais and spoke. Next I said a few words and paraphrased:

> "Her heart was woven of human joys and cares,
> Washed marvellously with sorrow, swift to mirth.

The years had given her kindness. Dawn was hers,
And sunset, and the colours of the earth.
She had seen movement, and heard music; known
Slumber and waking; loved; gone proudly friended;
Felt the quick stir of wonder; sat alone;
Touched flowers and furs and cheeks. All this is ended.

There are waters blown by changing winds to laughter
And lit by the rich skies, all day. And after,
Frost, with a gesture, stays the waves that dance
And wandering loveliness. She leaves a white
Unbroken glory, a gathered radiance,
A width, a shining peace, under the night."

Rupert Brooke had long ago captured the spirit that was my mother.

At the end of the service, the minister bade the occupants of the first row to follow him to a nearby hill that Mother, years before, had selected for her final resting place. Under the trees, he handed Olivia a box. She scattered a handful of ashes, then silently passed the container to me. After I held the last tangible essence of my mother in my hand, I passed the box to my daughter. The day was drawing long shadows upon the woodland path.

Thus I said good-bye forever to my mother. As for Olivia, I had no words at all.

EPILOGUE

So THERE YOU ARE, DEAR MOTHER (I WOULD NOT HAVE DARED CALL you Lilian either to your face or your friends) . . . here are the recollections of the life begun one Saturday afternoon in Tokyo from the hurly-burly of your chaise longue.

From my earliest memory, I worshiped you, feared you, felt insignificant beside you. As a small child, unless you were near, I felt bereft, an abandoned puppet unable to move without you beside me to pull the strings. The moment you reappeared, I felt safe again, but awaited your commands, your approval, your judgments.

You with your lilting laughter, you could destroy a budding friendship of mine in a phrase or two, caricature a neighboring family in one sentence, reduce my whole school class to ignorant yokels at a glance. I never questioned you. Taste, discrimination, good manners, love of the arts, intellectual clarity, the highest morality in all things . . . respect for these I learned at your knee. In our fifty-seven years together I never once saw you slip from your own standards.

Now that you are gone, the most remarkable of your many qualities seems to me to have been COURAGE. It must have shattered you to find yourself, the mother of two small babes, supplanted in your own home by the Japanese maid, to voyage to a strange land, uncertain of financial assistance from your husband, alone to build a makeshift nest in which to rear your brood of two.

Had you been less Victorian, less impulsive, less emotional, would you have ousted the interloper, won the day, kept your family intact? Was it injured pride, vanity, concern for appearances, or an uncompromising sense of morality that made you leave our house in Tokyo forever? Perhaps it was a broken heart that caused your children to be wrested from a life of comparative luxury, the "right" schools, the "right" friends . . . that took you from the city in which you were very popular in both musical and theatrical circles to a land where you knew no one, where you had to start a new life in your midthirties without much money, no connections, no family ties.

You chose to raise your children in California. You chose to marry an American businessman, totally unlike you in temperament, but similar in ethical standards; an atheist like yourself. You and he wrote your own bible for your daughters. The laws were strict, the way was hard, punishment awe-ful. God-the-Parent was wrathful. "Love one another" was omitted. The milk of human kindness flowed not at all. Parents were Parents. They were not meant to be friends.

I remember making your bed one morning when I was nine. Being uninitiated in the vagaries of the female body, when I found a spot of blood on your bottom sheet, I was convinced you were dying. I kissed the dried blood, finished my chores, and streaked off to hide under the honeysuckle hedge. I cried for days whenever I could find the luxury of solitude.

It was then that I began the habit of putting baskets of flowers (usually nipped from the neighbors' hedges) over the front doorknob. Ringing the bell, I would then hide behind a bush. You'd open the door and in a stage whisper exclaim, "There must be a fairy in our garden." My pleasure was ecstatic. Whistling nonchalantly, my hands thrust into the pockets of my blue jeans, I would enter through the back door. Neither you nor I would ever acknowledge the incident. Sentimentality was bad taste.

You didn't mind, years later, when I began to telephone you on my birthdays . . . to thank you for giving me life. I'd always felt that October 22 was *your* day, not mine, the one on which you'd given birth in that Tokyo house to your second daughter. Eventually, you were to say to friends, "You'll see. Before this day is over, I'll hear from Joan!" This was a respectful, amusing form of sentimentality which you could condone.

Only once was I your confidante. You'd just returned from the local grocery store in Saratoga. Something in your diction, your impersonal, polite way of addressing shopkeepers, had annoyed the clerk. His "Who the hell do you think you are?" stunned you. I happened to be alone in the house when you arrived. You were shaking. No one had ever spoken to you like that before. Sitting at the dining-room table with your panacea cup of tea in front of you, you looked me straight in my momentarily grown-up eyes. "I'm *not* a snob. I'm *not* undemocratic. It's just the way I was brought up to behave!" We were briefly the same age. Before I had finished my cup of cambric tea, you had extracted my oath never to buy my penny candy at that store, never to set foot inside its door. I kept my word.

When I went to Japan the umbilical cord was cut, but not without pain. Your letters would arrive ten to fourteen days apart. At school I would daily scan the morning papers to learn when the latest ship from San Francisco would be docking at Yokohama. When your letter was delivered, I would steal up the wooden stairs of our dormitory, lock myself into the lavatory cubicle. Here, in privacy, I could read, reread, every line of your graceful handwriting, examine the stamps, smell the notepaper, hoping that your scent would have crossed the Pacific inside the envelope.

When I returned to California the following year, we had grown apart. You would never again be the ministering angel who took my temperature when I came home ill from school, who would climb the stairs to my sickroom with trays of medicine and invalid's food, who would correct my grammar, my diction, my manners. By now you had started lecturing on current events, reading plays at women's clubs, teaching drama at San Jose State and Stanford University. You were no longer the mother of a skinny, freckle-faced, taffy-haired duckling. I had begun to think that I might just be turning into a swan. Did I only imagine that surprised you, did not altogether please you?

I do not remember one time when you said I was pretty, that my figure was acceptable, that my clothes were well chosen. I do not remember one time when you discussed my wardrobe or my hair-style. I do remember the night in Hollywood when I was to attend my first Academy Award dinner. The makeup man at R.K.O. had taken great pains trying to make me as attractive as possible. When I arrived home to dress, you made me wash my face with soap and water. "You look like a painted hussy!" I was nineteen . . . I would not have dared disobey or question your judgment.

Did you want me to marry Conrad to get me out of the way, or to see me with a home of my own and with financial security? Were you afraid I would go astray among the wolves of Hollywood, or was the tension between your two daughters more than you could cope with? I never knew why you didn't try to make us kinder, more understanding, more forgiving of one another—or did you prefer us at each other's throat? Somehow, I felt that you were afraid of Olivia, that she could berate you and, under the onslaught, you would always retreat, even as you did with Father.

How pleased you were when I married Brian . . . an Englishman, my father's build, almost looking like him. I think you were a little in love with him, being nearer his age than I, as you erroneously pointed out (not until I read your obituary did I learn you were born in 1886). You certainly bestowed upon Brian all the charm and coquetry at which you were so expert. And he delighted in you. I felt very much in the role of "I" de Winter while you were playing Rebecca to Brian's Maxim.

I could never understand why you weren't with me in Santa Monica when my daughter was born. You never suggested it. When I telephoned you from my hospital room after Deborah's birth, your only concern was that you shouldn't be called "Grandmother," but that "Gams" would be acceptable because of your beautiful legs.

Debbie was five weeks old before you saw her. She never interested you much and you seldom inquired about her when she was growing up. Of your three grandchildren, only Olivia's daughter, Gisele, born in Paris, captured your heart. When her son, Benjamin, became seriously ill, you admired his courage and remembered him generously in your will. You left not even a trinket to Deborah.

Down the years I stayed with you in your various places in California. You came to stay with me often in Brentwood and New York. Three times we traveled to Europe together. Our conversations were mostly about food and restaurants. (I am still turning up recipes in your distinctive handwriting as I sort out drawers or closets in my New York apartment.) I knew you cared about your appearance and I often tried to compliment you on your clothes. You would dismiss my remark with "Oh, it's last year's" or "It's on its last legs." We seldom discussed my husbands, my lovers. You had little respect for the stronger sex . . . dismissing men like your dresses as though they had served their usefulness, seen better days, and the sooner they were condemned to the dustbin the better.

I asked you once after Mr. Fontaine died if you thought of marrying again. You said, "Heavens, no! Men are too much trouble!" Except for Brian, you never were more than mildly amused by my male attachments . . . usually saying, "Oh, *that* one . . . what can you expect?" or, "You can have the whole lot of 'em . . . they're not worth the powder to blow them up!"

Do you know I can't remember your ever admitting to me that you'd ever seen a film of mine or asking about any aspects of my career? You only sketchily mentioned Olivia's and then with more criticism than praise. In rereading your letters, signed "M" or "Mater," never have I found any allusion to my public life, to any honors or awards I might have received. You wrote mostly about the parties you'd been to, the food that was served, how you dressed.

During the last year of your life I arranged to bring my poetry reading to Santa Barbara—"The Romance of Elizabeth Barrett and Robert Browning." At the Sombrero Theatre, Alexander Scourby and I gave the evening recital to a packed house. You said you were not well enough to attend. You didn't. Next morning I brought you the orchids the management had been kind enough to present to me after the program.

You were loved, respected, and admired by your friends, by the students and artists you worked with . . . acting, directing, teaching. To this day strangers will come up to me and boast that they knew you in theatre, on campus, in films. They feel their lives are richer for the experience.

During the last summer of your life, I took a house in Pebble Beach to be near you. You had always loved its windswept coast, often taking your young daughters there for holidays and Christmases. "It reminds me of Japan," you often said. You even lived there for several months before making your final home in Santa Barbara. You spent the Christmas of 1970 with me in the same rented cottage.

On a hot August morning in 1974, I drove down the coast highway in my station wagon to fetch you. We were going to have ten cozy days together by the sea. We were going to walk on the beach, sit in my garden under the pine trees, and say all the things to each other we'd meant to say, neglected to say, refused to say during our many years as mother and daughter. I was excited at the prospect, hopeful that I might be adult enough to conquer my emotions, to be objective in my views. Most of all, I wanted to ask a thousand questions about you that I had never dared ask. Had you loved my father? Why had you hated your mother, cut yourself off from all ties of England? What had you been like as a child? What moon had you cried for?

In Santa Barbara that evening, I drove you through the hills of Montecito, along the palm-fringed coastline. My dear, chic, gay, laughing mother, you were now wearing bottle-bottom glasses, a hearing aid. Your stockings sagged around your once shapely legs. Your cashmere coat was too short for your dress. As I looked at your withered body, my throat constricted, my ribs ached.

After dinner, which you hardly touched, and a mundane conversation that I directed into your hearing aid over the din of the restaurant, we drove to the cinema. During *Daisy Miller*, the boys behind us kept kicking our loge seats. Halfway through the film I escorted you out.

That night I slept on the couch in your living room, finding myself curled in a fetal position on the floor when I awoke the next morning. You had already stepped over my slumbering body on your way to make our tea.

After I dressed, I opened your bedroom door. You were naked, sitting on the bed trying to reason with a silk stocking you held in your hand. "I can't, Joan. I can't go with you to Pebble Beach. I simply haven't any strength."

Though we had intended for the resident nurse to give me a ten-day supply of insulin for your daily dose, I knew you were right. I did not try to jolly you, persuade you, convince you that the holiday would do you good. It was obvious that part of you had already embarked on the final trip.

Never having seen you undressed since I was a small child, I felt I should avert my eyes as I helped you into the bathtub, dried your shrunken body with a towel. Once you were back in bed, I fled.

Thirty miles north of Santa Barbara, I pulled the station wagon off the highway. Sitting in the car in a eucalyptus grove, I wept. It was not yet nine o'clock. I'd had no breakfast. By one that afternoon I reached the Pebble Beach cottage, locked the doors, closed the curtains, and howled like a wounded animal.

Flowers die . . . even sunsets. Friends have left me, love affairs have crushed me, but you, Mother, were indestructible, made of the substance that lives forever. You had immortality about you.

For the next six months, your doctor and I kept from you the nature of your final illness. I saw you two more times before that February day in 1975 when, in your sleep and with your infinite sense of dignity and decorum, you left this planet.

The last time, in December 1974, as I was leaving your Santa Barbara apartment, I told you that I was embarking on a tour of *Cactus Flower* but that I had arranged with the producer to take the Easter week off and would fly to California to spend it with you. Your face went blank. Your voice suddenly seemed weary. "Oh, Joan, that's such a long way off!" Both you and I knew we were saying our last good-bye.

Your final words to me, during our last telephone call, were "Remember how much I loved you."

INDEX